Jim Moginie was raised in Sydney's northern suburbs and attended high school in the city, where he befriended future Midnight Oil drummer Rob Hirst. Together with another friend, Andrew James, they formed the band FARM before recruiting singer Peter Garrett and Martin Rotsey and changing their name to Midnight Oil. Jim is best known as a songwriter, guitarist and keyboard player for the band, but his career has also spanned dozens of less well known creative adventures, from playing traditional Irish music with Shameless Seamus and the Tullamore Dews and creating soundscapes for eight guitars under the banner of Jim Moginie's Electric Guitar Orchestra, to playing with punk-edged cerebral rock band The Family Dog and surf instrumentalists The Break. Jim has also collaborated with prominent artists such as Silverchair, Sarah Blasko, the Warumpi Band, the Living End, Kasey Chambers, Neil Finn and the Australian Chamber Orchestra.

The Silver River

Jim Moginie

HarperCollins*Publishers*

HarperCollins_Publishers_
Australia • Brazil • Canada • France • Germany • Holland • India
Italy • Japan • Mexico • New Zealand • Poland • Spain • Sweden
Switzerland • United Kingdom • United States of America

HarperCollins acknowledges the Traditional Custodians
of the lands upon which we live and work, and pays respect
to Elders past and present.

First published on Gadigal Country in Australia in 2024
by HarperCollins_Publishers_ Australia Pty Limited
ABN 36 009 913 517
harpercollins.com.au

A catalogue record for this book is available from the National Library of Australia

ISBN 978 1 4607 6585 2 (paperback)
ISBN 978 1 4607 1748 6 (ebook)
ISBN 978 1 4607 3798 9 (audiobook)

Cover design: Design by Committee
Front cover image © Andrzej Liguz/moreimages.net
Back cover image by Christabel Blackman
Author photo by Robert Hambling
All internal images courtesy of Jim Moginie or the Moginie family archive, unless
otherwise noted
Typeset in Sabon LT Std by Kirby Jones
Printed and bound in Australia by McPherson's Printing Group

MIX
Paper | Supporting
responsible forestry
FSC
www.fsc.org   FSC® C001695

For the mothers

For the love of music
Is sweet and dangerous
To lose yourself to the love of all
Pray for the partner bound to be lonely
Pray for the player that has no child.
– Shane Howard, 'The Love of Music'

Therefore, since we are surrounded by
so great a cloud of witnesses,
let us also lay aside every weight,
and sin which clings so closely,
and let us run with endurance the race
that is set before us.
– Hebrews 12:1

The Silver River

CONTENTS

There is a town I was born
It is a place I've never been
Don't even know where it is
Don't even know my name

Where is home? Where is my home.
I'm searching far and wide

It is a bastard song
It's the feeling that everything's wrong
We are alive, we that have wings
We have devices that do anything

Where is home? Where is my home?
I hear my spirit cry.

Midnight Oil, 'Home'

How can you mend a broken song?

Thunder grumbles overhead behind blankets of grey cloud. The air is thick and the barometric pressure is falling fast. The wind stops. Wattlebirds make bell sounds in the banksias and the sea sighs in the distance. Mist obscures the headland, a swirling blur over a troubled sea.

I've been coming to the South Coast of New South Wales ever since I was a child. The national park runs south from here all the way to Batemans Bay. Miles of deserted beaches and rocky outcrops, reefs full of salmon and blackfish. Whales give birth in Kitten Bay, just outside my window. Local fishermen say that everything taken from here is below legal size.

When you climb up the hills of spotted gum and burrawang, Montague Island appears and disappears like a phantom to the south. Native heath and pea flowers stretch to the edge of the cliffs and scratch you as you pass. The smell and cathedral roar of the ocean snaps me out of my reverie.

I wish my parents had written down their life stories. I asked my adoptive father, Paul, to do it. His eyes glazed over, a faint smile appeared and he changed the subject.

When I finally met my biological father, Brian, he told me my mother had changed her name from Susan to Anne sometime after her birth. No wonder I hadn't been able to find her. Brian and I sat on plastic chairs among the weeds masquerading as lawn outside his house. Brian was talking and smoking, warming up to his subject. He said that after I was born he drove to the hospital in Sydney to bring her back. They didn't go straight home to Queanbeyan. Passing the Canberra turnoff, they drove towards Yass. He told me they stopped the car and considered going back to get me.

Like a river changing course, everything that followed in my life was determined in that moment of indecision.

A rainy
night in
Yallah

It's 2007 and I'm in Bali on a holiday with my children, Alice and Sam. I'm playing ukulele a lot. I adore ukuleles. They're easy to carry on a plane. No one searches you for drugs, people leave you alone.

We're staying at a beach resort with no beach. They detonated the coral reef just offshore to get the lime to make the concrete to build the salmon-pink resorts along any bit of coastline available, and the beach disappeared overnight. Someone should have remembered their beach-erosion and sand-dynamics geography class from school. Karma, greed ... sounds like a potential Midnight Oil song, if the band still existed.

My new band, Jim Moginie & The Family Dog, have had an interesting year. After huge sellout tours of stadiums in the eighties and nineties with Midnight Oil, I released my first solo album, *Alas Folkloric*, onto an unsuspecting world in 2006 for the re-education of Oils fans, introducing them to my music without its charismatic dervish-dancing frontman and long-time bandmates and collaborators. These are my baby steps, learning to perform, lead a band, be a frontman, manager, booker, paymaster, to win hearts, minds and a new audience after living and breathing within the walled city of rock aristocracy for as long as I can remember.

At the local Balinese money changer/laundromat/internet café, I log on to the sleepy dial-up connection. An email arrives from my manager, Arlene Brookes. It says there's a date available at the Yallah Roadhouse near Wollongong.

'Book it,' I type.

*

Three weeks later there are just thirteen pre-sales at the 450-capacity venue. For a Saturday night, that's a bad sign. The email from Darren, the venue manager, is edgy. 'It's not happening. Do something.' Maybe it's the price, but $15 seems reasonable to me. Is it my tendency to downplay my involvement with Midnight Oil? I'm reluctant to trade on the band's good name. I'm striking out alone, letting the new music be judged on its own merits.

Three hours before the gig I want to rewrite the sign out the front of the Yallah Roadhouse to say 'Jim Moginie's Midnight Oil Show'. I should have done more publicity. More posters, maybe a nude parachute jump with IMAX cameras off the top of Mount Keira. Why didn't I date a *Neighbours* star, or sashay down more red carpets?

At an interview the day before, ABC Radio Wollongong played two songs from *Alas Folkloric* and a Midnight Oil song. An article appeared in the *Illawarra Mercury* and there was a competition through Wave FM for a support band. The venue bought generic advertising – TV, print media, an ad in *Drum Media*. My manager and publicist have pulled out all the stops.

I've travelled up and down the Princes Highway to the South Coast since childhood, passing the Yallah Roadhouse on the side of the road, but never played here. Dapto Leagues more than once, Shellharbour Workers repeatedly, Wollongong Uni, Mount Pleasant Sports, Port Kembla RSL, WIN Entertainment Centre, the Collegians Club, Waves Nightclub, but never the Yallah.

It sports a big 'What's On' sign out the front. International acts like Gene Pitney, Don McLean and Glen Campbell have played here. Rose Tattoo are on next week, and I've spotted the names of Kasey Chambers, Gina Jeffreys, the dynasty of Kernaghans and Josh Pyke.

It's an odd place for a venue. No houses nearby, in the middle of a dusty paddock with a few masticating horses. I imagine the set of the American television variety show *Hee Haw* with Buck Owens and Roy Clark recreated inside – hay bales, gingham-clad blondes and upturned wine barrels for tables. Donkeys with gap teeth and straw hats. I grew up with Australia's own versions: Chad Morgan, Reg Lindsay's travelling show and the mighty Slim Dusty. Playing at the Yallah should be a career highlight for me, but I'm having an existential crisis, like the character in the Bread song 'The Guitar Man', or Kevin Johnson's 'Rock and Roll (I Gave You the Best Years of My Life)'.

In my new band are Tim Kevin, who has played in a bunch of inner-city bands, and Kent Steedman and Paul Larsen Loughhead from cult heroes The Celibate Rifles. They're no strangers to big venues themselves, and the Rifles' punk-surf rock lineage is known here and overseas.

We've gathered a solid repertoire of tunes through much rehearsal, a six-week residency in Sydney's Newtown and playing for fun in garages – not precious note-for-note renditions but free-wheeling, turn-on-a-dime extemporisations that, on the one hand, could peel the paint off a Korean trawler and, on the other, offer a subtle psychedelic interplay that breathes life into the music. It's a band where people really listen to one another.

After soundcheck, we head outside for a band photo in the late-afternoon light. My girlfriend, Suzy, aims the camera and we strike some half-arsed poses. Getting four people looking good all at once in a photograph is never easy, especially at our age. We stand in front of the fluorescent yellow Starbus, the shuttle used to convey the hundreds of potential punters from distant Wollongong, lying dormant on the tarmac like a ruined ghost ship. Someone is always looking off to the side in these band shots. Rob Hirst did that very well and often in Midnight Oil. I was always hiding up the back, or the one caught with his eyes closed.

The venue is an L-shaped room with a pool table at one end and the stage at the other. The wide lanolin-soaked floorboards and rusty tin roof remain from the original woolshed. The upturned half-cask tables are there, a few lounge settings strewn about, a bar with galvanised iron features, beer on tap and a brightly lit fridge full of fluorescent cooler bottles and cans of Bundy and Coke. Darren says they've sold three more tickets over the phone. Things are looking up. I ask if it's a walk-up venue. 'No one can walk here. It's miles from anywhere,' he says.

It's 7.30pm and insufferably hot under the tin roof. The crowd heads outside with beers in hand to watch the sun set over the Great Dividing Range. Clouds blacken the sky, but the blazing Australian sun bursts out between them like light rays in a Renaissance painting. Paul, our drummer, is telling me about his wish to get a block of land when there's a thunderclap. It's about to rain. There is something great about being on a veranda in Australia when a storm is approaching. Negative ions. There's a Gang Gajang song about it that became a Coke ad.

Two punters, Lee and his partner, come over to chat. They're from England and are big Midnight Oil fans. Lee tells me he had a lot of trouble buying our 1980 EP *Bird Noises* and had to fork out $140 for it. As the sky darkens and crackles around us, he says his sixty-five-year-old father is also a big fan. He saw us playing the Aston Villa Leisure Centre in Birmingham in 1993 on the *Earth and Sun and Moon* tour. I remember that gig. A big sports hall, not exactly full but not exactly empty either. We had come off the peak of the previous two albums' dazzling success. I tell Lee I've got some copies of my new record here and he says he'll buy one to send to his dad. But he hasn't heard us yet, and it's another band he's a fan of.

Some of our early gigs have been shaky, but we're getting better. We're using in-house PAs and lights and local sound people to keep costs down. Gone are the high production values of the Oils. But the passion is flowing; the band is starting to cook. Last night's show at the Cat and Fiddle Hotel in Balmain was hot.

The rain increases in intensity. Suzy prowls around with the camera as the light fades. It starts to bucket down and everyone heads inside as Pettibone, who won the Wave FM support band competition, fire up. Three girls and a boy, they have cut their teeth at South Coast folk festivals. One of the girls, Jamie, sings, plays guitar and has a strong voice. The other two girls play harmony lines on fiddles, and the boy, James, plays both banjo and double bass.

'Well, with this rain, those that might have been thinking of coming will stay home,' says Darren. A cruel but fair analysis. My hearts sinks. There are maybe twenty-five people here. It's going to be an intimate show.

Through the windows, lightning illuminates the sparse paddocks outside. The rain on the tin roof sounds like the roar of applause for The Beatles at Shea Stadium in '66. It's a deluge over which Pettibone are becoming inaudible, even though they're playing through the PA. But the atmosphere is upbeat. People who know who I am are giving me sideways smiles and shy looks. A few leaks in the roof spring to life. Garbage bins are hastily put beneath them by the staff. 'We thought we'd fixed the leaks but they just moved to different places,' says Darren.

Then the volume drops suddenly. Dave, the sound man, looks askance at his mixing console, to the stage and back again, perplexed. It's a brownout. Two hundred and forty volts has dropped to around one hundred. The lights dim to gaslight intensity, like the interior of an inner-city terrace house in Ultimo in the 1890s.

Another thundercrack. Lightning hits the end of the veranda and we're in darkness. Pettibone smile nervously in the dim green glow of the emergency exit light. The power flickers, but hope is dashed as it snuffs out again. The drink fridges flick on and off like fireflies and then die. People start shuffling about. Everyone is suddenly in the moment, marooned in a monsoon, afloat in a woolshed of dubious occupational health and safety standards. It's exciting.

I suggest Pettibone come down to play beneath the one emergency light where most of the audience are. The band are used to playing acoustically and happy to oblige, but the rain on the tin roof is cacophonous. Even Jamie's strong voice can barely be heard unamplified. Only the banjo cuts through.

While Pettibone play and the crowd claps along, I go to the band room to get the box of CDs. Selling your CDs is the difference between profit and loss when you're playing to a small audience at a venue on a door deal. I set it on a table and a fellow named Lincoln comes over. He's a Midnight Oil fan, a drummer himself, and within thirty seconds he scribbles down his website and contact details and offers his services. He buys a CD and another Oils fan comes over. Let's call him Doug.

Midnight Oil fans are sweet and love their music, but that was then and this is now, and 'then' is usually all they care about. Maybe, years ago, perception and emotion crossed over for them in a 3D moment of crystal clarity while listening to some record I'd been a part of, divining and solidifying their place in the universe as only music can. But Doug has had a few drinks, and I've gone from rock god to journeyman, with no security guards to micromanage such encounters or choreograph strategic exits.

Darren and I walk over to the windows and look out on completely dark paddocks. The lights of Shellharbour are extinguished. The whole district has gone off the grid. It's starless and bible black outside. We will have to cancel the show or play acoustically – no amps or microphones. I announce to those there, 'You can get a refund, and we'll make good by doing another gig. But in the meantime we'll have a go at playing.'

Pettibone are happy to loan us their instruments. Kent, normally anatomically connected to his Epiphone Crestwood guitar and juiced-up Echolette amp with custom four-by-ten quad box, gets the double bass – an instrument he's a stranger to – but he's only momentarily flummoxed and quickly finds his way around it. This band would rock if we were playing xylophones and paper-comb harmonicas. The first song is 'Halfway Home'. The rain has stopped and you can almost hear the words: '*Halfway Home, everything's been set in stone / Halfway Home, give the man a microphone.*'

Tim sings like a bird and plays a borrowed acoustic guitar, then grabs the double bass and Kent switches to guitar. Kent and I break strings at almost the same time, bashing away to be heard. Mick, the roadie, does a quick string change. I attempt a harmonica solo of Cold War proportions, skidding along the hem of catastrophe, but the audience are getting into it. Candles are lit and set atop barrels; beers flow. The audience can hear us curse under our breath and laugh when new instruments appear. The staff hand around buttered bread on gingham doilies in wicker baskets. There's a bit of Country Women's Association in all of us – it's turning into a driver-reviver caravan or afternoon tea with the ladies at Lifeline.

Then Midnight Oil's long-time accountant, tour manager and minder sweeps into the dim light of the room. Craig Allen, a karate black belt, shaved head and dressed in black with a knife, phone and Maglite torch in his utility belt, is like a white pointer sniffing the air. It took him ten minutes to find the entrance to the venue in the dark and he's scanning the room for fire exits and working out strategies to deal with potential threats. He assumes a position by the back wall to assess and calibrate 'the crowd' for any security risks to my personage.

Paul, our drummer, is trying to figure out which drums to play, decrying his lack of light sticks or brushes as he clatters around disconsolately through the first few songs. I borrow James's banjo to cut though on the solo for 'Stand Your Ground'. The tuning is unknown to me but its volume and clarity could penetrate the ears of the hearing impaired a few suburbs away in Jamberoo. I silently pine for my ukulele.

Doug, to my left, is firing up. Between calls of 'Wedding Cake Island!' and 'Oils!', his blood alcohol is reaching prisonable levels. 'Hey, Jim. The power's back on,' he jokes, and the audience groans. Craig takes a few steps towards him. If the elimination of a potential threat is initiated, Doug could be in for a quick karate chop to the back of his neck, a charge of 20,000 volts from a cattle prod hidden in a utility belt or a deft shot of horse tranquilliser. I don't think I'm insured for this. But Doug's mate tells him to shut up and Craig retreats into the shadows like a hooded cobra.

We break into an impromptu cover of 'Who'll Stop the Rain' and the crowd sing along. At last, a song they know.

We play some songs from *Capricornia,* the last Midnight Oil album, which not many bought, although three people in tonight's crowd swear they have it. *Alas Folkloric* was avoided by commercial radio but has gone 'indie platinum' – 2000 copies – which is fine for a new artist, but not a pinch compared to a Midnight Oil record.

Suzy has the camera. Determined to capture the event, she uses the flash. Each blinding burst is like a Mundine punch. I stagger like Raymond Burr playing Lars Thorwald in Alfred Hitchcock's *Rear Window* as the room swims back into view. I'm surprised

Craig doesn't try to eject her – there was a strict no-flash policy at Midnight Oil gigs, but this is not the Hordern Pavilion or Wembley Arena; it's Yallah Roadhouse in a blackout, and she's my girlfriend.

The humidity and folk electricity in the air is building as the gig is coming to its climax. 'Say Your Prayers' includes a clap-along verse. I'm getting the hang of this audience-participation thing. I finish with a solo version of 'Shakers and Movers'. Doug moves close to me on the floor and, like a new but unpaid band member, starts to dance, Garrett style, all stomping feet and cyclonic arms – a sozzled grasshopper moving in for the kill. I move towards him and dance along, looking into his eyes and singing: '*I can shake / I can move / But I can't live without your love.*'

*

We pack up by candlelight. Craig's torch lights up the stage as I try to put all the fiddly little bits into their cases. The moment all the gear is offstage and wheeled out, the lights flicker on. A collective 'ohhh' goes up. The audience has just left.

Darren asks me to sign a photo and a Cascade bottle for the venue. It's a tradition. We climb into the rent-a-wreck one-tonne van and I say goodbye to Dave the sound man. 'The best mix I never did,' he says.

I have been humbled. I'm the man who fell to Earth.

One

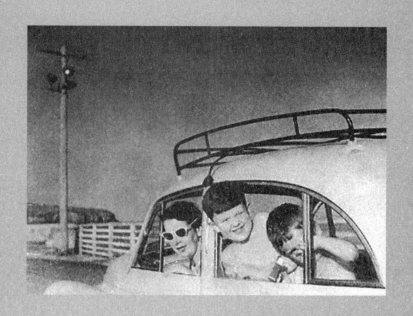

The smell of sparklers

I grew up in the suburbs of northern Sydney, listening to the sounds of cicadas, magpies and kookaburras. In the late 1950s, the Moginies lived on a half-acre block in Wahroonga, a bushy and sleepy hamlet near Hornsby, dozing beneath an unforgiving Australian sun.

My first memory is of me walking along a pier holding my father's hand and feeling a deep sense of belonging and safety. My dad, Paul Moginie, was someone strong who was going to look after me for as long as he possibly could.

As well as my dad there was my mum, Betty, my older brother, Kim, and various dogs, including Rhani the labrador and later Benji and Otto the basset hounds. We lived on a street lined with magnificent London plane trees, a long straight rabbit run where people could drive fast in cars without seat belts, multi-speaker stereo systems or airbags. I spent a lot of time on my Sunbeam bicycle in nearby Wahroonga Avenue, a promenade not unlike those in Savannah, Georgia, but instead of oaks and Spanish moss, native eucalypts towered overhead.

If our house at 62 Burns Road had a style, it was Californian bungalow with a dash of Tudor. Called 'The Lodge', it had been the gatehouse of an estate, long subdivided, that once belonged to a family called Snow. Painted rose-petal pink, it was set close to the road, leaving a huge backyard at the rear. Inside were dark, chunky mahogany beams with walls of austere white plaster. In the lounge room, English fine bone china plates were displayed on wooden picture rails. Possums would often descend the chimney and run madly around the plates and we would catch them like jugglers as they spun earthward.

The lounge led to a sunroom furnished with armchairs upholstered in a floral Sanderson print – pink and green on a sea of dark grey. Hazy, handmade glass windows overlooked the garden. It was as if you were in the pages of *Country Life* magazine, or in Sussex, England. It wasn't long since the end of World War Two and we were still the staunchest of allies. Bob Menzies was prime minister, worshipper of the Empire, and the Union Jack was the epitome of cool. England was a country for which no sacrifice was too great.

Undermining this superimposed idea of monarchy was the birdsong – cackling kookaburras and the chortling of magpies floating across the soft sound of sprinklers on lawns. Peewees and bulbuls, small birds like finches and wrens, the night calls of the mopoke and distant droning flies. The warm air was filled with the airborne pollen of wattle, melaleuca and bottlebrush from the omnipresent bushland just a mile away. Australia crouched like a beast under a thin veneer of King and Country.

On one side of the house was a deep garden bed with huge trees and European plants: elm, sycamore, pine overhead, and oyster plants, azaleas and rhododendrons everywhere beneath. It was a playground with never-ending possibilities. The driveway of the battle-axe block next door had a bamboo grove on either side where a child could believe they were fighting in the ever-escalating Vietnam War.

Dad tended to his buffalo lawn with pride, shovelling loads of superphosphate on it, year in, year out, which almost but not quite killed it each time. Superphosphate was the wonder chemical of the era, a carcinogen in sheep's clothing. We couldn't play on it for weeks after. It would burn our feet, Agent Orange–style, but he was protective of his green and even turf. He used a concrete bowling club roller to level it and another spiked roller to aerate it. When bandicoots dug it up looking for insects, he threatened them with certain death and every expletive in the book.

In the centre of the lawn was a huge vegetable garden but the only vegetable was a monster rhubarb plant. It made the best dessert ever and we plundered its juicy stalks, which somehow made it grow faster. Mum boiled it to a pulp and dolloped it out with lashings of brown sugar and Peters ice cream.

Cracker night was all dizzy excitement. Throwdowns, tuppeny bungers, Roman candles and Catherine wheels would create eye-watering clouds of sulphur dioxide and metal salts, and a furore of whooshes and explosions. I liked the slow burn of sparklers best. Their metal and magnesium smell got on your tongue somehow, and their meteor showers of tiny particles tickled your hand without burning.

At the rear of the half-acre was a low hedge, and behind that the incinerator. You could burn off back then, and I have memories of my father making huge fires on a Sunday. It was usually a conflagration of damp grass clippings ignited by a splash of petrol. After the initial explosion rattled the windowpanes, he would stare into the flames for hours on end. I always wondered what he was thinking, if that's what he was even doing.

The things you couldn't burn went to the tip, which was really just a huge sandstone valley where rubbish was dumped and bulldozed in. Scavengers prowled the periphery and swarmed in when cars arrived and opened their boots. One day my parents threw out all of our old 78 rpm records and they were mercilessly swooped upon. I didn't have the good sense to rescue them, being too small and unaware. Mum and Dad replaced a few with 33⅓ rpm vinyl, but this was the music of my parents' heyday, the roaring twenties through to the beginning of rock and roll, and would say so much about them. I would dearly love to have those 78s now.

I spent a lot of time sitting on the back step. I'd spit watermelon seeds onto a narrow patch of soil between the house and the sandstone flagging and was amazed when watermelon plants sprouted up a few weeks later. I didn't know that seeds grew into plants. It was the beginning of my interest in the magic of botany.

Nights were spent looking at the southern sky. My grandfather James Noble had been a World War One infantryman who served in Europe. The night he died, Mum took me outside and we saw a bright star. We were convinced it was him, ascending into the heavens, and wrote this information down in our old family Bible. I was named James after him, but everyone called me Jamie.

Kim, twenty-six months my senior, was the extrovert. I was withdrawn and skinny, and Kim was highly social with a broader build. He left me to my own devices and I to his. We were different people with different aesthetics and few interests in common, but our relationship was, and still is, warm and kind. We each respected the other for being other. He was mechanically minded, like Dad, forever stripping cars or motorbikes or putting together Airfix kits from Hobbyco of World War Two airplanes, like the B-52 known as the Flying Fortress that ended up on the hedge, being shot to pieces with the family air rifle.

School was just a zebra crossing away from the house, named The Bush School because it was spread out under skyscraper-high eucalypts with their understorey of wattle and scrub. Gumnuts, leaves and twigs crunched underfoot on the grey asphalt playgrounds, which were ruptured by tumescent and rampant tree roots. We drank milk from small glass bottles delivered to the main quadrangle daily in wire racks, warmed and soured by the sun. Free milk was a scheme introduced by the Menzies government to give children healthy bodies and minds.

The classrooms were a mix of demountables, tin sheds, fibre-cement and brown-brick structures. The desks had inkwells where we'd dip our nibs to write 'the quick brown fox jumps over the lazy dog'.

My family didn't trouble churches on Sundays, so when we were asked what religion we were at school and told to join a line according to our denomination, I didn't know what to do, and I still remember that feeling of tightening panic. I had to decide on the spot whether I was Catholic, Presbyterian, Anglican, Muslim or Jewish. I joined the Church of England line because I'd read the name the day before on a sign outside a local kindergarten.

Betty, our mother, was a constant presence. When a tiger caterpillar dropped from one of those giant trees into my blue short-sleeved school shirt, I felt an itching sensation and went home covered in angry welts that she looked after with soothing creams. Once she got mad with Kim and me, threatening us with a wooden spoon, but she broke it in two on the kitchen bench instead and we fell about laughing. She was always smiling or giggling about something. When she'd had a gin and tonic she'd sing The Beatles' 'I Wanna Be Your Man' to our father to get a reaction. But they weren't physically affectionate with each other. I didn't know why they slept in separate beds, like in old movies. Despite the deep sense of security I felt, and the affection that my parents shared, it was not a cuddly kind of household. Mum applied herself to her job as housewife with zeal, keeping things on track for Dad, the breadwinner, and for us. There were very rarely raised voices. Kim spent more time with Dad and I more time with Mum. That's how life played out.

When Mum took me to the city on the train, she wore a veil — see-through black lace with embroidered black dots. It made this familiar woman mysterious, a Greta Garbo or an Ingrid Bergman, someone from antiquity, or the ruling classes. I suppose she was teaching me how to shop, so we shopped and then went for a sandwich in the Strand Arcade. Funny how a lot of Australian placenames are from England, like locations on a Monopoly board. I had a ham sandwich and thought it was the height of fine cuisine if the crusts were cut off the refrigerated white bread and there was a sprig of parsley on the side.

Dad was a more distant and moody figure. Born in 1917, he was stubborn and ornery. He'd never change his stance on an issue. When he said something, well, that was all there was to it. When he did smile it was as if the sun had suddenly shone through the clouds and the world was altogether a better place.

He was an early-onset diabetic and had to inject insulin twice a day, a medical reality that started for him at age fifteen, but he ate and drank whatever he pleased – not making history there in being a naughty diabetic. In those days, insulin came from the pancreas of pigs and he injected it with a huge glass syringe like those used on horses. Sometimes I would watch him do it from the darkness of the hallway. He had a rounded shape to him, forty-four inches at the waist, due as much to the insulin as his love of a cold longneck of Reschs Pilsener when he returned home from work.

He was at his most vocal in front of the television set. If a Labor politician said anything, he would explode with 'He should be bloody well shot!', 'Shooting's too good for him' or 'He's a waste of a good bullet'. His most definitive and commonly used line was 'Poppycock!' Sometimes we would call him Cocky Pop.

During World War Two, diabetes had excused Dad from overseas service, so he enlisted in the Volunteer Coastal Patrol operating out of Neutral Bay. On his ten-metre yacht, *Moana Lua,* he and other civilians tracked rogue Japanese submarines infiltrating Sydney Harbour. Dad was also completely car crazy.

He had a car dealership, Brownhill-Moginie Motors in Kings Cross, and he raced in endurance rallies. During the war, he would parade around Sydney in shiny American convertibles from the dealership, sculling Coca-Cola while American big-band jazz blasted out of the radio. It was the era of the Battle of the Coral Sea and Sydney was overrun with US Marines. They were the heroes of the day, helping to save our country from the maw of Japan's onrushing march southwards.

Dad first met our mum, Betty, on a double date at the fashionable Princes Restaurant in Martin Place during World War Two. The war was on their doorstep and lights had to be kept low to avoid potential bombing from above. On another night, Dad walked out of Princes in the early hours to see the spectral vision of a Japanese Mitsubishi Zero flying low above, a spotlight trained on it as it hummed and moved slowly across the night sky.

In my childhood, I discovered many unpolished and dusty trophies from Dad's car rally heyday languishing in the garage. These time-trial events involved driving day and night down unsealed bush tracks like a total maniac around places in country New South Wales such as Molong or Hill End. Dad's heroes were legendary but lunatic drivers like 'Gelignite Jack' Murray, Donald Campbell and Jack Brabham. He subscribed to *Wheels* magazine and was a keen follower of journalist and race-car driver Peter Wherrett. We often found ourselves at the speedway at the Sydney Showgrounds or at Warwick Farm for the car-racing fixtures. Formula 1, demolition derbies, the annual day-long TV coverage of the Hardie-Ferodo 500 at Bathurst with the gladiatorial Peter Brock Holden and Allan Moffat Ford clashes – anything with wheels, we were there.

Dad also loved Märklin train sets and had amassed them since childhood, stockpiling a huge collection. It had swollen to include miniature people, trees, platforms, houses, livestock and bridges, as well as miles of track – a virtual world. A blue rheostat controller shaped like a cube with a black chicken-head knob for speed (graduated in 10km/hr increments up to 200) and a red bezel light governed the motion of the trains. There was the distinctive smell of ozone from the arcing of the brushes or wheels on the track as the engines got hot, along with the hum of the rheostat and the clatter of the rolling stock. Dad built a room on the back of The Lodge, just off the kitchen, christened it the playroom and proceeded to nail pale reddish-brown Oregon shelves to the walls to run the trains around on, like a 360-degree multi-storey car park. It was a rough build and Mum must have told him to take it all down after a while, but the trains were always set up on the floor somewhere, along with a basic Scalextric slot car set that Kim and I would scurry our Mini Coopers and Lotuses around. Sometimes we headed to Waitara to the pro-level slot car track where we could experience how it was really done. It had an eight-lane banked track and a smaller, but wickedly challenging, ten-lane flat track, both coin-operated at twenty cents for fifteen minutes.

My father's job description was 'businessman'. When I was very young he sold 'Filter-Ray' blinds that protected the goods in shop windows from fading in the Australian sun. They made everything displayed in the window a muddy yellow colour, like looking through the end of a Lucozade bottle, and didn't exactly set the country ablaze. But his next company, called Karbonkraft, manufactured carbon paper – the magical stuff you sandwiched between sheets of paper to make carbon copies on your mechanical typewriter. It was a successful enterprise, and the typing pool was run by women who didn't like typing things twice. There was no chance of revision once a letter was dictated; it may as well have been inscribed in cuneiform tablets. The business grew and it soon moved into a factory at 4/10 Hannon Street, Botany, where it flourished for the next decade.

Watching
the test
pattern

Music was a big part of our family life, yet no one played an instrument. There was a Chrysler radiogram in the dining room, out of which blasted my parents' favourite records: Della Reese, Louis Armstrong, Duke Ellington, Artie Shaw (whom Dad had seen at The Trocadero in 1943) and the Latin sounds of Herb Alpert & the Tijuana Brass.

We also had a bamboo tiki bar with a built-in turntable. *Blue Hawaii*, an LP by The Polynesians, was invariably playing, featuring songs like 'Sweet Leilani' and 'The Hawaiian Wedding Song'. There were always parties and people drank more in those days, mixing hurricane-like cocktails. A trolley groaned under the weight of bottles of whiskey, brandy, cognac, vodka and crème de menthe, and soda siphons with their CO_2 chargers. Everyone smoked constantly. The war was still fresh in most people's minds and all my parents' friends and families had been involved in it. Maybe that's why they drank. To forget, or to remember. But they would laugh and drink like there was no tomorrow. These were lawless times before seat belts, random breath testing, speed cameras and all the security checks and balances we enjoy today.

Black and white television arrived in our house in 1961. When we switched it on, there was an audible thump, then the picture appeared through hectic horizontal lines and drizzled down onto the screen. We would always be fiddling with the vertical hold to stop the picture from rolling as the valves warmed up. And when we switched it off, the picture compressed into an intense white dot before vanishing off into infinity like a UFO.

TV could weave magic spells. Even the test pattern was a thing of wonder, but the first thing I saw that really caught me off-guard was The Beatles, around 1964. Their music was so upbeat and comforting, the combination of sounds completely joyous. I unpicked the staples of their centrefold in *TV Week* and glued it carefully inside the lid of my Globite suitcase to impress my school friends, but I don't recall them being impressed. Beatlemania caught on like the bubonic plague just weeks later.

Every year we'd go to the Easter Show at the Royal Agricultural Showgrounds, now known as Fox Studios. We always tackled the task in a clockwise direction, starting from the Paddington end. First stop was the woodchop competition, where giants of men made matchsticks out of huge tree trunks. Tasmanian champions dominated, especially members of the Youd family, moustached and heavily tattooed, with barrel-like bodies. They seemed heroic, like they were on an odyssey of some kind, strapped onto their massive upright logs, heaving into those giant eucalyptus trunks like vicious termites.

Next was the pavilion of wondrous new cars, shining under bright lights, all chrome and fins on rotating carousels adorned with beautiful and be-gloved female models who rotated along with them. Then we'd make a hasty trip through the farm animals' exhibitions and their stables of hay and manure, first prize for best chook or pig noted and quickly forgotten, followed by the art made from the fleece of sheep and goats. In the largest pavilion, massive fruit and vegetable displays were arranged like giant mandalas, often in the form of a multi-coloured map of the state of origin. These were judged like a beauty pageant in which all the states competed. In the cake- and scone-making competitions, pastoralist Queensland would always win.

The showgrounds were built around the Sydney Cricket Ground Oval, the SCG, which was where the most grandiose spectacles happened. One year we watched a man parachute in from the sky above. Another time someone with a jetpack buzzed around like an insect. But the high point of every year took place in the Hordern Pavilion: the show bags. With a budget of only a few coins, I rushed in a panic around the cavernous hall, seeking the one with the most lollies, comics and junky trinkets, until I was exhausted and had to be carried back to the car, always parked miles away, asleep on Dad's shoulders.

Our cars were Leylands, Holdens, Valiants and Fords that Dad would trade in every couple of years, and when he was in the motor trade he was hip to auto customising and got himself the numberplate KO 111. He said KO was for 'knockout' and the numbers a tribute to Lord Nelson, who sported one eye, one arm and one leg at the end of his life. Mum's car at one point was a white Ford Falcon 500 wagon with a customised BGM 505 – her initials, Betty Gwendoline Moginie.

The weekends were spent very much as a family, often exploring the countryside by car, sometimes bringing along one of our cousins or a school friend. We'd find out when the steam trains were running and stand on the railway bridge at Hornsby as they roared beneath us in a clamour of heat and noise. Before it was illegal, one of Dad's favourite things was to make a barbecue on the side of the road. Through Windsor, the Blue Mountains and Kangaroo Valley, where there was little kerb and guttering, he would steer the Leyland, Holden, Valiant or Ford into the scrub and we would be despatched to collect bits of rock to make a low, three-sided structure, onto which he would drop some chicken wire and some petrol to get the kindling going. After the explosion, on would go the snags and the chops. Potatoes and bananas would be thrown straight into the ashes, everything blackened in the ensuing conflagration. The best trips would also include a stop at the Golden Fleece service station in Mittagong, where the restaurant served chicken in a wicker basket with crumbed onion rings on a crisp gingham napkin.

A big night out for our family was going to The Coachman Restaurant on Bourke Street, Surry Hills. I had to get dressed up in my red velvet suit with bow tie and cufflinks. There was a live band with accordion, guitar and drums taking requests. Once I asked for Jimmy Webb's 'Macarthur Park', a big hit for Richard Harris at the time and an epic and difficult song, but I didn't know that then. The band members deflected, avoiding eye contact. 'Volare' or 'Delilah' would have been best.

Next door to us lived Harold and Yvonne Halvorsen. Originally from Norway, the Halvorsen boat dynasty went back generations in Australia. They built leisure boats, America's Cup boats, navy boats, any kind of boat. Harold drove a Bentley with 'HH' on the numberplate down to their boatsheds in Ku-ring-gai Chase National Park every single day until well into his nineties. Their son, Harvey, played the trumpet very loudly in the backyard during my infant years. Fortunately he became a notable boat designer instead. Boat fever ran through the family. At the age of eighty, one of Harold's brothers, Carl, was commissioned by the Norwegian government to hew a mast out of a huge Sitka spruce delivered to Bobbin Head. Carl, stripped to the waist, stood astride the huge tree trunk savagely brandishing his axe with the precision of a surgeon's scalpel. It took him three months to finish the job. He was a man of iron with seafaring genes but he could mix with both the hoi polloi and Hollywood stars, like Bob Hope and Alfred Hitchcock, spruiking his family's boats in California. We would visit Bobbin Head on the weekends to look at the boats. In the office there was a large framed photograph of Hitchcock, eyes agog, bottom lip extended theatrically, with a Halvorsen life buoy around his neck. I wondered about Hollywood, and how a celebrity like Hitchcock could even imagine his picture hanging in such a far-flung corner of the Earth.

Mount Alvernia Seminary and Retreat was up the road from our house and an episode of the television series *Whiplash* was filmed there with Peter Graves, star of *Mission Impossible* and *Flying High*. I saw him in the box seat, with his mop of blond hair, flicking the reins as he deftly swung the coach and horses off Burns Road into the grounds, with a Hollywood film crew to capture it on celluloid. At the age of five, I felt like I was witnessing magic.

From Year 6 onwards I started to commute to and from school and I would always take a shortcut through Mount Alvernia to get to the train station. It was like a Southern mansion with deep verandas, but hewn from Hawkesbury sandstone, with huge grounds and heavily shaded. I would run for fear of being caught, turning left through imposing gates and high-tailing it along an interminably long Tuscan red gravel driveway. It was the longest shortcut and it got my adrenalin going to trespass in this way. I'm sure the monks knew. With all those hours spent cloistered in there, they wouldn't have missed much.

Kim and I were enrolled to go to the exclusive Sydney Church of England Grammar School (commonly known as Shore), the boys' school in North Sydney that our dad had attended during the Depression. I started in the last year of primary school. Shore was Etonian in appearance, but I immediately took to it. I would get a pink card most Fridays, a sign of excellence, and came first in most subjects. There were good teachers and I felt really supported.

Before I started high school, the family took the Falcon 500 wagon down to Tasmania on the ship *Empress of Australia* for our summer holidays. I was seasick as soon as we cleared Sydney Heads and stayed that way all down the eastern seaboard. It was a rough voyage, ploughing and rolling across the whitecaps of the Tasman Sea, but sweet relief to sight land and cruise into the placid waters of Devonport a day and a half later.

I carried my first camera in my bag, a Kodak Box Brownie, which would take as many as eight large-format black and white photos per roll of film. It had to be wound on mechanically and I'd often expose the film accidentally by opening the camera when it hadn't latched properly onto the sprockets, leaving only a few photos intact.

On Tasmania's east coast at Bicheno, Dad got a massive seafood platter delivered to our room. I had never seen anything like it. Scallops, lobster, crab, bugs, oysters, all fresh from the pristine local waters. Towards sunset, I crossed the road down near the wharf and climbed a forty-foot-high mountain of empty scallop shells. I still remember the crunch underfoot.

We motored down the east coast to Hobart, where the traffic reports routinely said, 'No traffic today.' Road kill littered the highways. I counted 144 dead animals as we circumnavigated the island. Wedgetails and crows spiralled down and alighted on their carcasses.

We were there in the aftermath of the 1967 Black Tuesday bushfires. Whole towns had vanished. The village of Snug only had a few chimney stacks left standing as we drove solemnly through the ruins.

Despite all that, this was a beautiful holiday. We stopped at every 'strawberries and cream for 25c' stall by the roadside, and it was the first summer of daylight saving. The days seemed endless so far south and the light was different to Sydney – cold and clear.

I was now eleven-and-a-half years old and had a kind of confidence going. I was coming out of childhood and becoming more aware. In Tasmania things seemed to be in living colour for the first time, raw and vibrating with Antarctic clarity. But driving across the island westward into Queenstown was a shock. Copper mining had deforested the place. It resembled the pictures of Hiroshima we'd seen in *National Geographic* in the doctor's surgery waiting room. There was a threatening atmosphere. I thought there must be bad people, mad people, out there who had done this, until I found out that part of the reason for keeping the place denuded of vegetation was to bring the tourists in.

After traversing the west coast, we motored up to a motel just outside Burnie and across the road from a wild surf beach. We were biding our time for two days before the ship took us back up to the mainland. I experienced my first lava lamp in the motel lobby, mesmerised by its writhing fluidity – red blobs evolving and dissolving in a yellow liquid.

Luckily the weather was better for the return voyage, dead calm the whole way. One of many water dispensers on the ship was mounted on the wooden wall near our cabin. I was obsessed by the way the water came out so neatly when you pressed the shiny blue button, flowing into indigo-coloured paper cups embossed with the Australian National Line's 'ANL' logo on a yellow ship's wheel.

In the afternoon, my mother found me there, playing with it. She approached me and said, 'Jamie. I have to tell you something. You're adopted.'

I fiddled with the little cups.

'Are you okay?' she said.

I nodded, looking away, still fiddling with the cups, and she walked off.

There was no lightning bolt or trumpet voluntary, but questions began to scamper through my mind. Why did my people give me away? Was there something wrong with me? Did they give me away without a fight? Wasn't I good enough for them? I probably deserved to be abandoned.

I felt like a fake, a mistake. My aunt wasn't really my aunt, my cousins weren't my cousins. My brother wasn't my brother, and my parents weren't even my parents.

No questions were asked by me or explanations offered by my parents then, or for many of the years that followed. All I knew was that I had to get on board with the new paradigm.

Sinking
in a
straight line

We arrived home and I went straight into high school, having been accelerated a year. The buildings were big and cold with linoleum floors, high ceilings and draughty staircases like hospitals. Class sizes doubled, tripled, and there were many new boys who were older, and smart and loud. Some came from wealthy families. I was daunted by their brashness and self-confidence. I fell silent and shut down. Nothing external seemed of any consequence. Daydreaming became my whole world.

My newfound identity – or absence of identity – made me feel as if the rug had been pulled from beneath me. In the classroom, my work went into freefall. I was suddenly last in the class – thirty-third out of thirty-three. I started to stutter if asked to speak. And the work was much harder. We had languages now: Latin and French. Puberty was coming on like a locomotive, the body's chemicals and unfamiliar rhythms whizzing about inside. Discipline was tougher and dispensed liberally. Parents sent children to this school to toughen them up for the brutal world ahead. The school was rugby union mad and the sporting field was violent and bloody. I was always a forward or a lock in the scrum, bashed, bitten and thumped. Any idea of sport as a way of learning fairness and team spirit was lost on me. I had few friends, and with so much going on in my head, I'd retreat to the library at lunchtime to hide.

Although my adoption wasn't mentioned again by my parents or by me, in the tuckshop queue one day a boy hissed, 'You and your brother are bastards.' I assumed Kim had been told about his adoption and had confided in someone, but the two of us had never discussed it. Kim was in the year above me at school, a well-liked and confident boy with many friends. Though he didn't ignore me, he didn't exactly seek me out at school either. We were very different as people, but both of us were trying in our own ways to survive the competitive environment and the ever-present threat of violence that existed day to day within the playground, as well as the disciplinary code of the classroom. The tuckshop incident was a typical kind of brutalism that passed as normal behaviour – from the headmaster, the teachers and the students.

About that time, we moved south of Wahroonga to a double-storey Cape Cod house at 8 Ormiston Avenue, Gordon, so Dad could be closer to work, even though it only cut down his commute to Botany by eight minutes. It also meant Kim and I were a bit closer to school. The house was in a cul-de-sac beneath towering blue gums and jacarandas. There was a public golf course down the road, an abandoned dairy at the end of the ridge, a creek, and acres of bushland that I could wander around in freely.

We had a Seventh-day Adventist neighbour called Mills, and a family lived a few doors down in a doll's house version of Tara, the home of Scarlett O'Hara in *Gone with the Wind*. I was interested in their daughter but way too shy to say boo. I had no sisters and went to an all-boys school. Girls were alien to me, but I somehow knew I was wired heterosexually.

I had a small bedroom upstairs, deep in the roof of the Cape Cod. I chose the smallest room because it felt safer. There was a dressing room off Mum's bedroom, and that became my music space. I always loved music when I heard it, especially The Beatles. At age nine I was given an instrument called a Clarina, made of red plastic and with multi-coloured keys, which sounded like an oboe. I used to serenade the family from the back seat on car trips. Luckily no one seemed to mind. Emboldened, I progressed to a battery-powered organ, also with coloured keys, bought from Woolworths in Canberra on a family holiday. Once more inspired by The Beatles, I asked for and was given a steel-string Kapok guitar that someone had put nylon strings on. I loved the feeling of it buzzing through my body, and I learnt a few shapes from a chord chart from Tarantella, a music shop in Gordon.

I became interested in recording my organ and Kapok guitar, so I commandeered a portable National R2-503S tape recorder that Dad no longer used at work. I loved threading the empty spools with fresh tape, the smell of the oxide as it spun past, the caramel colour as it rotated, the magic of the sound of playback through the little speaker. Soon an H.G. Palmer fan-powered chord organ arrived, sounding something like an accordion. One of the windowed alcoves in the Cape Cod formed a booth with a tight sound in which I'd play guitar and use the bathroom scales as a foot stomp box. Later I bought a Grundig valve tape deck for $20, with a valve 'Magic Eye' level meter and no case, just the metal chassis. This was soon replaced by a stereo Sony TC-377, which was much cooler and easier to handle. The equipment nut in me was born. I did many recordings on this beast, even attempting a version of The Beatles' 'I Am the Walrus', overdubbing sounds by bouncing from track to track until the original sounds became inaudible.

Once I borrowed a Minimoog synthesiser for a week from a friend who I found out later was a drug dealer from Paddington.

I made a mountain of wild experimental recordings learning to use this marvellous thing. I fell in love with synthesisers. Taking me aside when he came to collect it, my friend reached into his coat and asked, 'What are you into, man?'

'Music?' I said innocently.

*

I got quite bored in my music room at times, but that boredom would always turn into something creative. Teaching myself to play and record music helped me make sense of the world, and as I clung to it, my outside world seemed to shrink. Maybe it was puberty, the adoption news or the rugby school, but I didn't want to know about anything apart from music, and I couldn't relate to anyone who wasn't into music. It became my refuge, a language I wanted to express myself in. The rest of my adolescence was like a fog. I was biding my time, waiting for something else to happen.

I didn't socialise or come downstairs if visitors arrived. I could see them walking up the path to the front door from the window. When uncles from either side of the family would demand my presence, Mum would say, 'He's okay. Leave him alone.' They were all returned World War Two veterans who felt life had to be lived to the full and had little time for shyness. They talked loudly, sonic booms amid raucous laughter, which I found terrifying, but their general unruliness may have been covering up the after-effects of war, including depression, nightmares and other psychosomatic disorders commonplace among returned soldiers. Uncle Bruce had served as an infantryman in Europe and worked the rest of his life for Legacy, the charity that looks after veterans struggling with health issues and families widowed by war. Uncle John had been a corporal in the 2/5th Commando Squadron in Kokoda from 1943 to 1945. He was a big man who came back weighing just thirty-five kilograms. But the most boisterous was Uncle Sydney, named after the city, who had served as an officer in Europe. Syd had given me a silver cup when I was a baby, inscribed with 'Mates Forever'. He had a snow-white moustache and a purple-pink face, the colour of magnolias in spring. None of these men would ever mention what happened to them or what they had seen.

From Tarantella I collected the weekly Top 40 chart and occasionally the *Boomerang Songster*, containing the lyrics of popular songs of the day. I was addicted to the Top 40 hit radio on 2UW and 2SM. I'd call up the station to win records with my knowledge of rock trivia. I knew Johnny Winter had been born in Texas, so they sent me Jose Feliciano's single 'Hi-Heel Sneakers / Hitchcock Railway'. In 1968 and 1969, pop, psychedelia and rock were crossbreeding, and singles could be over seven minutes long.

*

Dad loved Rudyard Kipling, and there were many of that author's books throughout the house. I suspect my brother was named after the character in his novel of the same name, *Kim* – Kimball O'Hara was the orphaned son of an Irish soldier. We had a printed version of Kipling's poem 'If', contained in a broken brown frame without glass, the paper faded to a coffee colour. Dad left it lying around the house and often recited it by heart.

If you can keep your head when all about you
Are losing theirs and blaming it on you,
If you can trust yourself when all men doubt you,
But make allowance for their doubting too;
If you can wait and not be tired by waiting,
Or being lied about, don't deal in lies,
Or being hated, don't give way to hating,
And yet don't look too good, nor talk too wise.

I would read it over and over, for its meaning but also for its metre. It was like a good song lyric that hit you between the eyes. I'm sure Dad left it around for his sons to absorb. There were a lot of life lessons in there, and the poem made plain that pitfalls lay in wait for me on the road ahead.

I made sure I didn't stand out at the rugby school, keeping my head down. A loose conglomerate of bullies and their acolytes who called themselves 'The Mob' would often pick some lone individual at random to bash up at lunchtime in the basement of the Benefactors Building while the masters turned a blind eye. One of 'The Mob' asked me to show him if I could play the F chord in 'Julia' by the Ted Mulry Gang. Like all tough guys, he was okay when he was on his own but not so much as part of the group. He handed me his guitar and I went *BRANG!*, playing an F with ease. They didn't pick on me after that.

Academically, I was an underachiever during high school and wasn't pushed by my parents. They weren't ever involved in me getting homework done, even after they discovered that I'd intercepted a damning school report at the letterbox and burnt it in the backyard incinerator. They seemed to see that I had some kind of promise, albeit one they couldn't quite grasp. This benefit of the doubt meant I was, thankfully, left to my own devices. But Wilbur Sawkins, my maths teacher in the last years of high school, insisted students keep notes on his lessons in an exercise book, just copying down what he wrote on the board. I found that writing it down helped me learn, as if the information went to my brain through my hand, and soon found myself at the top of the class.

I regret that I didn't take art at school. The art teacher, Ross Doig, had taught the great Australian painters Garry Shead and Tim Storrier when they were at Shore. The two would later take him out to lunch when he was an old man, a repayment for his mentorship. I had always drawn and doodled, and the art room looked intriguing – gloriously chaotic, cluttered with every kind of artwork, and it stank of turps and oil paint. Art seemed a luxury to me then; it was otherworldly. Across the hall from the art room was the woodwork room. I chose that instead. We made utilitarian things like wobbly pencil boxes with sliding lids and dodgy doorstops, learning to wield PVA glue and fretsaws and to nail timber.

In 1970 I brought a copy of The Beatles album *Let It Be* into music class. The original pressing was accompanied by a deluxe book of photos of the band. The teacher denounced the whole package as blatantly commercial, over-hyped and pretentious. That was upsetting, but otherwise music at the school was good. The teachers were accomplished English organists, in both the church and the classroom. I was complimented on my singing voice and became a short-lived treble in the choir until my voice broke. We sang from worn-out hymn books a few times a week. I loved the effect 'Jerusalem' had on me, a composition as deep as the ocean, with words by William Blake and music by Sir Charles Hubert Hastings Parry. It was great to sing en masse, and I grooved on the echo of the school chapel.

Most of us had to go to cadet camp every year in the last three years of school. It was compulsory, as was conscription, under the 1964 National Service Act. Like our forefathers, we believed we were all headed to the war in Vietnam at age twenty, a threat that was repeated like a mantra throughout childhood. When I learnt to strip and reassemble a Bren gun, I really learnt to strip and reassemble a Bren gun, believing I would need that skill when I was crawling around the jungle in Long Tan.

'What you people need is a bloody good war' could have been the school motto. Something that was echoed by Dad, who directed it at Kim and me more than once.

Cadet camp was always held in December in the blast furnace of the Australian summer. One year, on the day before we left, I was at St Leonards train station when a fellow student smashed his toe with a hammer in an effort to avoid going. He was surrounded by a circle of traumatised bystanders. He still had to go, mutilated toe and all.

The Australian Army had a base in Singleton that we reached via the long and winding Putty Road. As soon as we tumbled out of the buses there was a 'meat parade' to check us for venereal disease. Having to present our genitals for inspection in public to unsmiling army personnel was clearly designed to dehumanise. This is how they thought they could make men of us, or transform us into fourteen-year-old killing machines.

There were night exercises where we crawled on our bellies for miles through dry grass to take a hill from an enemy (another group of boys), sliding over ant nests and stones, gripping our Lee–Enfield 303 rifles for dear life. Sometimes we'd even encounter unexploded grenades and mortars. The area was frequently used as a bombing range by the Australian Army, and if they had shelled us I wouldn't have been surprised.

During the day flies swarmed, always there in our eyes, mouth and ears. On bivouac, we had one pint of water to last the day in face-melting heat. Dust was everywhere and we had to keep our rifles, the brass on our uniforms and our gaiters spotlessly clean and ready for random inspections conducted at all hours of the day and night. When a bushfire came over the hill towards us, we were evacuated not by army trucks but on foot. Mother's boys were fainting randomly as we route-marched our way from the flames. I dreamt of getting home and eating SPC tinned peaches in the bath.

At night, members of the school army band, for sport, would throw tins of rations into the fire and watch them explode, and then we had to jump over the flames in time to avoid the flying metal shards. I should have joined the band because they had the least to do and didn't have to crawl around with guns at all hours. But, as potential infantrymen, we were allowed to blast a car wreck with the Bren gun from the other side of a huge paddock.

The noise was extreme and the recoil against my shoulder was thuggish and violent, leaving bruises and stretched tendons. That actually was fun.

As a reaction to all this discipline, people would do crazy things, like laugh loudly when things weren't funny. I remember being picked out of the parade to clean out the latrines. 'Thunderbox Detail' was to be avoided at all costs, but it was better than standing at attention for hours in the 40-degree heat until there was a thump on the ground as some poor soul passed out.

In the final year, I had the good sense to join the Signal Corps. All that was required was to sit by the radio day and night taking messages. One day we were flown up in a Hercules aircraft with the rear cargo door open, hanging by our webbing seat belts, when the pilot put us into a vertiginous climb. All I could see was the Fred Williams–like Australian bush rotating steadily, thousands of feet below. For a moment I couldn't hear the engine at all, and a silence fell. Everything was suddenly big, like I was being shown the world in all its glory for the first time.

Gone
fishin'

Throughout high school I rode my pushbike on weekends and afternoons around the bitumen streets and clay tracks of Gordon. In summer the air was filled with the blue mists of eucalyptus oil. The soundtrack was primarily The Beatles, followed by bubblegum like The Archies, The Royal Guardsmen and 1910 Fruitgum Company. Also 'Build Me Up Buttercup' and singles from Atlantic, Motown and Stax. Songs like 'Patches' by Clarence Carter, powerful voices with smart arrangements, great backbeats and extraordinary bass lines, along with horns, strings and lots of backing vocals. When I ventured downstairs I would listen to records on our Pioneer stereo, which my Uncle Ted had obtained from David Jones. Apparently, it had fallen off the back of a truck when he was working there as a storeman and packer. Married to Dad's sister Betty, Ted was a Cockney who adored my mum and her gentle, light-hearted ways.

Mum would always read the *Australian Women's Weekly* for women's business and Maggie Tabberer's fashion column for style tips, as well as Charmian Clift's column in the *Sydney Morning Herald*. We'd tune in to *Beauty and the Beast* on ATN-7, where the women panellists always bested the grumpy and outnumbered male host. One day, on King Street in the city while driving the Valiant, we nearly ran over one of the Beasts, a jaywalking Stuart Wagstaff.

Every year we would go south to Lake Tabourie for holidays and stay at one of the shacks owned by the Gillies family, who owned many houses there, as well as the shop and real estate franchise. It was a six-hour drive in those days on serpentine roads that seemed endless. The car would routinely overheat or tyres would blow. We would always stop at the pub at Milton for a pink lemonade. Kim and I knew we were getting close when we spotted the distinctive shape of Pigeon House Mountain. Captain James Cook gave it its name on his journey along the eastern seaboard, but for some reason we called it Mame, perhaps after the woman Louis Armstrong was so obsessed with in the song of the same name that Dad had on heavy rotation in the house. In fact, the mountain resembled a woman's upturned breast. The local Aboriginal people must have thought so too, calling it Didthul, which means the same thing. The journey ended when we reached a sun-bleached wooden bridge, where the bolts nearly jumped out of the beams as we drove across, and saw a particularly monstrous golden Leyland cypress conifer standing like a sentinel, welcoming us to Lake Tabourie.

The shacks were mostly fibre-cement or weatherboard. We often rented one by the lake called 'Gone Fishin'. Tabourie was idyllic and time seemed to stop. The ever-present threat of bushfires filled the nostrils – there was always one happening somewhere nearby – along with the whiff of septic tanks leaking into the lake. One year they opened the lake to the sea to wash out the muck, an event heralded with much pomp and ceremony in the *Milton-Ulladulla Times*. A big crowd watched as the bulldozer dug the channel. The lake was a freshwater ecosystem. Australia in the sixties was not an environmentally aware place.

Kim and I were given a plywood canoe for Christmas one year. Dad lashed it to the roof of the Holden with octopus straps to take it down to Tabourie and swathed it under the family's omnipresent weighty green canvas tarpaulin. We set off on Boxing Day and it all slid off about fifteen kilometres into our trip, near Carlingford. I'll never forget the sound as the entire payload hit the concrete surface of Pennant Hills Road. Miraculously, no one was hurt, and we bundled it all back and continued on, Dad and Kim managing to repair the canoe later with much fibreglass and epoxy.

Tabourie had no fences so we could roam freely across anyone's grass, trimmed short by local kangaroos. Most days we would walk the grey sand track alongside bracken fern and burrawangs to the surf beach. I loved the South Coast's tall eucalypts and empty beaches; they all seemed untrifled-with. But once we'd reached our place on the sand we were constantly strafed by low-flying aircraft from HMAS *Penguin* in Nowra, swooping so low we could see the faces of the pilots and bombardiers as we lay on our beach towels. I crossed over the sand bar to Crampton Island one day on the low tide, but the tide rose and on my way back I was hit by two rogue waves approaching me from opposite directions. I thought I was going to drown. I told Mum and Dad when I returned, but they didn't seem too concerned. I wrote a letter to my grandparents about it, complete with a hand-drawn map of the island and adjoining coast, arrows depicting the direction the waves were travelling, and a stick figure representing myself.

The days drifted by as we paddled the canoe on the estuary or walked to the shop for lollies. I liked to wander around wearing my duffle coat and desert boots with a pair of binoculars around my neck, a would-be nature watcher. Sometimes we'd go for a drive south through Termeil State Forest and I'd count the termite mounds I'd see from the car.

We'd head to Bawley Point, a desolate lump of granite jutting into the ocean. From the Gantry, the remains of the old timber wharf put there to get the cedar out of the area by ship in the mid-1800s, you could see stingrays and grey nurse sharks circling in a dance in the clear water below.

Dad loved boats just as much as cars and toy trains and was a life member at the Royal Sydney Yacht Squadron at Kirribilli. When we weren't at Tabourie, we'd take out a Halvorsen cruiser closer to home, navigating Cowan Creek and surrounding waters north of Sydney. We'd head out in the afternoon from the long wharf that hugged the northern shoreline. These days the whole thing is a marina full of million-dollar vessels that are rarely used, but then it was a boat-building and vessel-hire mecca with rows and rows of gleaming Halvorsen cruisers with their teak or maple topsides and spotted gum hulls. We would take out a 26-footer that slept five, or a 36-footer that slept eight. While he was still alive, my grandfather James would come with us. In the evenings we'd drag up a mooring or drop the pick in one of the many bays and inlets, Refuge Bay being the most protected from the weather. Dad would fish and often pull up mulloway, yellowjackets, a bream or a flathead, his lines rigged accordingly. Pulling up catfish would always traumatise me as he would bash them to death against the hull with his longneck of Reschs Pilsener.

Kim and I would row the dinghy about and swim. We'd always eat onboard and play Scrabble, or games like draughts or Squatter, which was like Monopoly for pastoralists – those with the most sheep at the end of the game won. The cliffs of the Hawkesbury River rose majestically on either side as we headed upstream, massive ramparts of golden sandstone thrusting up into the sky in the afternoon light. Under the waterfall at Refuge Bay, icicles of cold water fell from so high that it hurt your head. At night we would find a calm berth and drift off to sleep with just the gentle undulations and sloshing of the boat.

One summer we rented a house on the coast at Hawks Nest. Dad beach-fished for whiting and I walked the endless sandhills. We spent the nights listening to The Beatles' *White Album* on a portable Sanyo turntable–stereo combo with only one speaker working, the one with the vocals in it, and peeling mountains of prawns for dinner while killing hundreds of flies with a plastic fly swatter I was given for Christmas.

After that summer we returned to the South Coast and concluded that we preferred it to the North Coast. We rented a house on the beach at Culburra, a three-hour journey from Sydney, and in the shack behind us we met the Thorley family. Judge Barrie Thorley was an important man of letters in legal circles and his fellow judges came down over Christmas to drink insane amounts of alcohol once they'd hung up their robes for the year. Not a sober judge in sight.

Our family hung out with the Thorleys and their two daughters, Sara and Rachel. I got *Sergeant Pepper* for Christmas and it was the soundtrack of that summer. I played guitar at nightly barbecues – Beatles songs, requests or made-up little tunes.

'You know, you're really good at playing that thing,' said Sara.

No one had said that to me before.

Eventually Dad bought a block of land at Culburra and designed and built a house, with a barbecue made from local bush rock to cremate our food. Number 201 Penguin Head Road had a killer view south from the headland over a huge expanse of water for seven miles. A southerly could gain megatons of ferocity before it jettisoned itself into the house. Any tin shed we built on the block got blown into the stratosphere, but the house, in essence a brick monolith, never budged a millimetre.

We could see Currarong way in the distance. At night, the Australian Navy used to bombard the bushland outside the town from Jervis Bay as part of their regular naval exercises. With all of its surreal descending lights, detonations and flares, you could imagine what Dresden was like in 1945.

My nylon-string guitar continued to be my constant companion. I'd discovered Julian Bream and his Bach Lute Suites Nos 1 and 2 at Tarantella, and I was teaching myself to read music by listening to his RCA recording and playing along by ear with the score open in front of me.

Building
a fire

Late in the first year of high school, John Royle and I were out on the asphalt beneath the sandstone and brick edifice emblazoned by our school motto, *Vitai Lampada Tradunt*: 'They hand on the Torch of Life'. John was a Mosman boy, a bit nervous but more serious than the others in our year. And he played the flute.

'The flute is such a shithouse instrument,' I said.

John knocked me to the ground. WHACK! I passed out momentarily, but I had more respect for him after that and, as can happen, we became good friends.

The next year I met Chris Hodgkinson. Chris had intense eyes under dark brows, and a nose with a bit of a ski jump on the end of it. He was skinny, blond, affable, a relaxed sort of character. He played guitar, and John, he and I hung out together and formed a loose musical alliance. We were the misfits of the school, unlike the rugby, cricket or rowing superstars that graced the front cover of the school magazine, *The Torch Bearer*, or the lawless ones of 'The Mob'. I had discovered music was a friend to me, and now music was becoming a way to make friends.

Our headmaster, Basil Holmes 'Jika' Travers, was a brilliant sportsman back in the forties and fifties, a handy cricket all-rounder who also played rugby for England. Jika was sports mad, and neither he nor his school administration embraced the pop music and long hair of the late sixties and seventies that was overrunning the world. If your hair touched your collar you could be caned. It was cane law at Shore. There were drills, which meant running around the quadrangle for forty-five minutes on a Friday afternoon and being struck hard on the back of the legs by the baton of a sergeant major, and weekend detentions (simply called Saturdays) deployed as a way of controlling undesirable behaviour. We were all being prepared to lay down our lives in Vietnam and no discussion would be tolerated. The school represented the old-world view at a time when society had split in two. Our fathers and uncles had been shaped by battle in their formative years as well. Young people like me couldn't communicate with those who were obsessed with war, especially such a tone-deaf one as Vietnam, but new bands like Country Joe and the Fish were singing songs that denounced it. I was definitely against it on conscientious grounds; it seemed more about destroying the ideology of communism than anything else. But there was self-interest too – who wants to die young? Chris, John and I were estranged by the school's relentless pursuit of excellence on the field, in rowing and in the academic world, where good marks meant you could ascend to the rank of doctor or lawyer, or become as wealthy as Croesus in business. We really couldn't have cared less about all that. We were all about music.

*

John, Chris and I formed our own schoolboy band. I was still playing my H.G. Palmer organ. After I politely queried Chris over his fudging of the C to G7 chord change in 'Chewy Chewy' by 1910 Fruitgum Company he said, 'Well, if you think you can do it better, play it yourself!' I figured it out that night at home on my guitar and by the next day's rehearsal I was the superior guitarist of the two of us. I bought a $20 Westone electric guitar from Tarantella and we became a twin-guitar band overnight.

In the second year of high school, Chris introduced me to Andrew James, whom he had met at tennis coaching. He lived not far from me in the oddly named The Chase Road. Andrew was a wizard on the bass, with fingers that flew nimbly up and down the fretboard. We christened him Bear. Even though we went to different schools, we were in the same year, two shy boys who would seek each other out, walk the leafy streets and talk music. Bear's parents, May and Bob, were British to their bones – £10 immigrants who had upped stumps for the promise of jobs and the sun and sand of 1950s Australia.

Bear and I listened to the prog-rock warlords on cassette. Yes were a favourite. These bands could play, and we got used to their overly complex arrangements, which helped our guitar fingers to get moving. For band practice we'd go to my house, Chris's place in Bangalla Street, Warrawee, or across the road to Rob Stevens's house. Rob had a piano in another room, where I would escape to improvise soft dreamy pieces. I loved the overtones, the density of sound, the clangorous voice of pianos, and played whenever I could get my hands on one, in between making a caterwauling hash of Rolling Stones and Easybeats numbers with the band.

One day, John said, 'Hey, I know this guy with glasses. He sings and air-drums his way around Mosman.'

Rob Hirst, age fifteen, was soon lugging his Star drum kit up the stairs of the Cape Cod. His drums were a lava design, all reds, blues and greens. From the first whack, he had a great beat. We played whatever popped into our heads – Creedence Clearwater Revival songs, The Who, The Beatles, The Monkees. Bear and I looked at each other in amazement, enjoying the din of it, and Rob's uncontrolled laughter, hollering and general abandon. We were now dealing with a hyperactive child extrovert, but he could really play, unlike others we had jammed with – essentially blokes who just owned a drum set. He'd learnt the rudiments of rolls and paradiddles from being in his school cadet band, rather than electing to be cannon fodder like me with my .303 rifle and gaiters. He said the band unit in cadets at his school, Sydney Grammar, was a complete bludge. I could still barely play guitar (it sounds like cats being tortured when I play the tapes I made at the time) but it was a start, and our band was born. We called ourselves Schwampy Moose, a Creedence-inspired bayou reference.

We rehearsed again at the Cape Cod, which Mum and Dad tolerated, but the neighbours quickly put an end to it. There was no money to book rehearsal rooms – we didn't even know what a rehearsal room was. Any living room would do, so we'd get together at someone's house in Pymble, Killara, Vaucluse, Avalon – anywhere. Friends would ring up: 'Quick, the folks are out. Come around for a few hours if you wanna make some noise.' Other times we'd go to Rob's house at Balmoral Beach in Mosman. After practice we'd set up our amps on the veranda, directing them and our nascent repertoire in a spray across the whole suburb, pretending we were The Beatles on the Savile Row rooftop.

Chris's place had fewer distractions for rehearsing, but a neighbour once walked in and quietly insisted, in his polite North Shore way, that if he had to listen to us we should at least tune our guitars, and he patiently helped us to do so.

When Rob joined we became a real band; the whole thing lifted. Previously, anyone would join in on our jams. Neighbours would yelp into crappy PA systems, friends would ride around the room on bicycles. But now it was starting to sound good and everything else became peripheral. There was attrition as we made headway. Chris soon got the boot because he would turn his amp way down and use a music stand onstage. John was dropped after a while, as we didn't need flute. Such vaulting ambition and much collateral damage, but somehow we still remained friends.

Rob became singer and drummer and Bear had an angelic voice for harmonies. I did a little reluctant backup singing but was getting way more into guitar, and we could play on the fly, winging it without any conversation or explanation. We wanted to be a power three-piece somewhere between Mountain, Cream and New Zealand band the La De Da's.

I was terrified at our first gig – a small party in a house on Eastern Road, Turramurra. By now the three of us were all between fifteen and sixteen years old. I thought everyone was gawking at me and that my ears were too big. It was an odd phase, like my stuttering episode. But I was thrilled with the experience of playing in a band more than I was embarrassed by it. There was something monastic and deep about the whole thing. It wasn't about being an entertainer; I felt needed, part of something. Being in a band meant belonging.

Rob was good at getting us work and we played a few school dances. My sex education was a ritual observed from the stage: buses of girls were dropped off at the boarders' dance followed by the inevitable gyrating and groping of the girls on the dance floor, usually in the dying minutes before the buses whisked the girls away again.

Schwampy Moose did a lunchtime concert at the assembly hall at my school and the boys seemed to like it, but during our version of The Beatles' 'I'm a Loser', Jika Travers ran up onstage and turned off the power to our amps, then ran back off as fast as he could. He didn't say anything. It must have been a silent protest of some kind. We were schmucks to him and the school. We switched our amps back on and continued, somewhat deflated.

My parents bought me a Weidig upright piano for my seventeenth birthday, from an ad in the *Trading Post*. It cost $110 and came from a house in Cammeray. It was lugged up the stairs to the music room of the Cape Cod, where I spent even more of my days and nights figuring out chords and songs on it. I had been asking for a piano for a few years but hadn't realised how magical a thing it really was until it finally arrived. All possible music was now at my fingertips, like a puzzle to solve, and it was as if I was being swallowed whole by it.

It dawned on us that Rob couldn't sing and drum at the same time the way he wanted to, and we all agreed we needed a frontman. We had no luck until Ian Chambers turned up for a couple of rehearsals after reading an ad Rob had placed in the classifieds in the *Sydney Morning Herald*. Ian was into Black Sabbath, Deep Purple and Dio, and sounded a bit like Ozzy Osbourne when he sang. But he soon stopped showing up, and we sat, demoralised, waiting for him to arrive. Still, we used the delays to write our own music, and early songs like 'Gettin' Gone', 'Country Stomp', 'Do Me a Flavour', 'Blue December' and 'Crystal Radio' came out of these times.

We christened the band FARM, unaware there was a psychedelic band with the same name plying their trade in Illinois. It was an acronym for Fucking All Right Mate. Rob duly designed a business card with the name at the top, a doctored image of Blinky Bill the koala walking along purposefully brandishing the Eureka flag below that, and the logo 'Collective Ego' and his home phone number at the bottom. In the meantime, our ex-guitarist Chris and school friend John Garrett were putting together a tour for us up and down the coast of New South Wales. It was the summer of 1973–4. I was pleased Chris still wanted to be involved after being turfed out of the band. Determined to find a singer for the tour, Rob put another ad in the *Sydney Morning Herald* classifieds. Peter Garrett – no relation to John – was the only person who responded. A band putting together a trip up and down the New South Wales coast in summer was right up a surfer like Pete's alley. He wanted a summer job and our ad ticked all the boxes.

Rob's alma mater, Sydney Grammar School, was less averse to rock than my school, and we were granted permission to do the occasional concert or rehearsal in their Science auditorium in College Street, Sydney. Late in 1973, that is where we first set eyes on Pete. Three years our senior, he had long since left school. He sat in the audience at a safe distance while we fiddled around with our amps (nothing much has changed). He looked intimidating, his gangly limbs draped over a couple of seats, long white Johnny Winter hair, monstrously tall with piercing eyes under a heavy brow. He appeared to be snarling, and I thought he was going to kill us.

We launched into a couple of songs and he sang along in a kind of high-pitched voice, one leg thrust forward. If we were expecting John Fogerty, this wasn't it. A kind of trilly stream-of-consciousness improvisation emanated when he couldn't remember the words to 'Locomotive Breath'. However, when we embarked on a free-form blues he was clearly in his element, rapping and improvising convincingly over the top.

Afterwards, Rob and I went behind the curtain.

'What do you think?' he asked.

'It's unusual, I guess. Maybe he's got something.'

Pete was in. He was the sole applicant, and he conveniently owned a large white PA system. I don't think we thought about it for more than a few seconds, but those few seconds were the beginning of an odyssey and countless years on the road together.

Pete must have liked what he heard, too. He understood that there was something in the raw sound of the band. The blast of Rob's kick drum, the quirkiness of the two mother's boys on guitars, and the seriousness we projected. He told us he'd been driving trucks in Canberra, delivering domestic heating oil, and doing a degree at ANU, and was up in Sydney to visit his family. His musical pedigree was a Canberra blues-rock band called Devil's Breakfast. It comprised our future accountant, Damian Street, on bass, and future bus driver, Richard Geeves, on drums. Someone called Trevor played guitar, and Pete sang and played harmonica – a power three-piece plus singer in the mould of Free or local heroes Hush. Their act culminated with Pete and Damian jumping off the PA stacks simultaneously and colliding mid-stage on the final crashing note of their set. I never saw them but was told, probably by Pete, that they were seminal.

That summer tour began at the Corrimal School of Arts Hall, though no plaque dated 1973 dignifies this sacred site. After the show, Bear and I slept in sleeping bags in the public toilets at Bellambi Beach, with the perfume of the White King deodoriser blocks in the urinals. We didn't have any money and hadn't thought through the accommodation concept fully. Pete and Richard Geeves slept at a safe distance in a tent out on the idyllic headland. The next night Bear and I discovered the best system was sleeping 'head in' underneath the front of the Hillman Hunter on the soft sand of the beach. Once I woke suddenly and banged my head on the sump. Another time we woke to a blazing sun with crabs crawling all over us. Sometimes we'd try to sleep in the hall after we played a gig. On one occasion we made it until 7am before we were evicted by the janitor. Another time, an elderly woman from the hall committee arrived at dawn and started to shriek at the sight of our sleeping entourage. Pete's deep voice growled theatrically from his sleeping bag, 'Now listen, sweetheart …' He sounded more menacing than intended and she ran away, alarmed.

As it rolled on, the tour was well attended. In summer holidays, these normally sleepy seaside hamlets were full of adolescents with nothing to do at night, and 'Top Sydney Rock Band FARM', as our poster boasted, was the only noise in town. We'd charge $2 at the door, Chris would take the money and my technically gifted school friend Craig Alexander did lights with his home-soldered lighting panel – a Year 11 woodworking project – and a bunch of par cans on stands with coloured gels over the top. We played covers: 'Locomotive Breath' by Jethro Tull, 'Jumpin' Jack Flash' by the Stones, 'Take Me Down Easy' by Jo Jo Gunne, 'Race with the

Devil' by Gun, 'Yours is No Disgrace' by Yes, and anything else we could get from the start to the end of.

We played Nowra, Batemans Bay, Bermagui, Tathra. I learnt to bodysurf under Pete's guidance. No bathing or showers for us, just a surf. After the tour, Pete was studying law at the University of New South Wales (UNSW) and none of us was sure if he was going to return to the fold.

When I left school at the end of 1973, I didn't know what I wanted to do with my life. Kim had repeated his final school year and then opted to study winemaking, but I hadn't given it any thought, not for a moment. I was still in my teen daydream, blissfully unaware of everything. So, like Rob and Bear, I chose the ultimate delaying strategy – university.

I spent an agonising night before enrolment day sitting at our wobbly circular dining table, studying the university literature, thinking that the courses I'd qualified for with my mediocre marks weren't for me. The next day, I randomly chose a psychology degree.

Mum was concerned: 'Only mad people do that.'

TWO

That lost Australian guitar sound

I ended up moving across to a straight Science degree, majoring in Physics and Mathematics. After three years at Sydney University, I'd be able to do a qualifying year to get into Architectural Acoustics at UNSW and learn to design buildings for good sonics, thereby pursuing my passion for sound, music and noise.

University involved a long commute, with my briefcase and umbrella, from Gordon to Redfern station, and then a walk to campus. I wasn't your typical student living in Newtown sharehouses eating instant noodles. Science students had to be sitting in the auditorium by 9am sharp, Monday to Friday, for the Maths lecture. The professor had been frantically chalking hundreds of formulas up on a massive multi-panelled blackboard since 8.30 and we had to scribble it all down by hand before he rubbed it all out. We couldn't amble into a tutorial at 2pm half pissed and then go to the pub like a good Arts student.

There were often well-known bands playing at the university. I saw Stevie Wright on the Front Lawn and Billy Thorpe, Mother Goose, Ayers Rock and Blackfeather at lunchtime shows at the Union Theatre. Aussie bands were loud and raw. They had long hair, beards and 100-, 200- or 300-watt guitar amps with slope-fronted quad speaker boxes stacked on top of straight-fronted quad boxes. Guitars weren't supposed to go through the PA system so they weren't miked up, just the bass drum and vocals, usually. The guitar tone was clean, powerful and bass-y. It sounded tough. That particular Australian guitar sound of the seventies has been lost. All local amplifier manufacturers died out, killed by the lifting of tariffs in the eighties. Names like Lenard, Strauss, Vadis, VASE, Phoenix and Goldentone live now in the sentimental landscape of ancient times. But that un-finessed and thick guitar sound has never left my heart. When Deep Purple came to Australia in 1971, Lenard built hundreds of speaker boxes as part of the band's production demands, then sold them for $5 apiece without speakers. I needed these desperately so bought two. To get the money I had to raid my coin collection and sell my sterling silver threepence pieces from the George V era for their face value. Christmas puddings were never the same again.

Hornsby Police Boys Club hosted all-ages gigs with spandexed, long-haired prog-rock bands whose guitar and drum solos and general wizardry were their calling card. Whether with Bear or Rob, I would go along to whatever was on as long as it was free to get in. I also saw The Masters Apprentices and Zoot playing at the Showgrounds, also in spandex, but these bands sounded brilliant. Doug Ford from The Masters impressed me greatly as a guitar player, as did the whole band, and with Zoot (in a heavily Who-influenced phase), the sight of Rick Springfield throwing his white SG guitar into the air was unforgettable.

Around 1973 I had discovered Dutch band Focus. Their double LP *Focus III* was mostly instrumental, the singing more like yodelling, but Jan Akkerman's machine-gun bursts of wiry guitar made me go crazy. I'd try to copy these unhinged and blazing phrases by slowing down a tape I had made of the record. It was on high rotation daily. I really caught something in Akkerman's playing. He was different from the usual rock-star guitar players of the day, not as blues-based. He had a gypsy soul like Django Reinhardt, the technique of Julian Bream and the pure abandon of Jimi Hendrix. Bear and I saw him at the Hordern Pavilion on 16 July 1974. I was eighteen. The place was foggy with marijuana smoke and we were thirty feet from the stage. Akkerman came on in leather pants, holding a glass of red wine, and my jaw was on the floor from the first note. He was loud and confident and played with so much expression, feeling and speed if required, but with that gypsy roughness. I felt like I had been to the mountaintop and received holy orders. Playing guitar was what I was going to do for the rest of my life.

Bear bootlegged the gig on his National Panasonic cassette recorder with a microphone hidden in his hat, and it is still the most amazing concert I have ever heard. You could fairly pigeonhole Akkerman as playing European progressive music, but it was highly melodic and presented in a simple four-piece format. If the yodelling got too much I would ignore it and just listen to the guitar. It was pure, with so much feeling when he swelled and bent the notes, but also gnarly and ragged. He seemed to enjoy his mistakes, and that was a big part of the appeal for me.

What I heard in his playing was the confluence of influences in the geography of Holland, sounds reaching him from Britain (Bream, Hank Marvin), France (Django), the USA (Wes Montgomery) and Spain (Paco de Lucia, Andrés Segovia). He put it all together in his own unique way. He switched me on to those other players, too, and I'm forever grateful. (I got to tell him this when I was lucky enough to meet him in Holland in 2011.)

Punk came along and wiped the floor clean of progressive rock in the ensuing years, but to me Akkerman transcended shifting music fashion. He was a player who could breathe fire, above Hendrix, Page, Clapton, Rory Gallagher or any of them. I was playing with my fingers on the right hand, classical style. Thinking I was a bit of a hermit and an anomaly anyway, I locked myself in the music room and intensively taught myself to play from listening to the radio, the Bach Lute Suites sheet music, and Akkerman. I'd buried any thoughts about where this mysterious passion for music might have sprung from, and no one in the family, or extended family, showed interest in playing any kind of instrument or could show me the shortcuts. So off I went to Robertsons, a local music shop, where the guitar teacher got me onto some Carcassi studies for my right hand, which he adapted for plectrum style. I just wanted to be more like Akkerman and get his speed and clarity. After three lessons I was on my way.

*

We toured the next summer, 1974–5, but Pete, now undertaking his bar exams, couldn't do all the gigs, so we enlisted Rob's motorbike-riding friend Nigel to fill in on singing and another blow-in, Peter Edwards, to play really good blues harp and be our roadie. Our specialty was a killer twenty-minute rendition of The Doors' 'Roadhouse Blues'. I grew my hair and sported a wispy beard, a reaction to the years of the militaristic short back and sides of school. Bear and I spent time playing lots of music in his Hillman, mainly prog rock, that Jan Akkerman bootleg from the Hordern Pavilion. On a night off in Moruya we saw Company Caine play the School of Arts Hall. The guitarist, Dave Caine, looked really bombed, but he had magic in his fingers. I had my first beer in the pub before the concert, but people kept handing them to me and I ended up having six. I was completely pissed for the first time ever, so that might have coloured the experience as I stood swaying wide-eyed and open-mouthed in front of Dave's amp.

Touring was my first taste of freedom. It was so innocent when I look back: it was all about the music. Drugs, girls and adulation weren't important. Neither was money – no one got paid. If it went over well with the surfers and holidaymakers, that was enough for us.

By the time we played Port Macquarie, Pete had returned to the fold. His white Devil's Breakfast PA blew up early in the set and we refunded the money to the few punters there. That night the Hells Angels gave Bear and me shelter in their clubhouse across the road from the hall. They drank much beer but abided by the moral code of their colours, looking after their own and others in need. We slept on the kitchen floor, me with my head next to the garbage bin.

A well-known Newcastle band called Rabbit played the Port Macquarie pub the next day. Pete was staying there with his girlfriend and came downstairs to watch. He seemed to me like he was from another planet – studying law and driving trucks, he had attitude. He was articulate and loved to talk about the state of the world. A hedonist who liked a joint and a good set of waves, there was a stainless-steel quality to him, a lack of vulnerability. He seemed impregnable. I had never met anyone quite like him. I didn't yet know that he would become a father figure, a taskmaster and the voice of the songs we would all write. But that night, he was completely natural as he danced to the beat of Rabbit, with that long-limbed way he moved, still with thin white surfer hair hanging down. Our band was an unfolding story, but after getting his law degree, he declared, 'I'm going to put all of my eggs into FARM's basket.'

A dismissal
and a
tuning

Campus life at Sydney University was a bit daunting for me. It was a big university with thousands of people promenading about. At school I'd been socially awkward and would run in the opposite direction of parties, but in my first year of uni I went to one in Turramurra, close to where I lived. I had been dreading it all day. But when I got there, I realised everybody was struggling. Some talked too loud, or drank too much, or were bores that would pin you to a wall if you let them. Some were very cool and aloof, others seemed to want to talk about important things, like politics; others just said dumb shit. I realised that I was only as good or as bad as what came out of my mouth. So I learnt, slowly, to relax in that environment and be myself.

At the end of first year I'd had a girlfriend who studied Economics with Bear. I thought she was out of this world. I was in love, and she had no precedent. There was an unspoken reticence on both sides, a shyness or naivety. After a few months she'd emphatically moved on to someone from the more ordered and familiar world of economics. That was traumatising and, typically, I hung on in hope of a reunion. It took me way too long to figure out that the moment had passed. I had a lot to learn in that area. I promised myself I would do the abandoning in future.

One lunchtime I escaped into the sanctuary of the Union Theatre and saw David Lean's epic film *Ryan's Daughter*. The landscapes of the Dingle Peninsula in the west of Ireland took my breath away, as did the confronting lovemaking scene in the meadow lined with bluebells. A tantalising image that I had little knowledge of but yearned to experience for myself.

*

After a Physics exam on 11 November 1975, I walked out of Sydney University's Carslaw Building at 5pm to see the Whitlam dream had ended. Angry students were marching up and down with placards and megaphones. In the three hours the exam had taken, his Labor Government had been dismissed by Governor-General John Kerr. The far-reaching policies Whitlam initiated had cost a fortune and the conservative opposition blocked supply in the Senate. Kerr became a target for all and sundry on the left for his role in unseating a democratically elected government. He was the Queen's man on the ground, a staunch royalist and supplicant, often seen sporting a top hat, someone who belonged back in the Menzies era.

All hell broke loose in Australia. Whitlam himself had believed he would only get one term to rush through so many sweeping changes, and even though he was briefly re-elected in 1974, it was effectively what happened. Government was promptly delivered back to the conservatives in a landslide election result.

Before Gough had taken the reins of power in 1972, Vietnam had raged and Australia had snoozed for twenty-three years under a Coalition government. He recast the country from day one into a new world, creating a whirlwind of much-needed change that used up all of his political capital in that short term in office. Free medical care, free university education, women's rights, Aboriginal recognition, environmental safeguards, Legal Aid, buying Jackson Pollock's *Blue Poles*, the single mother's benefit, abolishing conscription and getting the country out of the Vietnam War were just a few of the things now enshrined in the national estate. There was a new pride in our country and a perceivable cultural shift, where it was cool to write songs and make films about Australia and not kowtow to overseas trends. Not just bush balladry and *Skippy* but the angular Melburnian wit of Skyhooks, followed soon after by the human postcard vignettes of Don Walker and Cold Chisel.

*

In early 1976, FARM supported AC/DC at Ryde Youth Club on a triple bill with Finch. It was an underground car park beneath the shopping centre, not a proper venue. AC/DC played in the late afternoon as thirty or so teenagers mooned around the cement floor doing ollies and kickflips on skateboards. With the original lineup including Bon Scott and Mark Evans, they blasted out a herculean set and made it look effortless. It was taut, disciplined and muscular. I watched Malcolm Young's right hand in wonder and heard how his rhythm locked in with Phil Rudd's hi-hat, the engine room underpinning the showmanship of Angus Young and Bon and the key to the swing and hypnotic groove of the band. They didn't care that the place was nearly empty, and seemed oblivious to their surroundings. They were also on their way to a double at the Bondi Lifesaver that night. Even so, they pulled out all the stops. It was an object lesson to any young player to convince the few that are there, even if it's only one person, and leave fast.

Keyboard players never lingered in our band. Rob's friend Peter Watson was a prime example, even though he suggested the name Midnight Oil at the Garrett home in Lindfield in 1975 (when we were pulling names we'd written on bits of paper from a hat). An Arts student, Peter Watson was Brian Jones–esque with manicured curly locks and a scarf, his shirt permanently unbuttoned to display a shaved chest. He was always laughing theatrically and was good with women. Murray Cook followed him into the keyboard chair. I had met Murray on the train going to university. He was the blond, dreamy archetype of a surfing hippie, but an enthusiastic talker who really knew his music. We had been a four-piece for a while and he could fill in on bass, guitar, keyboards or whatever was needed. He played the flute, too – surely an omen. But he was an adaptable, friendly guy. His time in the band would be short too, but for now he was in.

I was making headway on piano. I taught myself more moves and wrote a song called 'Lena' that had some offbeat chords in it, minor 9th and major 7th, all easy if you put your hands like a rake anywhere on the keyboard accidentally. This music had a certain magic or emotional weight that pulled at the heartstrings, like a Jimmy Webb or Burt Bacharach song. Pete's brother's girlfriend Lyndall really liked it, but it wasn't for a band who's forte was 'Jumpin' Jack Flash'.

*

Rob Hirst's father, Peter, was articulate, charming and physically fit, like Rob. Every morning, for decades, he would swim the length of Balmoral Beach multiple times and write the water temperature in the sand for the other bathers, a tradition that endured until the end of his life. He owned a property in Chatswood at 77 Albert Avenue. It was a single-storey Federation house with dark timber features and high ceilings, always cool in summer. Rob moved in directly from his childhood home and rented out the spacious rooms to all and sundry – students, itinerants or anyone who could come up with $15-a-week rent. This was to become our HQ, doss house and spiritual home.

There was a guitarist hanging out at Albert Avenue who had gone to school with Rob. I'd seen him play before at a school lunchtime concert in the Sydney Grammar School Science auditorium, where our band and his band, Gunja, did a double-header for a group of nonplussed students. Gunja, like their name, were heavy. Martin Rotsey had a great sound, with a Yamaha SG5 electric guitar he'd picked up while living in Japan when his father was working there as a scientist. His version of Hendrix's 'Red House' was astounding. He was a no-nonsense blues player who looked and sounded the business. The band were okay, but you could see in Martin's eyes that he was a gun.

Bear had been ill. He'd had a stomach ulcer operation and was sent off to a house in Bathurst to convalesce. I'm not sure Bathurst is a place I'd want to go to recover from anything. In 1824, Governor Brisbane declared martial law in the country 'west of Mount York', which effectively gave the soldiers and settlers the right to indiscriminately kill any Aboriginal people they came across. Many died in this place. It's always felt sinister to me, heavy with sadness and memory. Bear had been there for months when I ventured out to see him. He talked of barium meals and his spells in hospital. It seemed he had a weaker constitution than the rest of us.

While Bear was ill, Martin was initially filling in on bass, but Murray then offered to switch to bass until Bear got back in business. Martin moved back to guitar, and I played guitar and keyboard. So there was a lot of swapping around going on.

After some months in Bathurst, Bear returned, and we let Murray go. He didn't take it well, but sometimes something has to disappear in order for something else to materialise. The band's unerring instinct for survival had manifested itself again and was overriding friendships and loyalties.

*

My first-year girlfriend and I used to go to Narrabeen on Sydney's northern beaches for walks. It was a long beach that straddled suburbs and I always enjoyed escaping the manicured and leaf-blown gardens of the North Shore, where I lived. We would speed down Tumbledown Dick Hill onto Powderworks Road in my grandmother's Morris 1100. The view of the water that met us promised possibilities. A mile to the right across Narrabeen Lakes and down Pittwater Road was the Royal Antler Hotel. The Antler was a mecca for surfers, and when the band scored a weekly residency there through our agent, Jason Wilde, we started to build up a following, playing week after week.

When Martin moved to guitar permanently, we became a twin-guitar band, which focused the sound. I still had long hair and a beard, as did Martin. We must have looked like a pair of werewolves patrolling either side of the stage. But punk rock had arrived – The Saints, Sex Pistols and The Clash were on the turntable. There was a vehemence and simplicity to the sound that had been lacking as the progressive bands disappeared into Versailles-era pomposity with Persian carpets onstage and the trappings of wealth. Suddenly it felt like the excitement of Elvis reborn. Guitars were in, flutes were out.

Initially I had some reservations about being one of the guitar players instead of *the* guitar player, but I let go of that almost immediately. Martin's style and my style were so diametrically opposed that we complemented each other. We could play freely, and the distinct parts we dreamt up made the overall sound so much better. Martin was spiky, pushy and ahead of the beat, lifting the adrenalin levels of Rob's playing and Pete's movements.

Having another guitarist there took pressure off me and allowed me to start focusing on songwriting, and I could also play organ when needed.

We were drawing more people every week at the Antler, but one night we were all set to play when Jason Wilde decided to pay us less than our allotted $110. Pete addressed the crowd: 'Sorry, people, but our agent has decided to dock our pay so we won't be playing tonight. See ya.' He pointed Jason out and we left, despite his stammered protests. It felt good to stand up for ourselves like this. We kept our residency, with increased pay, and Jason respected us more. He even posed on the back of one of our album covers.

After another show at the Antler, we were approached by a tanned surfer. He spoke clearly and loudly in a messianic tone. Gary Morris Vasicek was fit, incredibly good-looking, usually shirtless and always in the company of two or three women. He saw something in the band and offered to manage us. A few days later I found myself eye to eye with him in one of the bedrooms at Albert Avenue. He lectured me as if he was hypnotising a chook. The subject of the discourse was a surfer's meditation on the middle section of our song 'Surfing with a Spoon'.

'The guitar bit sounds like you're in a tube, bent on making it to the end, flowing, sliding up and down, spiritual, you understand? And then the organ part is the total wipeout – you see the sky, and God. Like nature, you're weightless and adrift, no control, surrendered.'

I was, in Gary's words, being 'tuned'.

He stopped dead and looked me directly in the eye. 'Understand?'

I nodded, not understanding a word. And that is pretty much what happened for the next twenty-five years.

Gary and Pete were from different galaxies but somehow on the same wavelength. One was a car and real estate salesman who had grown up wild in Papua New Guinea, a golf pro who had once caddied for Arnold Palmer on his Australian golfing tournaments; the other was an articulate and intelligent lawyer who loved to sing, surf and dance. What united them was a love of motor-mouthing, weed, surf, women, hustling the deal, and our music. And what was great about them was their complete belief in the band.

It was a relationship that would wax and wane for decades. Gary was more emotional and aggressive in his outbursts and would talk and talk until you surrendered. For every ten ideas, there would be two extraordinary ones. But at least he *had* ideas. Pete was more measured, careful with his words, ever the barrister, and would have the tenacity to query Gary on the finer points of his wild excursions. They needed each other to make it all tick. This is what greased the Midnight Oil wheel and kept it in motion for years. And that wheel was always moving, with lots of creative thought and business smarts refined by all of us in endless meetings. We all saw the power of the world we were manifesting, and the combination of personalities made for a heady mix.

After the first humiliating rejections by booking agencies, Gary saw that no one was going to help us. We would have to make our own path. He had a great philosophical sweep of the mind. He saw that the players in the music industry – the record labels, agencies and radio stations – were just gatekeepers between the band and our core audience. If we could go directly to our audience, we wouldn't need the industry.

Our music wasn't commercial; it was quirky in a lot of ways, similar to the progressive rock we had started with, but now sped up for the pub audiences that demanded it. It was delivered live with a commitment, power and punch that most other bands seemed to lack. Gary knew he had something to sell. The growing numbers at the Antler demonstrated this. He loved and believed in the band and, despite later fallings-out, we all knew we were lucky to find him.

*

I was never a star student at uni, but I saw the relationship between physics, music and spirituality. I noticed a couple of the more brilliant students would rhapsodise at the shapes of curves that fundamental subatomic particles made in a Wilson cloud chamber, then race up to the Great Hall organ and blast out Bach toccatas and fugues or some Messiaen. I had read Spinoza, who said the laws of the universe – gravitation, electromagnetism and the strong and weak forces that dominate the subatomic world – are proof of the existence of God, not the other way around. There was nothing wussy about this belief system, and no religious mumbo jumbo to wade through.

I had been doing my Science degree for three years and my marks were just good enough to allow me to go to UNSW to do an Architectural Acoustics degree in 1977. Some more engineering-related subjects were required, but it was only a few hours a week and I could teach guitar around my coursework at my friend Rob Stevens's shop, Turramurra Music, for a few extra dollars. Martin got a teaching job there too. I enjoyed it, and having a guitar in my hands for hours a day was great for my playing.

*

One day Rob called a rehearsal and, after lectures at UNSW, I arrived at Albert Avenue to see Pete crouched on the floor in the kitchen, head in his hands. He had red eyes and cuts, bruises, ash and burns all over his body, and was rocking backwards and forwards on his haunches with his hands on his head. Fire had engulfed the upper part of his house in Lindfield the previous night and he hadn't been able to get through the flames to save his mother. The place burnt to the ground while Pete paced up and down the street, howling helplessly.

He was quiet for months afterwards. He shared a house with some people who told me they were concerned about him. He punched holes in the walls, raw with frustration and anger.

He had already shaved his head for a gig at Leumeah and in the ensuing months his onstage performances became increasingly intense. One night we played at Selina's at the Coogee Bay Hotel, which had a white perspex dance floor in front of the stage, with lights under it that typically flashed out of time with the music. It was a weeknight and the crowd was just a ragamuffin smattering of people. Pete walked briskly onstage and laid waste to the plastic dance floor with the blunt end of the microphone stand. It was utterly destroyed in a matter of seconds, before we even played a note.

Pete became more serious and focused about everything in his life. Grief and fury made their way into his onstage persona, and the punters, oblivious to where it was coming from, couldn't quite believe what they were seeing or hearing alongside the increasing attack of the music around him. Word about the band was spreading, especially in our spiritual homeland, Sydney's northern beaches. We had Gary's management, a record deal was being sought and agents were sniffing about.

On 10 December 1977, we decided to 'go professional', throwing away any idea of alternative employment, and lash our minds and bodies to the Midnight Oil wheel. It was our first gig at the Bondi Lifesaver, a rock and roll club where everybody who was anybody in the music business used to drink. Renée Geyer pinched my arse while I was onstage as she walked by.

But I had just landed my dream job. It was at the Experimental Building Station in North Ryde, part of the CSIRO, and had taken years of study to qualify for. I wasn't quite ready to give it up, unsure that the band was the way to go. So, into 1978, I thought I could do the two careers simultaneously, the CSIRO during the day and the band at night. It was my first full-time job – Technical

Officer Grade 1 in the public service, on the handsome wage of $70 a week. The laboratory work involved looking at the acoustical properties of materials and measuring how soundproof they were. We blasted white noise into one room and then measured the difference between the sound reaching the microphones in that room and the sound reaching the microphones in the adjacent room, on the other side of the material being tested. We'd compare the difference at certain frequencies and distances and come up with a figure measuring sound transmission loss for bricks, glass panels, timber, fibreboard or anything that came across our desk. The data was telexed to Honeywell in North Sydney and fed into a state-of-the-art computer, and then the results were telexed back later in the day, which was frustrating and time-consuming. I figured out that the little HP scientific calculator in the lab could do the same job, wrote a simple program that saved the hassle, and was applauded for my efforts.

The lab was littered with weird and wonderful equipment, including a Nagra tape recorder, to this day a thing of beauty and engineering perfection. The sound of the Concorde's first flight to Australia in 1972 had been recorded passing left to right in stereo and we played this back on the Nagra regularly at thunderous volume.

We designed the windows for the High Court in Canberra so the judges could gaze out at Lake Burley Griffin from their chambers and make their deliberations in complete silence. The windows had to meet a very demanding specification, so we used three layers of 10-mm glass at various angles with air gaps in between. They were witness to many historical judgements, like the Mabo case in 1992 and the 1996 *Wik Peoples v Queensland*.

Coming back late from shows in places like Newcastle, I was supposed to front up to the lab bright-eyed and bushy-tailed every weekday at 8am. As a young man I could handle it physically, but one day I felt so desperate after a 4am finish at the Mawson Hotel at Caves Beach that I resigned. The bosses were kind enough and said, 'Come back next year after rock and roll leaves your system.'

The band had achieved a kind of critical mass, feeling more solid every week due to playing so much. We were all obsessed with it, and that was making a believer of me.

Five against the world

Clare O'Brien moved into the share house at Albert Avenue early in 1978. She had moved from Brisbane and was working as a psychiatric nurse, and she was down-to-earth, smart and beautiful. She was twenty-two and I had just turned twenty-one. The attraction soon took hold. It might have gone to the next level when I brought her some of my tomato plants for the Albert Avenue vegetable garden. We got together on a night when the band played Flicks in Manly.

Flicks was an old cinema turned into a venue, with a stage that raked down on a fair slope to the audience, and we played there many times. It was run by Larry Burton Danielson, who would later become known as one of the Woolworths bombers, convicted of attempting to extort money from the supermarket chain after a store was bombed in Maitland in December 1980.

The music industry at that time was rife with criminality – part underworld, part anti-establishment – and we were starting to come across many of these people – Gary's 'gatekeepers' – drawn in by the magnetic pull of a cash economy and zero accountability.

No rules applied, so you could invent your own, and this outlaw status was worn like a badge of honour.

One night at Flicks we supported the hugely popular soft-rock male duo Air Supply. We had our own following by now and Air Supply's music wasn't the audience's speed, but I was still surprised when they were booed offstage by an extremely vocal northern beaches crowd. Singer Russell Hitchcock responded with 'We play real music!' and then fled the stage as the first glasses were thrown.

*

Double Jay, or 2JJ, founded by Marius Webb and Ron Moss, was another Whitlam initiative – a government-funded youth radio station that came to represent the changing of the guard. A 24-hour non-commercial rock station like this had never existed in Australia. And it was the only one outside of a few community radio stations that was fully supportive of up-and-coming Australian bands. Skyhooks' 'You Just Like Me Coz I'm Good in Bed' was the first song played on air on 19 January 1975.

In May 1978, we played a 2JJ-sponsored concert at St Leonards Park with The Angels and Cold Chisel. These bands became the lynchpin of Oz rock for years to come, thanks to Double Jay, and we all benefitted greatly from this relationship as our destinies entwined.

That day the band played well, and Clare was with me. It was wonderful to have someone I loved by my side to share the experience. I was still a bit awkward, with a moustache, lugging around a Yamaha YC-25D organ and a heavy wooden Leslie 147 cabinet, with acoustic screens I'd built at the lab. I made them from white pegboard, Caneite and yellow fibreglass, to stop spill from other instruments leaking into the organ microphones. One of the stage crew said, 'That's the best live organ sound I've ever heard.' But once we got proper road crew, the screens were somehow 'lost'.

George Wayne, one of the DJs at Double Jay with a popular afternoon show called *Cooking with George*, was holding court backstage in his signature overalls at St Leonards Park. He was a lovely and complex man who simply worshipped local music. He'd play four or five tracks of a band in a row, or even whole albums. He was funny, opinionated, anarchic and forever editorialising the nightly gig guide, the 'What's On', which could take him an hour to get through. Live music was happening all over Sydney; it was a vibrant and dynamic scene. George and many others – Chris Winter, Gayle Austin, Holger Brockmann, Russell Guy, to name a few – played whatever music they wanted and became our very own pirates of the airwaves. True radio freedom without demographics, market research or second-guessing, unburdened by the formulaic playlists of modern radio.

I was now a professional musician, which meant I was broke and still living with my parents. It also meant I had time for thinking about writing songs. I read an interview with Don Walker in *RAM* (*Rock Australia Magazine*) where he talked in a measured way about writing with Cold Chisel. He had a great lyrical turn of phrase, with songs about our country and not some cod-Americana, which many local bands were parlaying on commercial radio at the time in an effort to make it overseas. The lesson for me was to forget that and write what I knew, something meaningful about my own place, my own country.

Midnight Oil were starting to work interstate more and more, and I moved out of home at Turramurra into a small flat in Goodchap Avenue, Chatswood. Clare had moved from Albert Avenue to rent a room at 43 View Street in Chatswood, a big old Federation house with leadlight windows, pressed metal Wunderlich ceilings, fireplaces in every room, wide verandas and a slate roof on an enormous double block facing west. She didn't want me to move in with her straight from home until I could cook and clean for myself. 'I don't want to turn into your bloody mother,' she said. She bought me a copy of *The Commonsense Cookery Book*.

Eventually I did move into View Street with her. Clare and I were very relaxed and happy with each other. I was getting to know love, the give and the take of it, what it was all about. Life in the big old house felt new and uncharted. The moustache went and I cut my hair short. I learnt to cook. It was peaceful there, apart from the possums in the roof, and I wrote many songs in the quiet rooms. I was lucky; ideas seemed to come out of thin air without too much coaxing.

*

Midnight Oil signed a recording deal with 7 Records early in 1978. Tony Wade-Ferrell was the A&R man and Ken Harding was the boss. We were given our own label, Powderworks, to be distributed by RCA. We named it after the road we drove down in Narrabeen to get to the Antler. (Our fan club also eventually became known as the Powderworkers.) The contract was buttoned up with a lunch at the Black Stump restaurant in Frenchs Forest. The suburban steak restaurant seemed a house of haute cuisine to us, a culinary nirvana. We signed the deal happily over dessert, Frogs in the Pond as I recall. Our in-house bush lawyers – Pete, Gary and Rob – had weeded out any dodgy clauses and effectively rewritten every word of the thing in our favour.

The previous year we'd made some rough recordings on my TEAC 4-track reel-to-reel in the living room at Albert Avenue before progressing to a demo studio across the back lane, above the Save the Children shop. It was then a huge jump to a proper studio with engineer-producer Chris Neal, who owned Airborne Studio in Brookvale. Chris was a fine musician with a successful career in film soundtracks and was a sweet and funny bloke with industry insider status. Generous with his time and studio hours, he loved the band and wanted to help out in any way he could. He counselled us with wise words about the idiosyncratic music business, so alien to us, often with hilarious discussions over a beer or two.

In early 1978, 2JJ asked us to do a radio broadcast as part of their 'Live at the Wireless' series in the labyrinthine ABC studios at 201 Forbes Street, Darlinghurst. There was a sizeable studio audience and it was our first-ever live recording. In-house engineer Keith Walker got us a strong, powerful sound. It was wilder and more live-sounding than anything we had recorded before. Keith demystified all the ins and outs of the recording process for me and was a very friendly character and good communicator. So we decided to record our imminent first album with him instead of Chris Neal. Chris took the news very hard. He had really helped us and put in a lot of time, but once more we had to go with our gut. Every band gets these decisions thrown at them in their lifespan, risking everything to get to the next level.

The recording was pure joy. We were set up in a room at Alberts Studio in Boomerang House, King Street, Sydney – the Alberts of the *Boomerang Songster*. It consisted of white rendered walls with a big mirror along one wall. There was no acoustical treatment, just a small living room–sized rectangle. It was the same room where Harry Vanda and George Young had cut all those great AC/DC records, plus their own productions – Flash in the Pan, JPY, The Angels, Rose Tattoo, Cheetah and William Shakespeare.

As the songs for the first album went down, I stood near the door, speaker box facing into the wall. I've subsequently seen pictures of Malcolm Young doing the same thing in the same spot. I used a borrowed Marshall head with my quad box, bought with three months' wages from the CSIRO. The Yamaha YC-25D organ with Melos echo unit on top was in front of me to the left, perched on its S-shaped tubular steel legs. Rob was at the far end of the room to my left, facing the control room. Bear was across from me. Martin had his amp in another room at the end of a long lead but was in the room right next to me. Pete was in another room singing along. Willow, our roadie and mate, was whispering something to Pete that we weren't supposed to hear about how we were all doing individually under the pressure of the red light, but there were microphones everywhere and we could all hear through the headphones. We were textbook studio rookies.

After shows we'd go back to the studio and do midnight-to-dawn mix sessions on the cheap. We used the adjacent studio with a new-fangled MCI computerised console that kept breaking down. I'm not sure about the others, but I was really happy with that record, which we simply called *Midnight Oil*, and it forever holds a place in my heart. More to the point, I found myself comfortable in the studio environment and mesmerised by its possibilities. After the final midnight-to-dawn mix session, I went home so excited that I stayed awake all the next day, a man possessed, recording new ideas on the TEAC in my parents' basement, wildly inspired.

Now we had the album done, Gary's idea was to hit the 'four points of the compass' every week. South could mean Wollongong. West: Parramatta. North: Newcastle. East: Bondi. The next week would be Melbourne, and we'd hit Carlton, St Kilda, Geelong and Ferntree Gully. The next week we'd drive to another capital city and do the same thing, while still playing in Sydney once a month. The gigs were coming thick and fast. In my mind, it's a blur; there's nothing I can recall except the din of it, the sweat, the roar of the Marshall amp and the attack of Rob's cymbals. The hearing in my left ear has never recovered.

Pete made the call that he needed some support onstage visually and emotionally from the rest of us, so rather than gazing at our shoes and playing our licks, each of us did something to lift our game, to match his cartwheeling and intense persona. Martin developed his bop, prowling around the stage puffing on a cigarette and charging at the audience. Rob had a whole show of his own going behind Pete, comprising water on the tom toms, Keith Moon–esque stick-twirling and lifting his arm high above his head before driving the stick down onto the snare drum with terrifying intensity. Bear became more animated. I took Gary's suggestion and stood still and stared intensely down at the audience, a more minimalistic approach, perhaps a tip of the hat to the deadpan and stationary stage persona of Rick Brewster of The Angels. In any case, we would always leave the stage having given our all.

Our fans were growing in number, but in the suburbs and regional centres there were still lots of blank looks as the behemoth did its thing. Our biggest and most consistent audience was still on Sydney's northern beaches: the Royal Antler, Flicks Manly and the Manly Vale Hotel. French's Tavern in the inner city was strong but very small and we soon outgrew it, opting for more reach in the suburban beer barns.

On our first sojourn to Melbourne, we drove from Sydney down the Hume Highway without stopping. I was a twenty-one-year-old non-smoker, wedged in the middle in the back seat of a Holden FC with three smokers and the windows wound up. At 2am the next morning we arrived at our hotel, the Car-O-Tel in St Kilda, to see the road crew of Ol' 55 pissing off the balcony in unison, aiming their volley in our direction. But Jimmy Manzie of Ol' 55 and Greg Macainsh from Skyhooks befriended Pete. Like Chris Neal, they offered lots of helpful advice about the industry, wise mentors in a sea of opportunists and diminished brain cells. We were outside the industry and liked it that way, distrustful of anyone beyond our inner sanctum unless they proved themselves worthy.

Melbourne was a revelation. It was the first time I tasted pizza and Lebanese and Greek food. My childhood was one of meat and three veg, where tinned food, Deb Instant Mashed Potato and Surprise Peas were the norm and Kentucky Fried Chicken was a delicacy. We would go up to St Kilda Road every night to play the brand-new Space Invaders arcade machines for hours on end. Martin was the champion. On the minus side, I couldn't relate to the flatness of Melbourne and the focus of the town being a muddy river. I was Sydney-centric, too ruined by the seductive beauty of the harbour and the endless stretch of surf beaches to notice the cultural richness of Melbourne.

Melbourne's community radio station 3RRR was a great support to us. Only seven people turned up to our first show at Martini's in Carlton, and most of them were from the radio station. We became friends with all of them – Diana King, Geoff King, Dorland Bray, Nadya Anderson and Deborah Conway. They supported and played our music just like 2JJ had done.

The feeling in the band at that time was that we were 'Five Against the World'. With Gary it was really six, but we used that byline with some effectiveness in the media. Everything around us in the business was lightweight and poppy and we were anything but. We were a flesh-and-blood, live-rock juggernaut in the act of creating itself.

We were booked to appear on *Countdown*, the antipodean version of *Top of the Pops*. Gary and the band had some thoughts about changing our presentation to distinguish us from the other bands that would appear on *Countdown*'s flashing plastic dance floor, with shampooed hair as long as their scarves and white satin or lycra trousers highlighting their well-proportioned bottoms. They would mime their latest single to a mob of psychotic teenage girls who screamed on cue. Above them a chocolate box of lights would flash on and off, and every band, no matter who, became the Bay City Rollers in a sea of hair dryers. This was not what we wanted at all. No one had told *Countdown* about the arrival of punk.

The night before taping, we played at the Bondi Lifesaver supporting Rose Tattoo. We got out of there at 3am and were booked on a 6am flight to Melbourne. When we got to Melbourne we checked into our accommodation, the Majestic Hotel, a boarding house in St Kilda, and proceeded to have a quick nap. Gary went in to *Countdown* ahead of us. Our request for special presentation didn't help win any ABC hearts and minds so the gatekeepers of pop cancelled our slot. Ian 'Molly' Meldrum was the host. We saw him as the devil incarnate, with his stammered introductions, his embarrassing and unwatchable interview with the then Prince Charles, and his kingmaker status in the industry.

That night, all slightly relieved and blearily nonplussed by the rejection, we played a show where we were rained on with spit from the audience, who got the idea somewhere that we were punks. As nasty as that was, it felt closer to where we wanted to be.

Countdown did champion Australian music, so I would watch it in spite of myself. It was said that if you were on *Countdown* on a Sunday evening you would wake up on Monday a star. We took stock of the *Countdown* situation and opted to go to the people directly, turning up in their towns and convincing them of our worth, one by one, on their own turf. Not that we had much choice. But that way we collected a live following that was more loyal than a pop audience. It made things a lot harder for us and would take years, but we were up for it. There was a work ethic emerging among us that would later scare the pants off many, including some of our own band members.

In radio-land 1978, not much of our music got airplay, except for 'Run by Night' and some other tracks on 2JJ and 3RRR. Commercial radio avoided us and continued on with their soft-rock barrage of LRB, Air Supply, Dragon and the like. We decided that if the industry wouldn't have us, we would align ourselves with worthy causes that would. We did benefit gigs for Greenpeace, Save the Whales and any charity or organisation we could get behind as a band. Gary organised themed concerts like the Before the Bomb Ball and Death to Disco with military precision, featuring bands like Radio Birdman and Jimmy and the Boys, and these actually made money. Multi-band bills drew more crowds. The shows also bypassed the agency system, sold out venues and made the whole industry sit up and take notice.

'Aussies Destroy Venue'

Despite our emerging popularity, some might say notoriety, my father seemed to think that Midnight Oil was a dead-end career for me. Mum never questioned anything I did, but back in 1976 Dad had chased Pete and Rob out of the house with his walking stick, yelling, 'Get out, you long-haired bastards.' It was only in 1979 when I brought home a gold record for 20,000 album sales that he changed his tune. Nothing succeeds like success. 'Oh, now I see,' he said. 'Keep going with it, son.'

Rob and I had established a songwriting rapport – 'Cold Cold Change', 'No Reaction', 'Naked Flame' to name a few. Rob was brash, funny and super intelligent, contrary to the clichéd view of drummers. He was organised, articulate and highly driven, loving the band with a passion that was to remain undimmed. That big-picture view was matched by an ability to create and get inside great melodies and lyrics, which suited Pete completely right from the start, but was a thing that took me years to get a handle on. Rob was the band's engine room, onstage and off. We all had ideas for songs and would all contribute parts, and I could do music;

there was no shortage of that. I loved to make cassettes full of ideas and give them to the band to see what got a response, which was pretty much what I did for the whole of the band's career.

Those songs ended up on *Head Injuries*, our second album, produced by Les Karski and engineered by Peter Walker. We sent Les a demo tape and he came back with a letter full of critical and funny comments. For 'Profiteers', he wrote 'too much hippy waffle'. For 'Cold Cold Change', he parroted the lyrics of the chorus, just saying 'have a significant time'. He was brutally direct, all for tightening up arrangements and cutting out superfluous sections, and had a punk-pop ethos.

I had been secretly listening to American band Boston because I appreciated their concise arrangements and melodic guitar playing, a bit like the soaring 'Telstar' by Joe Meek, and had written a long song called 'Is It Now?' in that style. It was a bit of an epic by punk standards, with lots of moves worked out on my piano and then taken across to my trusty TEAC reel-to-reel to add guitars, drums and voice. In the kitchen of Pete's place at West Street, Crows Nest, he and I worked on the lyrics, our first collaboration. In rehearsal we sped it up, and Les had inspired ideas for key changes for the end section. At that point it would just lift off and go into orbit. It was always among my favourite moments when we played it.

We worked long and hard on *Head Injuries*, with weeks of pre-production and recording time and lots of midnight-to-dawn sessions after shows, often stumbling into the daylight exhausted. This was to become our great advantage, honing songs and arranging them well, all the while playing to the band's strengths. I could see that if we had the right people around us and worked hard, we could make great records.

*

Straight after recording *Head Injuries*, Gary sent us on a tour of New Zealand. It was late 1979 and soon-to-be manager of INXS Chris Murphy and his sister Charne tour-managed us through it. We had twenty-five shows in as many days and travelled around in an eight-seater bus with no suspension. The promoters had stencilled our name on the side in big letters using electrical tape, so we were reluctant to get in the bus at all.

It didn't take long to get into the New Zealand newspapers. 'Aussies Destroy Venue' howled the front page of the *Auckland Star* after our first show at a club called The Gluepot, where Pete ripped down the curtains, Martin thrust his guitar into the ceiling and left it hanging there, feeding back, and Rob smashed up the kit and rammed his sticks into the low roof.

Whether it was adrenalin, pent-up excitement or the result of watching too many Who performances, Kiwis turned up to our subsequent gigs expecting more of the same. But rock destruction can't be faked; it must come from the heart.

Audiences at the other gigs were funereally quiet. At the Hillcrest Tavern in Hamilton, there was an immovable pulpit in the middle of the stage that had to be incorporated into the show somehow. We did four nights in a row there with the audience seated on chairs. A bell rang after we completed our cyclonic set, the lights came on and everyone left as one, as if braindead and joined at the hip. No encore was requested, considered or delivered. Hamilton seemed like the most boring place on Earth, but Bear berated us for our opinions. 'You can do anything here you could do anywhere on a Saturday night,' he said. We stared back at him aghast. The shops and cafés closed early and the fare was hogget (old lamb) and parboiled frozen vegetables. Television stopped transmission at 10pm with an animation of a little Kiwi climbing up a ladder into bed and flicking off the light. That meant a long night of nothing ahead for us, except maybe a game of cards. It was depressing.

Napier was better, a hot surf spot with a black sand beach. A friendly bohemian woman ran the hotel, which was like an old boarding house. We loosened up there, having a couple of beers after the show around a big pool table. I enjoyed the game even though I'd never played. New Zealand in 1979 is where we all learnt its finer points.

Our crew was Colin Lee Hong on lights, Ali Emmett on sound and Glen 'Pig' Lloyd doing stage. Pig was a rock and roll warrior, a man with a sweet soul and love of music, but an alarming capacity for violence. He had worked with bands we looked up to, like Split Enz, and could get any job done, like building a stage where there was none. He pulled out all stops to make the gig happen. Wild-eyed, straggly haired, with a mouthful of bad teeth and battling addiction, he would wield a heavy stainless-steel pipe that he named the 'wombat basher' if punters, or even bands, got out of line. When an unknown hand came around the dressing-room door trying to gain access before our show at Wellington Town Hall, Pig reduced it to a bloody mess before it was hastily and silently withdrawn.

Bear was out of his comfort zone and unhappy on this tour. I'm sure ongoing issues related to his ulcer had a lot to do with it. Once the band had nonplussed the North Island, he flew from Wellington to Christchurch. He didn't want to do the Cook Strait boat crossing because of his delicate stomach. We had a hellish sea voyage with most of us seasick, and then drove full bore all day to get to our hotel rooms in Christchurch at 11pm. When we arrived, we discovered our accommodation had been cancelled. Mightily pissed off, we had to continue driving to Dunedin, where the first gig was, a further 360 kilometres south. No service stations were open after dark in Timaru, so we ran out of gas on the hills above Dunedin. We were now utterly exhausted and Pete nursed the bus and literally rolled it in on petrol vapour to make it to the hotel as the sun rose.

After weeks of cramped travel in the bus with no suspension, those of us with the longest legs were in deep need of some back re-alignment. Pete and I went to a chiropractor in Dunedin, a guy who also treated horses. The result was that Pete blacked out on the table and the resultant spinal maladjustment made him as stiff as a board. I also came out feeling like I had an ironing board instead of a spine. The punters were expecting us to annihilate the stage that night having read the headline 'Aussies Set to Destroy Dunedin'. What they got was Pete standing rigid and immobile, like a department store dummy.

But there were many stellar moments on that tour, like flying over Lake Wakatipu and The Remarkables to Milford Sound in a daredevil single-propeller plane, and the sight of Double Cone peak as we flew close to moraines and the walls of glaciers. Waterfalls thundering down the steep sides of fjords, creating ethereal mist. Riding up a mountain in a bubble-shaped cable car in Queenstown, snowploughing down Coronet Peak on rented skis wearing our jeans, meeting strangers, eating bluff oysters and getting pretty drunk. On the last night of our residency at the Hillsborough Tavern in Christchurch, there was an egg-throwing competition between Colin the lighting guy and Martin across the heads of the audience, and Pete invited the whole crowd back to the hotel. As the proceedings wore on we festooned the outside of the building with rolls and rolls of toilet paper, cast out the windows so they looked like streamers.

After a tour like this, we felt we could take on anything. We learnt to be a band and that we could be stoic in the face of hardship and still enjoy ourselves. It was a crash course that stood us in good stead for what lay ahead. The landscape was widening like the vista from the Milford Sound airplane, the world below stretching to infinity, beautiful and limitless.

In the meantime, word came back to us that Gary had found God. Many stories were circulating regarding his conversion. One was that he saw a dead dog on the side of the road and pulled over. Laying his hands on it, he prised open its jaws, breathed into its mouth and uttered the words 'May the Spirit of the Lord Jesus Christ be upon you' and the dog got up and ran off. Then he hitched a ride with some Christians in a Kombi van. In any case, he was now a born-again, and it rapidly dawned on the rest of us that no one was looking after the shop. Back in Sydney, on the stage before a show at The Family Inn in Rydalmere, there was no road crew, to which Gary said, 'The Lord will provide.' Maybe He or She would have, if we'd been believers, but we needed something else. Another manager.

Gary recommended Zev Eizik, a promoter from Melbourne. Zev was very successful at promoting overseas touring acts in Australia with his company ACE. With fuzzy hair and big owl glasses, he was extremely likeable. Constance Adolph was deputised to work with us as tour manager. As a child in the USA, she had been Little Connie on *The Mouseketeers* TV show. Upfront, sassy, tough with intemperate promoters and innkeepers, and a mother to all of us, Constance was an ever-present companion on the road. On days off she would send me to Woolworths at Town Hall in Sydney's CBD to buy her false fingernails.

Zev, Constance and the ACE team were much more 'industry' than Gary's inspired thriving-on-chaos methodology, but they were reassuringly efficient and professional. The band's trajectory was still on the ascent and Zev's company knew all about touring, so, predictably, our touring increased exponentially. There were now endless trips up and down the Hume, Sturt, New England and Pacific Highways, all the capital cities and regions serviced repeatedly.

The band always preferred cars to aeroplanes, despite the yawning distances. I remember driving with Bear in Gary's old Humber Super Snipe, which sat at fifty miles an hour on the speedo, after a show at the Pier Hotel in Frankston. We inched to Sydney in one go, delirious at the dawn breaking over Yass. Another night we drove from the Jindalee Hotel in suburban Brisbane back to Sydney non-stop, arriving around midday. Another time, on a stretch of road driving south from Kempsey, I was driving the hire car, probably a Holden Commodore, with the whole band. Some were asleep in the back seat, heads nodding. The old road was single-lane, and I'd been sitting behind a truck for what seemed like hours. I pulled out to overtake when another truck reared up out of a dip, right there in front of us. Pete was in the passenger seat and grabbed the wheel from my frozen hands. His quick reactions saved everybody's life. Many people had died on that bit of road. Luckily, Pete did most of the driving, another time saving us from a blowout at 180 km/hr just south of Warwick.

Despite suffering the dangers of the roads as a result of the time we spent on them, we found that word of mouth was kicking in and the crowds were growing. The band were becoming more daring, more visual and louder, with massive intensity onstage. We had no time for the romance surrounding bands who wanted to be chic, take drugs, live in Melbourne squats or aspired to appear in indie films. Fuck that. We had a team ethos and were willing to do whatever it took. The aim was to blitz the audience and leave quickly. We stood united, and I was getting to love it.

On the days between shows, the adrenalin would subside and I would tend to the garden at View Street. The block was towered over by a massive angophora tree, all smooth bark and shapely pink-orange limbs that would glow softly as the sun set. A lone blue-tongue lizard lived in a terracotta pipe in the middle of the lawn, and there was a myriad of holes on a sloping section where a colony of deadly funnel-web spiders lived. When it rained, one or two would make their way into the house. Clare was by now working in the city in an office; she was the kind of practical woman who always needed the challenge of a daytime job, which also helped pay the rent. Things were really good between us, and we shared the excitement of what the band was building, laughing at the kitchen table about some of the more colourful characters that now surrounded us. It wasn't your typical long-distance relationship because I would return for a day or two every week before the hire car would pull up in the back lane, honk its horn and whisk me off again.

Bear, however, was finding the frenetic schedule impossible. Delicate constitution and ulcer aside, I found it hard to take him seriously when he drove miles across Sydney to find the cheapest petrol, and his running commentary was that the band were not in the best shape morally. He thought we were turning into animals, and in a way we were. But the band were really quite monastic, and the intensity of the shows meant no one could be self-indulgent or out of it. Or weak, in the Darwinian sense of the word. It was the survival of the fittest. Though his heart was in it, his body wasn't, and life on the road was simply destroying his health.

Bear left in 1980 after a gig at a Punchbowl pub appropriately called the Sundowner. It wasn't due to musical differences. Not many words were exchanged, but I knew it was the end of our road together. We were so close in the beginning, but I began to understand that people pass in and out of your life and that they always have something to teach you. I remember the feeling of sadness when he sauntered off into the dim night after the raucous show, straight into the arms of lifelong job security with the Commonwealth Bank.

We put word out on 2JJ that we needed a bass player. Auditions took place at Rhinoceros Studio in Kent Street in the middle of the city. Rick Grossman and Peter Gifford turned up, among a few others. Rick, a friend of Rob's, was someone we all liked and knew from his time with Eric Gradman Man & Machine and also with Matt Finish, but for some reason he didn't want to audition. The others all had their strengths and weaknesses, but Peter Gifford was as powerful and as fluid a bass player as you could ever hope for. We took him to the pub for a drink and a chat and offered him the job. He accepted graciously and we were off and running again.

Giffo had – still has – a great right hand, one that swings, and he could sing as well, which helped. He loved King Crimson's John Wetton, so he and I clicked. He equally respected and feared the scary maelstrom of noise he and I were capable of creating in what he referred to as 'our corner of the stage'.

Everything moved up a quantum energy level. Giffo was perfect for the pub environment that was nurturing us, and for the kind of ferocious live band that we were turning into.

Clamour
of birds

I have always cobbled together some kind of studio to tinker around in, ever since the one in the roof of the Cape Cod. In 1975 my parents had moved to Turramurra, further up the North Shore, and even though I'd left home my studio stayed there for many years. It was in a basement that was damp and often had inches of water on the floor, and you couldn't stand up without bashing your head on the floorboards and beams above, some with six-inch nails protruding from them. It was below the TV room, and Dad would bang on the floor above with his walking stick if things got too rowdy. But I was undeterred. I had the TEAC A-3340S 4-track, a small six-channel TEAC Model 2A mixer and a homemade patch bay sitting on a concrete shelf above the flood line, and a broken green swivel chair, two cheap microphones, a new pair of AR17 speakers driven by a Yamaha hi-fi amp, a beaten-up Star drum kit I had bought for $100, along with some of Rob's broken cymbals and old hardware. I was getting more adept at playing, recording and writing, with the tonality of the sound becoming part of the songwriting. I would demo quick sketches sometimes, or more involved recordings at other times. And I really had no concept of what would work with the band and always did it only for my own enjoyment.

In 1980, some of this basement music ended up in 'No Time for Games' and 'I'm the Cure', my paean to garage punk psychedelia and drug use, of which I knew little. Martin said he had an instrumental to throw in the mix so we put down a version of 'Wedding Cake Island' in the basement. It felt good to do something so laidback and melodic that featured surf guitar, acoustic guitar and a wailing Moog synth like a sea siren, an antidote to all that nocturnal cyclonic pub rock thrash.

I had discovered *Pet Sounds* by The Beach Boys and was fascinated by the chords and textures. Strings, sweet voices, marimbas, theremin, orchestral percussion. By day I would listen to that, and by night I would go to bloody and violent pubs like the Comb and Cutter in Blacktown to blast away at the audience with my Les Paul and Marshall.

In late July, after supporting the Ramones at Festival Hall in Brisbane (they looked like they'd landed in Queensland from another planet), we recorded 'Wedding Cake Island', 'No Time for Games', 'Knife's Edge' and 'I'm the Cure' for the *Bird Noises* EP at the Music Farm studio near Byron Bay, with Ross Cockle engineering and Les Karski producing. Cold Chisel, our contemporaries on the live circuit, popped over on the night before the recording. Don Walker was wry, Ian Moss dreamy, Jimmy Barnes engaging and funny and Phil Small was sweet and quiet. Drummer Steve Prestwich confided that he was also writing a few songs on keyboards, some of which made their later albums *Circus Animals* and *Twentieth Century*. They were such a diverse group of people, but I could see how all of the pieces made up a greater whole. After we had a few drinks, I ended up on the piano as a singalong burst into life. I wish I could remember the songs we played but The Beatles, ABBA, Jimmy Webb and Phil Spector were among them. Jimmy, never one to hold back, sat on the piano stool inches from me and sang into my right ear at tumultuous volume.

We recorded the songs quickly, but the studio was surrounded by hippies trying to sell us drugs. We mixed the EP the next week at Studios 301 in Sydney with Les, engineer Christo Curtis and me on the old Neve board in Studio 2 over two consecutive midnight-to-dawn sessions, and once more I found I loved being in the studio and the buzz of making a great mix. It was all hands on the faders, with no automation. My job was to switch on Pete's stream-of-consciousness rave briefly towards the end of 'Wedding Cake Island' and ride the guitar levels, but I was also the band's sole representative in the control room.

After hearing the assembled EP, I was as happy as a lark in the morning. At 9am the next day, completely spaced out, I bounced out into Castlereagh Street into a throng of peak-hour commuters on their way to the office.

Commercial radio picked up on 'Wedding Cake Island', feeling obliged to play something due to our increasing popularity. Finally, here was something that perversely complied with their laidback formats – an instrumental. It was a strange kind of vindication, but one that we happily endured. Perhaps Pete's voice didn't fit their narrow prerequisites, but whatever the case, we were now being played alongside Little River Band and Air Supply.

Five tall cedars

'*Brought up in a world of changes, part-time cleaner in the Holiday Flats ...*' I wrote these lines in a motor lodge on Glen Osmond Road, Adelaide, where Midnight Oil were playing the Arkaba Hotel for four nights. It was mid-December 1980. The Arkaba was a yurt-shaped room, dispensing little spirituality but all kinds of spirits.

The music came quickly, influenced in part by the snaky, wayward riff in Split Enz's recently released 'One Step Ahead', along with a stubborn desire to write a song in many different keys – F major, modulating via an E-flat flattened fifth to D flat and then a chorus in E and a slight return to an instrumental bridge in A minor. Apart from the opening lines and some of the chorus, the words were still unwritten.

Weeks later, I was sitting at Nobbys Beach with Martin. It was the evening before a gig in Newcastle. We were watching the leviathan container ships and coal loaders queuing up to get into port. A storm was about to hit and the mood was electric, the air charged with negative ions. The ship's lights had a ghostly sparkle to them. Goods coming in from other countries to promote our wellbeing, Australian coal heading out to destinations unknown to provide power for countless and nameless appliances and people. The vessels were huge and close and it was as if they were breathing in the heave and yaw of the swell.

A few weeks later again we were playing in Burnie, Tasmania. Budgets were wound tight and we stayed in the rooms above the venue with common bathrooms at the end of the hall. As is customary with bands on the way up or on the way down, I was sharing a room with Martin, who was always good at getting to the heart of things. He was steadfast, quietly insisting on the best, but he didn't have to say anything much; he just had to be in the room. The hotel overlooked Burnie's harbour and port where the Australian Pulp and Paper Mill pumped pigments and acids into the water, turning it chalk white in colour. Its chimneys belched clouds of industrial smoke and the smell was acrid, poison. It was a nightmare, a blotch on the beautiful coastline.

'You should write a song about it,' said Martin.

The words rang true, but pieces of the puzzle were missing. I had the music, but I wasn't much of a lyricist then. Pete tightened the focus of the few words I had and made them more universal. Then those ideas about wharves, harbours, coastline and pollution he fleshed out magically to become the Midnight Oil song 'Burnie'.

*

After more incessant touring, the idea of making an 'international-sounding album' was being thrown around. John Bromell, our publisher at Rondor Music introduced us to legendary English producer Glyn Johns. Glyn saw us at Selina's in Coogee on 21 February 1981 in front of a full house and loved the show. He met us the following night at a restaurant in Kings Cross, told us how great we were and regaled us with dazzling stories of recording

The Beatles, the Rolling Stones, Small Faces, Faces, Steve Miller, Joan Armatrading, The Kinks, The Who: all the people we loved. He had recorded *Who's Next*, the best rock record of all time. He was completely charming and enthusiastic. And he wanted to work with us at his studio in Sussex, England. At Glyn's instigation, A&M Records would be funding the sessions and were set to sign us to a worldwide record deal.

*

That year would see me make my first trip out of Australasia. First we landed in New Zealand for a few shows, which went well. I remember Clare doing a morale-boosting shimmy on the half-empty dancefloor in front of the band when we played at the Mainstreet in Auckland and thinking how lucky I was. After that we flew to Los Angeles, where, from our motel at Sunset and La Brea, we could hear shootings and helicopters and see searchlights strafing the neighbourhood all night. I had trouble with America: not the crime and the bombastic TV shows, but the thirty-five different types of milk and their crazy, five-minute-long delicatessen sandwich orders. At home we had one type of milk, and a ham sandwich just had ham on it. I couldn't understand how people could live with so much choice. The band were also scared of the insane traffic in a city where pedestrians are a threatened species. We would all hold hands as we crossed Sunset Boulevard.

After three days of have-a-nice-day surrealism in LA, during which the whole band went to Disneyland and queued up for the Matterhorn rollercoaster, we flew over the North Pole into Heathrow and caught black London cabs to a big house that Zev Eizik had rented for us in Warwick Gardens, Kensington.

A totally jet-lagged Clare and I got up at 4am and wandered the streets of Notting Hill and Shepherd's Bush. London is such a beautiful city in the dawn, with its ancient buildings, parks and statues in the soft light. In the ensuing days, we visited all the things that our colonialist upbringing dictated, including the Tower of London, Buckingham Palace and the Peter Pan statue in Kensington Gardens.

The band did some cursory rehearsals and writing for the album, but a lot of the songs still felt half written. I don't think we were fully focused on the job at hand. All our wide-eyed tourism, trying to adapt to and understand English people, and the time taken to kickstart our career overseas had become a distraction to the creation of the music.

A prestigious gig at the Marquee Club in London was booked. Rose Tattoo were there and they came back to our house after the show. Angry Anderson and Pete Wells talked about their gigs in Germany. They were softly spoken and great raconteurs, with dry senses of humour, as well as being covered in the most amazing tattoos. Our ebullient flute-playing friend Richo was there too. Martin and I played our guitars that night, battling through what we could of the album we were working on, with Richo egging us on. I remember him howling with joy when we played the serpentine riff from 'Brave Faces'.

Glyn's assistant, Sean Fullan, picked us up from the house to ferry us down to Glyn's new state-of-the-art recording studio in converted stables at Warnham Lodge Farm in West Sussex. It was a fully working farm with a big house, tennis court and separate accommodation for us with our own cook, an elderly Irish woman called Jean. On our first day, Glyn threw a big barbecue with members of English rock aristocracy in attendance – Andy Fairweather Low, Kenney Jones from The Faces and The Who, Ian Stewart from the Stones and, my favourite of all, Ronnie Lane. These were Glyn's neighbours and his pals. It was a bit of a shock to be among such exalted company.

Later that day, Glyn played us some music he'd previously recorded in the studio. It was Jools Holland playing some swing piano. The band stood as one behind Glyn as he sat at the console and played the track at deafening volume. We noticed there was blood trickling down the back of his neck. It remained a mystery but was perhaps an omen. With rising alarm, I wondered what we'd got ourselves into.

The studio playing area was a long barn with a high vaulted ceiling. The guitarists were arranged throughout the room, with the drums placed next to the control-room window, facing inwards. At the other end of the room there was a small, raised isolation room where Pete sang and where the acoustic guitars and piano were recorded. Martin and I had rented amps, a Marshall for me and a Vox AC30 for him with some minimal screen isolation. Glyn had a great technique for miking drums: three Neumann condenser microphones positioned just so. If the drummer had a good-sounding kit, as Rob did (having borrowed it from The Who's Kenney Jones), then it sounded brilliant.

Glyn would arrive in the morning and we would play him the song we were going to record. He hadn't heard the songs yet and hadn't really wanted to. The first was 'Burnie'. He got very excited, saying it reminded him of The Beatles. He inserted a bar of two beats with tape editing near the end, which threw the bar lengths unpredictably and very effectively.

He let us know that he hated overdubbing, proclaiming the oxide wore off the tape if it was played too often, which meant most of the record would be live takes.

'Why the fuck would I want to sit here overdubbing a fucking guitar solo with some fucking guitar player for two hours when he could have fucking blazed through it when the band played the fucking backing track?' he said.

Point taken. So discipline was required. We all had to play through the song from beginning to end, and everybody had to get it right at the same time. Glyn had a red light that he would switch on if he felt the performance wasn't up to it, and we'd have to back up and start again.

In the evenings, he loved to regale us over a balloon glass. 'Sean, bring me brandy!' he would command his assistant as he launched into another apocryphal and very entertaining rock anecdote.

His console was a custom-built Helios board with some valve electronics located in the first four channels. I asked him if the organ in 'Don't Wanna Be the One' could sound like the clavioline on 'Telstar'. Amazingly he had worked on that record at IBC Studios with Joe Meek so knew exactly what to do, overdriving the valves on one of these channels. 'Oh yes, Joe would come down and freshen up his tracks with an equaliser we had.' I was dazzled. The console was designed in a wrap-around configuration for evil-genius types, so no one could sit next to Glyn. The system overload lights on his huge Urei speakers were forever in the red, rarely in the orange and never in the green. When he played back the tracks, it was at such blistering volume that you couldn't really hear if it was a good take or not. It was very exciting though.

After this assault we would retreat to our cottage to recover and look at Glyn's gold records on the walls. And as we ate our Crunchy Nut cereal every morning, we'd look up again and think, 'How the hell are we ever going to get up there with that lot?'

Then we hit an inevitable obstacle: we started to get to the songs that we'd only half finished. Glyn would storm out of the room saying, 'I could be having more fun on my tractor!'

After one of these encounters, we didn't see him for a week and a half. Being mid-summer, it was hay-baling time, so we helped him get the bales out of the rain. Despite the conflict, it was fun and in our nature to lend a hand. Giffo even built him a wooden duck house, placing it on an island in a large pond where ravenous English foxes couldn't get at them.

Glyn was clever to leave us to it for a while. We were stuck in the English countryside without money or transport and it forced us to work on the remaining songs uninterrupted. Things lifted a few notches after that, especially with the song 'Lucky Country'. I manually played the song's changes using the sample/hold switch on a Micromoog synthesiser and we overdubbed everything from there. It had the feel of The Who's 'Baba O'Riley'. Even the drums were double-tracked and Rob performed them perfectly. We overdubbed a couple of Glyn's beautiful custom-made acoustic guitars at the end of the middle section, a moment on the record that still sends shivers up my spine.

Pete was in the habit of taking walks in the countryside to think over lyrics, and one particular day it was time to sing 'Lucky Country'. The vocal wasn't sounding that great at first. 'Right,' said Glyn, and he rewound the tape to the beginning and hit STOP. He disappeared into the studio and chatted to Pete for well over an hour, behind the vocal screen and out of earshot. The rest of us stayed in the control room, so I don't know what they talked about. Life, deep things, the universe, fears and desires – who knows? When he eventually came back in, Glyn said, 'Got it!' and pressed RECORD as he sat down. Most of what you hear of the vocal is that first take. Pete sounded amazing, intense and in the groove. That's real record production.

Glyn barked at me once or twice about overdubbing things, and the record seemed to be more about him than us; at least that's how I felt at the time. I wasn't a fan of the mood swings either, or the piercing stares through unflinching blue eyes. But *Place Without a Postcard* has become one of my favourite Midnight Oil recordings. We were captured pretty much live and raw, and the remastered version sounds brilliant. Glyn liked the sound of us, not us with lots of overdubs, and the job for him was to get the best out of us. He wasn't out to make friends; I was too young to really grasp that. But the songs are good, and when they're perhaps not as good, there's a great character to them that always gets them over the line. It's not contrived. It captured us on the pendulum swing somewhere between youthful naivety and songcraft.

*

There was a listening party at the studio once the record had been mixed. It was too much for the record label and their associates in this era of eighties hair, shoulder pads, Duran Duran and electro-synth pop. The last track faded out and was greeted with a bloodless silence. They all shuffled out awkwardly, muttering and stuttering in that painfully polite English way that Hugh Grant has since perfected.

Clare and I escaped to Paris with no warning, an Irish goodbye. We had hardly any money, opting to stay in the Latin Quarter at the modest Hotel Quartier Latin up on the fifth floor. It was a relief to have the record done. Pete and Martin turned up and we all met up with Richo, who busked with his flute outside the Louvre, making serious money. He normally worked London's Green Park tube station and had won the Greater London Council's 'Busker of the Year' award in 1980. His embouchure was impressive. I remember him blowing at deafening volume across the neck of an empty wine bottle, resulting in an explosive volley ricocheting off the Hôtel de Ville.

Being the weekend, we missed the bank (there were no ATMs in 1981) and had twenty francs to live on. It was enough for one baguette, a bottle of wine and two kebabs. Clare and I sat by the Seine drinking the wine, soaking up the atmosphere and the magical vision of Notre-Dame on the clearest of nights.

We returned invigorated to London. There was a problem with the Kensington house where we'd stayed. Zev hadn't paid the last few weeks' rent. The owners said we had scratched mirrors and broken furniture that had already been scratched and broken. They just wanted to keep the bond. Zev absconded with the rent money and was being chased by the police on behalf of the landlords. It was all very Inspector Clouseau.

But this was just background to the drama that was unfolding. A&M Records' co-founder Jerry Moss (the 'M'; Herb Alpert the 'A') wouldn't get back to us with his thoughts on the album. His people would say, 'Jerry needs the weekend to think about it,' or 'Jerry needs to go skiing in Aspen and he'll get straight back to you.' The signs weren't good.

Finally, we were summoned to a meeting at the plush Portobello Hotel to receive the news. Jerry wanted us to go back in again with Glyn. They 'hadn't heard the single' – meaning a radio-friendly 'hit' song. We said nothing. The Midnight Oil wall of silence went up. It lasted for minutes and was very uncomfortable. So they hadn't heard a single, they didn't like the record? They could take it or leave it. They left it.

Glyn was disgusted by A&M's decision. He utterly believed in the record. During the sessions at Sussex he had said, 'What are you going to do with all your fucking money?' as he passed crates of French wine into the kitchen. His answer to the label's search for a single was, 'Drop the needle down anywhere, guv.'

It was expected that we would deliver the record that would break us. Now that was not to be. Zev took the rejection hard. He thought this record was going to be everyone's one-way ticket to international stardom.

A&M ended up giving us the record, although we paid them for it later. *Place Without a Postcard* went straight to number one in Australia and we, like any Australian band that returns from overseas, went straight back out on the road to try to get back the fortune we had spent in the UK. The *Postcard* episode was very disappointing, but we took it in our stride because we completely believed in the band.

*

Whispers were circulating that Gary was re-emerging from his religious exile. We missed him and his inspired ideas, so after an eighteen-month absence he returned with a mighty roll of thunder. In early 1982 we had a show at the Myer Music Bowl in Melbourne and Gary organised a life-sized mannequin of Pete, a detonator and some dynamite. When Pete, in darkness, did his blood-curdling scream towards the end of 'Stand in Line', a spotlight appeared on the dummy, which was supposed to self-destruct. But at the crucial moment, the dummy wouldn't stand up by itself. Our stage manager, Michael Lippold, was despatched to crouch behind the limp doll and hold it. 'Blow it up,' he hissed like a maniacal Daffy Duck. 'Blow me up. Now!' It was detonated and a tiny puff of smoke appeared.

During 'Wedding Cake Island', Pete was lowered from the roof above the stage by a rope as he played an Ovation acoustic guitar. As he descended, the rope started to spin with increasing speed and he called out, 'Let me down, let me down!' and was hastily lowered in front of the audience of thousands. It wasn't yet dark and the drama played out in the dusk of a beautiful Melbourne evening for all to see.

Lippold 'knew people' and, more than once, he mentioned arranging Gary's murder that night. But the next day we played live on Lee Simon's *Nightmoves*, a late-night TV show. Gary insisted we use Vietnam War footage courtesy of Australian film-maker David Bradbury, superimposed on our moodily lit performance of 'Armistice Day'. This was a universe away from the mainstream cheese that was *Countdown*. Gary was back. This was 'Oil'.

A meeting was held with the band, Gary and Zev to resolve 'the Gary issue'. Zev later revealed that he'd eaten a hash cookie just before the meeting, which rendered him unable to speak. 'There was nothing I could do.' So Gary got his band back. And we him.

The final gig of the tour was on 28 March 1982 at the Sundowner in Whyalla, the industrial steel town in South Australia. After that, Rob and Martin headed overseas with their girlfriends to travel around Europe together in a little van. The rest of us were going to join them a couple of months later in London. After our false start with A&M, this really would be make or break for us. We were going over to the UK now to live for an indefinite time, and we were not coming back until we'd cracked it.

Goldhawk
Road

Around 1981, Dad retired and sold his Karbonkraft factory in Botany, gifting my brother and me $50,000 each. It was quite a sum back then. Kim bought twenty acres in the Southern Highlands to build a winery. Clare and I found a small Depression-era worker's cottage in Gladesville. It was the first house we saw and cost $78,000. I had $8000 in the bank and went to the band's bank manager at the ANZ in Chatswood to borrow another $20,000.

Number 25 Warner Street, Gladesville, was on a narrow and deep block, 40 by 200 foot. It wasn't much, but it was ours. It had two small bedrooms. The living room had leadlight windows, an ancient ceramic gas fire and my piano. The tiny dining room featured vertical lining boards and barely contained our old circular dropside oak table. There was a big sunroom out the back covered in seagrass matting and a lemongrass plant outside the kitchen window where bulbuls nested. I ended up insulating the ceiling and putting in French doors, a pergola and a new kitchen. Giffo came over one day and built a beautiful red cedar bathroom cabinet for us. Like the duck house he had built for Glyn, it was a piece of art. He loved working with his hands and having something to show for a day's work. Being in a band, you couldn't really ever say that.

We fixed the collapsing paling fence with star pickets, wire and youthful enthusiasm, and watched the choko vine go mad all over it. We put in a grapevine that scurried up to the top of the pergola. I messed around in the yard, putting in garden beds and smashing up the narrow concrete path that led up to the Hills Hoist with a sledgehammer. The Hills Hoist remained though, the most common and iconic sculpture of our country.

Clare and I were very much in love, and we had been together for nearly five years now. She mentioned the idea of having children. Children had never occurred to me, being so obsessive about my career. Clare said she was going to have them with or without me. 'With!' I said.

When I wasn't away, I'd have dinner ready for her when she came home from her new job as an environmental scientist. During the day I would motor up to the studio under my parents' house to record sketches of songs.

'Outside World' was constructed on my piano. The lyrics were a tone poem that started when I was lying in bed at View Street watching the gum trees sway gently in the breeze on the night of a full moon, conveying something of my own feelings, and not polemic, about disconnection and alienation from the world, and getting lost in nature. The sound of the song with its synthesiser pulse and string machine was inspired by a band called The Teardrop Explodes that I'd heard on radio in Melbourne.

Songs can come from anywhere. In 1981, US planes based on the carrier USS *Nimitz* shot down two Libyan jets over the Gulf of Sidra. The headline in the *Sydney Morning Herald* read 'US Forces Give the Nod'. I'd also been reading a book called *Multinationals Take Over Australia* by Len Fox, which inspired the other lyrics for 'US Forces'. The sound of that song was influenced very much by The Saints track 'Always', that idea of vocals answering guitars in a kind of round. The demo had my Eko 12-string acoustic guitar, an old bass of Bear's with the frets ripped out and four-on-the-floor drums with no backbeat in the verse, more like a traditional folk song. When the band heard those two songs, they liked them but said they weren't really Midnight Oil songs. Electronica and folk had never been part of our lexicon.

Before he went overseas, Rob came over and we sketched out 'Read About It', 'A Woman in History' and 'Only the Strong'. I had a demo of a song called 'Still Be the Same' that Pete liked. After some heavy surgery on the arrangement and a complete lyric rewrite by Pete, it became 'Maralinga', inspired by a book about the horrors of British nuclear testing in the outback that I had been delving into. Pete was writing lyrics that were either didactic or impressionistic, often from surf culture and his love of the natural world, or that took an issue-based idea like 'Maralinga' way further. As Rob and I had formed a songwriting duumvirate of sorts, Pete would come up with lyrics that Martin or I would add music to, or use orphaned ideas and riffs that he liked. Pete and the band could transform them into great Midnight Oil songs. 'Koala Sprint', 'Burnie', 'Knife's Edge', 'Tin Legs and Tin Mines' are a few examples. Alternatively, he would rewrite verses of Rob's lyrics to suit his own delivery, which sometimes caused friction, but usually I or one of our producers could resolve matters. Thankfully the best ideas would win, a democratic modus operandi to which we were all willing participants.

In May 1982, we flew to London with a guitar each and nothing else. Gary was with us this time. Through his Christian contacts he got us accommodation at The Foreign Missions Club in Islington, lodging for travelling missionaries. We didn't last long as we didn't join in morning prayer. We decamped to a crowded student dormitory in Islington with yellow fluorescent lighting but soon found a flat to rent above the shops in St John's Wood High Street, near Lord's Cricket Ground. This is where we stayed for months.

Gary and Pete were negotiating an international contract for us, which was another good reason to be in London. And we had an ally: Paul Russell from CBS Australia was now the head of CBS UK.

Initially there were no plans to make an album, just to play a residency in London and, through word of mouth, get people to the shows. It could have been quite depressing, waiting out the week for one solitary gig, but I was a young man in London with fifty quid a week in my pocket, so I went out most nights on my own. Culturally, London was way broader at the extremes than Australia. I perused *Time Out* magazine and checked out intriguing events of all descriptions. There were African, reggae, punk and world music artists playing every night. Rip Rig + Panic were popular and quite amazing. We saw The Clash at Brixton Academy when Joe Strummer had a Mohican haircut, just before guitarist Mick Jones got the boot, Talking Heads post *Remain in Light* at Wembley Arena and King Crimson at the Hammersmith Palais. I saw Mink DeVille, indie plays in the East End and Nureyev dancing, did all the galleries, design centres and loads of films. We stood side of stage for the seminal Stiff Little Fingers from Northern Ireland, and supported them at the Hammersmith Odeon one night. I was a sponge, playing catch-up on all the culture I didn't know I'd been missing. I was homesick but also kept occupied by writing out all the Midnight Oil songs in music notation for a songbook that our publisher had in the pipes. It wasn't like a normal songbook, as I included guitar tabs and proper guitar fingerings. I enjoyed reacquainting myself with what we had already written, with its little key changes and unpredictable lifts and shifts. I could figure out what made the songs tick, and I'm sure some of those insights ended up in the arrangements that became our album *10, 9, 8, 7, 6, 5, 4, 3, 2, 1*.

On 20 July 1982, a bomb blast by the IRA at nearby Regent's Park violently shook the windowpane of my bedroom at the top of the stairs. It killed seven soldiers and injured many others. I had never experienced horror so close to home. Anyone could be caught up in it, on the Tube, anywhere. One IRA statement was, 'We remind the British Government that as long as they maintain control of any part of Ireland, the Irish Republican Army will continue to operate in Britain.' I was from, in Barry Humphries' words, peace-torn Australia. No longer was I dealing with the antipodean bliss of my youth.

*

Nadya Anderson, our friend from 3RRR in Melbourne, was living in London, managing M (aka Robin Scott) who had a hit with a song called 'Pop Music'. Nadya's boyfriend was a skinny young Englishman called Nick Launay, a recording engineer starting up his career. We were starting to think about making a record in London now that the CBS deal was looking good and booked time at the Town House, a recording studio in Goldhawk Road, Shepherd's Bush. Gary liked the idea of enlisting The Police's producer, Hugh Padgham. He had come to one of the shows and seemed pretty keen. Nick had worked as his assistant before, and when they spied each other backstage, they both laughed and said, 'What are *you* doing here?'

We ended up with a weekly residency at the Zig Zag Club, an old theatre in W9. On the other days we travelled around London on the Tube, looking for amps and keyboards advertised in the back pages of *Melody Maker*. For the first shows we used the big Marshall amps we used in Australia. A lovely friend of Rob's called Nigel said it was too 'rock'. It was a barrage, with not enough musicality behind it. Martin and I had been listening to bands like XTC, Television and Gang of Four. Those bands had a really intelligent way of using guitars, with lots of cross-rhythmic interplay and textures. The very next week, we both found ourselves smaller amps. I scored a Carlsbro Stingray and Martin a Roland Cube-100. Odd transistor amps, but amps that suggested lots of other exotic possibilities. We were sick of that Marshall sound anyway, and they were too loud for most clubs. The next week the gig was more fun, both to play and to listen to. More exotic. Nigel approved.

One day, we went around to Nick's place in Fulham and he played us some of his work on a Revox reel-to-reel: Kate Bush, The Birthday Party and Public Image Ltd. He was clearly very talented and innovative. It was edgy, and it felt like you were being assaulted by the music rather than that honest band-in-a-room approach of *Place Without a Postcard*. He seemed a sweet bloke and I loved what I heard, so I was all for diving in with Nick. It turned out that he had worked exclusively at the Town House, the studio we had already booked.

Rob wasn't as enthused initially. It may have sounded too far out for him. He had been having a lot of anxiety at the time and was concerned we were going in the wrong direction. This cautiousness, admirable in many ways, is to stop the lunatics from taking over in the band, but this time I felt we needed to risk everything and push out past our boundaries.

'What do you guys want to do?' asked Nick.

'I want to get the biggest acoustic guitar sound in the world!' I replied.

'That sounds like a great idea. Let's DO IT!'

His enthusiasm was infectious, and he made interesting suggestions about the arrangements. The thing about the band was that if allowed the luxury of time, we would spend forever in a rehearsal room breaking down the songs, going down blind alleys and trying to turn things upside down just to see if it was better that way. We were in that mode for this album, upending the music while living constantly in one another's pockets.

*

One Friday night, after a week making demos in CBS Studios, I jumped on the train from King's Cross for a solitary weekend dash to Dublin to have some respite from the pressure cooker of band life. Living together, rehearsing together, we may as well have been sleeping together. We all respected what that intensity could create in the studio and onstage, but it could be measured at the expense of your own sanity. My train took me to Holyhead, Wales, where I jumped on the boat across the Irish Sea, with people seasick all around me, many drinking barrel-like cans of Carlsberg. After berthing at Dún Laoghaire, I found myself walking the streets of Dublin in the dawn. I had a camera and took some black and white shots of buildings, ducks in ponds and Tonge & Taggart drain covers. The city was pretty grimy and industrial-looking in 1982. That day I took a tourist bus down in a loop via Waterford, Kilkenny and Cashel, and scrawled my impressions with a biro all over a copy of *The Irish Times*. I was fascinated by the landscape and curious to know more about Irish history, especially after the Regent's Park tragedy.

That night I ended up in a little bed and breakfast in North Dublin somewhere off O'Connell Street. The chambermaid was coming up a dark and narrow staircase with an armful of sheets and towels as I was heading down. When she spotted me, she said, 'Are ye Irish now?'

'No,' I said.

'Oo, go on, yer a fine specimen of an Oirish lad, aren't ye?'

I didn't know what she was talking about but she seemed convinced I was Irish just from looking at me.

I enjoyed the camaraderie and happy atmosphere of the Irish pubs. Ireland seemed to be a country of lateral thinkers. I came back to London refreshed and ready to rejoin the fray.

More songs appeared. 'Tin Legs and Tin Mines' was a chord sequence and melody I had come up with that we glued to a joyous-sounding chord sequence from Martin, which became the chorus. Pete supplied lyrics and melodies. It all fitted.

There was a song of Rob's called 'Woman in History'. I had an arpeggio part that went well under the chorus. When Rob brought in his lyrics for 'Short Memory', I suggested scuttling the first song for the arpeggio and changing the chorus to his new lyrics, then breaking it down to a four-on-the-floor kick pattern and reciting a list of the atrocities of history over a simple riff in E. 'That can be the verse.'

I was reading some Irish history and argued for taking out a line about Irish bombs in London – clearly there were two sides here. With a few additions from Pete in the recording sessions, it was done.

Martin told me that Salvador Dalí never slept; it assisted his creativity. So I stayed up one night and came up with the 'Read About It' riff at 6am on my black Gretsch guitar and also the piano intro music to 'Tin Legs and Tin Mines' using a dreamy sound on a Korg PolySix keyboard that I'd bought by scraping together a bunch of traveller's cheques. We rehearsed in a facility that was a thirty-minute walk from the house, and when the day came I skipped through Primrose Park, spaced out and delirious, with the ideas ready to go straight into their respective songs. Thanks, Martin – and Mr Dalí.

Studio Two at the Town House was the place where Hugh Padgham, Peter Gabriel and Phil himself had discovered the Phil Collins drum sound, with Nick as assistant. The drum room was not large but was at least fifteen feet high, with stone walls. The kit sat atop a hollow wooden floor, with a manhole that opened to a ladder leading down to an empty swimming pool beneath. The Stone Room, as it came to be known, wasn't acoustically designed but a happy architectural accident that became the sound of the eighties. There was a prototype of a new console there, the first Solid State Logic 4000 B Series desk ever made.

Built in Oxford, these soon became the new industry standard worldwide.

Nick knew the room backwards. Rob was sent in first to get a drum sound, and when he played his cymbals they were louder than the drums, so Nick convinced him that he should overdub the cymbals later. This meant he could open up the room sound, primarily using an old BBC 'ball and biscuit' talkback microphone located high up, where the wall met the ceiling, to achieve huge tonality and resonance from the drums. Suddenly the drum sound became an explosive major player, and we added unusual textures to it. Three days into the record, we got the phone number of Maurice Plaquet Ltd, a West London music shop with an equipment hire business. The logo featured the 'M' written as a triplet and the 'P' as a down-stem quaver. If we needed an acoustic guitar like a booming Gibson J-200, a dobro, a xylophone, a Hammond organ or a brand-new Simmons electronic drum kit, delivery was only half an hour away.

Nick was all for messing up good sounds, especially the guitars, routing them through matchbox-sized amps and then running that through something else, or taping microphones to acoustic guitars to get more attack and clang out of them. A sonic terrorist on the desk, he didn't care about tradition. We were the same with the songs – we wanted to find out what was possible, and we happily demolished anything that wasn't working. The chorus of 'Read About It' had descending chords that sounded excessively poppy, so at the last minute we stuck it over a 6/8 version of the introduction riff, and it worked. Everything seemed to work in that session.

Sitting on the SSL console was a negative-ion generator, which we all believed helped keep us on our toes over the long studio hours, and a blue Smurf that we christened 'Phil', after Phil Spector. We burnt eucalyptus leaves to remind us of home and keep morale high.

I can't begin to describe how much I loved Nick's way of working, his eccentric and very English politeness and fantastic ear for sonics. He was on fire and, dare I say, so were we. We blasted the record out in a few short weeks. Though Rob had a nervous breakdown of sorts during the making of the album, he took all of his anxiety and anger out on his drums. That period in London was difficult for us all personally, with the homesickness and living in each other's pockets, but I remember it fondly. The record was well worth all the angst, warm beer and English disdain for anyone faintly colonial, Irish or foreign.

Due to Glyn's lobbying, we scored a support slot for The Who at the Birmingham National Exhibition Centre. Roger Daltrey came into our dressing room afterwards saying he thought we were great. I couldn't even speak when introduced to Pete Townshend; it was complete fanboy paralysis. The band and their crew were all very kind and offered us the support slot for their upcoming US tour. I heard later, unsubstantiated, that they wanted to poach Rob to play drums. Eerily, we used to call Rob 'Keith' because of his obsessive love of Moon's drumming. Rob worshipped him and had worn a black armband onstage at the Antler the night his hero passed away back in 1978.

The Who liked us. This was a dream come true. But we would have been driving in vans trying to keep up with their private jet as it zigzagged across the country. No US record deal had been secured at this point, meaning no records in the stores, and we would have been paid low fees with no record label to bridge the shortfall. And I missed Clare and was homesick and fed up with being in London living within the brotherhood. So I uncharacteristically spat the dummy and we all headed back for summer in Australia, except for Pete, who stayed for a couple more weeks and mixed the record with Nick. I felt we had made a great record and just might flip a few wigs with it.

Just before we came home, my heavily modified 1974 Les Paul

Custom guitar was stolen, so all I had now was my spare guitar, a 1972 black Gretsch Roc Jet. I had paid a guy in South Yarra $500 for it in 1981. I figured out a way to make it sound good by running the preamp of the Carlsbro into a Marshall amp. It had a sound that gave my playing a unique voice, so I stuck with it.

I was finding a lot of my 'Jimmy Webb' chords or textural colours were now being incorporated in the fabric of the band's sound. After London I felt more in control and more adult. And it set me on a path creatively that I would never really veer from again.

*

We had returned home with an album that was the much-needed jump in our career. We did a run of shows at the Capitol Theatre in Sydney. The band were playing really well and the new songs lent themselves to live interpretation, even though they had been confected in the studio. We went to an even higher level of recognition in Australia, playing bigger venues like Canberra's Bruce Stadium and the Sydney Entertainment Centre. With the advent of commercial FM radio after 1980, the Triple M/ EON FM stations were looking to find Australian versions of the album-oriented rock formats that dominated the USA at the time. Our *10, 9, 8, 7, 6, 5, 4, 3, 2, 1* was that 'right record at the right time'. Airplay followed for songs like 'US Forces', 'Power and the Passion', 'Read About It' and 'Short Memory'. We were shimmying up the greasy pole of success.

*

After a five-month separation, Clare and I decided to get married. Her parents were staunchly Irish Catholic and went to church every chance they got, so it seemed the decent thing to do, even though we thought it unnecessary to sanction everything with a piece of paper. The ring we chose was a beautiful Claddagh design from Galway. Two hands holding a heart with a crown above it: 'The heart is king.'

So all gathered on 19 March 1983 at St Martha's Catholic Church in Strathfield with Father Brian Titmus presiding over the ceremony. We walked down the aisle to the sound of a Celtic harp playing the 'Cliffs of Moher' and other Irish airs. A few Irish priests from the nearby college snuck in for a listen. After the ceremony, in the church's portico, our roadie Michael Lippold, also of Irish descent, gave me a shot of whiskey from a hip flask to calm my nerves. I was fond of him, and Irish people generally, because there was something cool in the way they were never cool; they displayed an upfront honesty, and always with a wink and a smile.

The reception was held under a rented marquee in our Gladesville backyard, with the band, aunts, uncles, parents, cousins, friends and crew. Everyone had to wear a hat, and we dined on pork pies and a three-foot-high profiterole cake. It was a huge, happy day. We were young and strong, full of boundless and infectious enthusiasm, and we stood ready to take on the world.

Skywards

In 1984 we made our album *Red Sails in the Sunset* in Japan. We had toured all through 1983 on the back of *10, 9, 8, 7, 6, 5, 4, 3, 2, 1*'s success and spent another six weeks in London. I felt our travel and business schedule was once again distracting us from our songwriting schedule, so *Red Sails* relied on a lot of weird sounds and effects to make up for it. It was fun to make – again with Nick – and had a few great songs, but Tokyo was an uncommon place to pick for an Australian band to record an album, culturally and linguistically. Perhaps that was part of the charm, along with our growing need to innovate. And the album certainly was perceived in that way. The studio was built over a disinterred cemetery, and the assistants suggested that there was an *obake*, or ghost, that strolled around the rooms after dark, as things would mysteriously move overnight.

After the band finished recording, Clare flew in and we visited the Hiroshima Peace Museum. We stood in front of a sidewalk silhouette, a haunting outline of a human being created by the atomic blast in 1945, etched onto the steps of a building. I looked around and saw a hundred Japanese faces looking at me as if I were the American pilot of the *Enola Gay*. On a train, an old man looked straight through me with cold eyes. He could well have been a *hibakusha*, a survivor of the bomb.

That same year, Pete had a nearly successful run for the Senate for the Nuclear Disarmament Party, and Midnight Oil were now a political entity in the eyes of the media. I was happy enough to be behind the scenes and make the music as good as I could. People in bands need to complement one another. Leaving people to do what they are good at was my way of dealing with it. I believed totally in our ideas and sentiments and putting them into song, but to me the world of politics appeared transient, alien and bereft, whereas a good song could live forever. Even so, I understood that to ignore the imperfect world of politics was to give up hope in humanity. Pete was born to it. Democracy is optimism in the face of despair.

The sinking of the Greenpeace vessel *Rainbow Warrior* in New Zealand by French terrorists on 10 July 1985 was fresh in our minds. Days before our third tour of the US in September we headed into the studio to cut the *Species Deceases* EP. It was all quick brushstrokes and good high energy, tracked live.

I had written a song called 'Valuable Thing'. The music sounded great, but the chorus lyrics weren't working. Minutes before Pete committed them to tape, Rob walked in and exclaimed, 'Oh, I know! This song is about the *Rainbow Warrior*!' And changed the lyrics:

> *Why wait for the planes to come*
> *When everybody's got you on the run*
> *South Pacific carry on*
> *Here come the Hercules, here come the submarines*
> *Sinking South Pacific dreams.*

Instantly the song, 'Hercules,' was a Midnight Oil song – it was about something meaningful and significant. I already had the middle bit, 'There is something I will remember', which would now fit perfectly. Pete changed and added to my verse lyrics and now the diverse parts were coherent. It felt like a miracle. We had a very good team, and that's what any good band is all about.

The EP did well in Australia, culminating in two sold-out shows at Kooyong Tennis Centre in Melbourne on 14 and 15 December 1985. The previous night in Geelong I asked the monitor engineer to turn something up or down. We were on a temporary stage built for the show, using scaffolding and timber with curtains around the edges. I pushed through one of the curtains and walked into a chasm, falling fifteen feet onto a road case with my Gretsch guitar strapped to me, fracturing three ribs. The show carried on as it must and I played in much discomfort. The band were unaware that I had fallen until the encore, when I was rushed to hospital. It was not the last onstage accident I would have.

Awakening the next day, I was cold, unable to move and in severe pain. Lippold, now our stage manager, visited me in my hotel room and said, 'That's what you get for changing your monitors.' My laughter hurt like hell.

That night at Kooyong stadium I went on bombed out on Panamax in front of 14,000 people and it felt like a blur, so much so that I went chemical-free the next night and at least felt like I'd experienced the show.

*

Earlier in 1985, Midnight Oil had toured the US supporting the English reggae/pop band UB40. Birmingham lads, they got up to play the horns on 'Power and the Passion' every night along with miscellaneous members of their entourage camping it up on toy saxophones. They travelled around merrily in a bus, grooving as one to deep reggae cuts amid a righteous fog of marijuana.

In New York, we found ourselves staying at the famous Gramercy Park Hotel. On our evening off we were whisked to a Manhattan loft for a photo shoot. There was a constant demand for publicity shots from record labels and PR people, trying to freshen up our image, week to week. We had some clothes from London's Kensington Market – a grab-bag of Doc Martens, skinny jeans and a hodgepodge of coloured shirts. Fashion wasn't really our area, but a few band members were experimenting with mullets.

We walked into a scene out of a Warhol film. Except it was more *Zoolander* than Warhol. There were bright lights, food, drinks and lines of coke everywhere. Models with long legs and men with permed hair mingled on upscale couches. Everyone was wired in some way – short-tempered and in a hurry. Decadent as it was, we were in New York, fashion centre of the universe, and the atmosphere was electric and all business. The photographer, I'll call him Henri, had just shot Duran Duran and was riding high. Gary watched the shoot unfold from up the back, drinking with the menagerie of beautiful people, while Henri arranged us in the frame. It may start otherwise, but the lead singer always ends up in the middle at the front. We were on little risers behind Pete.

'Smile, baby,' he said. 'Give it to me.'

More shuffling of positions and adjustments of hair. It seemed to go on for hours. We were not clicking with Henri. We were too straight for him, from a sunken world. We lacked the insouciance, and the nonchalance. But as obliging Aussies we did everything he requested, including pouting and sucking in our cheeks. But we couldn't feign the dispassion or summon the necessary disdain. It seemed we weren't real pop stars after all.

A makeup team whirled around us like a pit crew around a Formula 1 car. The more desperate Henri got, the more makeup they applied. Henri particularly didn't like my eyes. 'Your eyes are wrong, baby. They go down. They should go up.' A makeup artist was despatched repeatedly to fix the problem with much mascara. It was a strange kind of humiliation. I was never going to be one of the beautiful people.

Up the back of the room, the crowd were getting increasingly wasted and rowdy. Gary was having a ball, laughing at our expense.

'Who's a pretty boy then?' he said at the end of the session.

The photographic evidence exists in someone's attic, probably Rob's. He's our in-house curator who knows where the bodies are buried.

Warakurna

The feeling in the camp was that *Species Deceases* was all well and good, but we wanted to do something different now, more deliberate and song-oriented than the pub-rock thing. A kind of Australian music with space and texture that spoke of the country from the heart.

Early in 1986 we had been asked to contribute a song to a film called *Uluru: An Anangu Story* by the Mutitjulu community and recorded 'The Dead Heart'. The demo we made relied on two acoustic guitars, from Martin and me, a drum machine and bass guitar pumping out eighth notes and a sample that Martin performed on a bass guitar that went 'BROWWWWWW' every sixteen bars or so. We'd never used the drum machine and acoustic guitars together in this way; it felt fresh. It had beautiful, heartfelt lyrics by Rob. I suggested we speed it up and add the 'doo-doo' chant in between the verse lines which would shift from a minor to a major key to give the song a lift. The drum machine created a hypnotic groove and we recorded a sketch of it quickly. The Mutitjulu community heard the demo and approved the song.

The next week we went into Studios 301, Studio B, in Sydney, and recorded it with the band producing and Greg Henderson engineering. Acoustic guitars were to the fore, and Pete's ad-lib vocal and lyrics at the end took the whole thing even higher. We got it most of the way there using up all of the forty-eight tracks on two 24-track tape machines harnessed together, with various overdubs, including a glockenspiel, cello and a French horn, but it was Nick Launay, who happened to be in town, who rescued the whole thing by adding drum sounds and tom fills, and doing a consummate mix on the SSL console that straddled the control room in just one crowning day. That feeling of being so proud of what we had done was back again, the feeling I'd had after 10, 9, 8, 7, 6, 5, 4, 3, 2, 1. We made the film clip at Uluru with Ray Argall and 'The Dead Heart' sailed towards the top of the charts.

*

On 9 July 1986 we embarked on the *Blackfella/Whitefella* tour of the Western Desert, the Northern Territory and Arnhem Land. This was a joint project put together by Gary, Pete and the Federal Minister for Aboriginal Affairs, Clyde Holding. Along with the Western Desert's own Warumpi Band, we were to take our music out to Aboriginal communities, travelling into the heart of their civilisation. We'd heard about the problems out there and wanted to take a look for ourselves.

Charlie McMahon, a didjeridu player whom we had played with many times, knew Central Australia well. He had worked drilling bores and helped to establish the outstations that became the communities of Kintore and Kiwirrkurra, and he was to be our guide, our Western Desert road map. When Charlie said something, you listened, if only because he had a prosthetic arm with a metal claw that he operated by twisting his shoulder. It also doubled as a jaw-dropping tin opener. We first met in 1978 when he leapt up onstage to jam with us at French's Tavern in Darlinghurst, blowing the roof off with his didjeridu. He would menace the crowd with his 'log', narrowly missing our heads and the low ceiling as he swung it around in the air, sometimes firing pyrotechnics from it into the audience.

I first met Warumpi Band's Neil Murray as we were throwing our swags and guitars in the back of Charlie's ute at the Yulara Resort. His band was a bit late getting there, a day or two, but in the bush that's acceptable. Things happen, you know?

'Where have you guys been?' I said. He gave me a look that spoke of the frustrations of dealing with Aboriginal musicians whose first priority is family and culture, a career in rock a distant second.

*

The band hired a fleet of Toyota Sahara LandCruisers. Clare and I travelled with Pete and Martin in one; Gary, Giffo, trombonist Glad Reed and Stephanie Lewis, who ran our office, travelled in another. A documentary crew from ABC-TV's *A Big Country* commandeered another, and a journalist and photographer from *The Age* newspaper followed in yet another. The crew, consisting of Lippold and sound man Pat Pickett, carried the stage gear in a 4WD ute. Rob travelled with Charlie in his battered HJ45 Toyota. It was a veritable circus that headed out as one in a dust cloud for the four-hour drive west over red dirt roads towards the first show at Docker River.

As we passed Lasseter's Cave on the Hull River, eating the dust from the vehicle in front of us, probably Gary's, I suggested we call the album we were about to make *Diesel and Dust*. There were mutters of assent. The Petermann Ranges to our right looked ancient and sandblasted, with shades of pink, ochre and magenta as the light changed. The country was Namatjira exquisite – white river gums, clean and untroubled by European cattle or sheep grazing. Just as it always had been. In the words of the Neil Murray and Sammy Butcher song, it was 'Fine Open Country'.

I saw Warumpi Band play in their natural habitat that night, and it made so much sense. Their music was inclusive and about something – something good. Songs like 'Gotta Be Strong'. They had made just one album at that point, *Big Name, No Blankets,* with a punky, country, Oz-rock and reggae-influenced sound, but they had anthemic songs. Their lead singer, George Rrurrambu Burarrwanga, possessed an amazing presence, 'the Mick Jagger of the Western Desert'. I could relate most to Sammy Butcher, the guitar player who hid in the shadows, peeling off the sweetest country licks. With Neil's songwriting and guitar-playing, the solid metre of Gordon Butcher's drumming and Hilary Wirrie's deep-rooted bass, they were swinging like a barn door. It was the first gig of the tour.

We had left our dinner up on some soccer nets so the local dogs didn't get it, but returned to find it had been eaten by the crows, and when it was our turn to play, the Docker River audience was not accustomed to bright lights and roaring PA systems, so kept a healthy thirty or so metres from the stage. We had dropped in like rock warriors, a blaze of thunder and noise from urban Australia. The local people sat under blankets, huddled around campfires as dogs wandered around. They were so far away from us that all you could see were their distant forms. This was not our usual environment, which was drunk people and broken glass scattered on the floor of any number of suburban pubs and clubs. This was a dry community situated on red soil, with kids running everywhere. I'd say the members of the audience were completely nonplussed by the cyclonic noise that banged around their normally quiet community, though many shyly giggled at the sight of Pete's dancing.

The next day our convoy headed for Warakurna, just over the West Australian border. On the outskirts we saw where the Giles weather station had been established and a large chunk of space junk that had once fallen to Earth was proudly displayed.

Warakurna was a revelation. The language is Ngaanyatjarra and, like all of the Anangu Pitjantjatjara Yankunytjatjara (APY) lands, it possesses native title. A small population of around 200 lived there, primarily Aboriginal, with a few white teachers, medicos and administrators. The first thing we saw on entering was a scrawled notice on a car bonnet saying 'Strict Rules', and then a mountain of wrecked vehicles piled up in their hundreds in various stages of oxidisation and disintegration.

'Beat the Grog' was written on posters in the schoolhouse, which doubled as our change room. This was a concerted campaign by which Aboriginal culture could fight back against the domestic violence created by the alcohol that white people had introduced. We were playing on the school veranda and, around soundcheck time, some of us played football with the local kids on the chocolate-red soil in front of the stage, and some of the kids climbed up to bash on Rob's drum kit.

Phillip Toyne, environmental and Indigenous rights activist, lawyer and founder of Landcare, was travelling with us and suggested we play the gig, but we had picked the wrong day to come. The football had taken people off to Papunya and there weren't many left in Warakurna. Still, we previewed a version of 'Beds Are Burning', and with Glad Reed playing trombone it seemed to go down well. A camel joined us onstage, which seemed a good omen – the first but not the last live rendition of this song.

That night we made a fire and laid our swags on a soft and sandy riverbed. Touring with the Warumpis was a good move, but not just because we enjoyed their music. We were on their home turf and far from ours. Waking up in this dream landscape the next morning, I realised where we really were, in a country where English was not a first language, a country that had its own art, music and laws. Unknown in the big cities, but all within our country. We heard stories of white men in the early days handing pieces of poisoned bread to the historic caretakers of the land, to see them die like dogs. European settlers had conducted a murderous and sustained campaign of blatant land grabbing. We had wanted to see the conditions out there, but we were getting so much more.

Another travelling companion, journalist and self-professed hitchhiker Andrew McMillan, banged out his stream-of-consciousness impressions of everything around him on an early Radio Shack word processor powered by torch batteries, sitting cross-legged on the red earth of Warakurna, cigarette burning in one hand and car wrecks piled up behind him. He couldn't type the words out quickly enough. The next day we hit the Sandy Blight Junction Road heading north. Surveyed by Len Beadell in 1960 using a theodolite and carved out with a bulldozer, the road was named after the eye infection Len suffered during its construction. He noticed Bungabiddy (or Pangkupirri) waterhole and laid the road nearby for the benefit of future travellers. It skirted to the west of Lake Hopkins, a great salt lake with many muddy patches linked by narrow briny fingers. This journey took in brilliant views from the trig point on Sir Frederick Range. Our vehicle, with Pete driving as usual, would stop by the road every couple of hours. Someone would make a quick fire using twigs and boil a billy, getting right into the spirit of the pioneers and even Len Beadell himself. We threw Lan-choo into the boiling water and drank strong bush tea from enamel cups that tasted of ash from the fire.

We made it to Kintore later that same day, amazing considering the distance and state of the road. Kintore (Walungurru) had been founded as an outstation after bores were drilled (with the help of Charlie McMahon), and in 1981 many Aboriginal people returned there from the failed experiment of forced assimilation at Papunya. This was the beginning of what was called the outstation movement: the coming back to country. We arrived only five years after it was settled, so Kintore was only a school, a shop and a few other dwellings, sitting between a sacred men's mountain and a sacred women's mountain, known as the Pulikatjara. The language there is Luritja, different from Warakurna.

It was there we met Johnny Scobie Tjapanangka, a Pintupi elder who took us under his wing. In his green army surplus jacket, he knew everything that moved in his community. He saw that we could spread the message about the plight of Aboriginal people around the world and saw the significance of these particular whitefellas and their passing circus. In a men's ceremony in the shadow of the men's mountain, we were led blindfolded to an unspecified location where we were shown sacred objects of their culture. I can't speak of the things I saw and heard, but I was privy to a dizzying spiritual experience that linked ancient tradition to what was all around me in the living culture.

That night's concert was outside a tin shed near the store, and George joined us onstage for a majestically shambolic version of the Rolling Stones' 'Dead Flowers', arm in arm with Pete, both grinning from ear to ear.

Things had started to warm up between the bands and any initial wariness was being broken down. That night at our camp (always a few kilometres out of town so we could gather firewood), George, Neil and Sammy joined us, pointing out the Aboriginal names for the constellations in the sky, the Dark Emu, the Canoe in Orion. They told us the eastern hemisphere belonged to the Arrernte and the western half to the Luritja people. George had a great laugh and they all made us feel at ease. The next morning we woke up in our swag with frost in our hair, feeling pretty raw after a few cold winter nights out under the stars. It's still my preferred camp setting – swag, fire, no roof.

We would play our acoustic guitars around the campfire, which became symbolic of the tour, and work on our songs, jam with Charlie on Patsy Cline tunes, or play some Beatles or Rolling Stones. In stark contrast, some lads from Kintore came out to our

Kim, Betty and Paul Moginie at The Lodge, 62 Burns Road, Wahroonga, in 1956, looking sharp by the rose arbour while awaiting my arrival.

Mum in the early 1940s. Probably only this one shot, with its wonderful textures, really captures her gentle manner.

Me on a perfectly superphosphated lawn behind The Lodge, sometime in 1957, having recently arrived from the orphanage and probably wondering what it all means.

Left: Kim, me and Mum at Balmoral Beach, Sydney, in 1957. I tended to look clingy in photographs, whereas Kim always seemed to own the image.

Below: Buttoned down, dressed to kill and ready to blitz the education system, Kim and I prepare for a new year at school, in 1960.

Above: Kim and me with our Holden FC; note the number plate bearing Mum's initials. Roadside picnics were our thing. Dad used to polish his cars within an inch of their lives.

Me aged six riding Fancy, Uncle Bruce and Aunty Marg's Shetland pony, at their farm in Bredbo, NSW. Despite having the requisite jodhpurs and riding boots, I was petrified. Sensing this, the horse threw me to the ground seconds later.

Our first gig as FARM, at Sydney Grammar School, in 1973. I'm playing a $20 guitar through a Strauss Polka amp. There were twenty or thirty disinterested schoolkids in the audience.

Looking spritely, and in love, during one of my many trips to the NSW South Coast, this one with Clare in 1979. *(Clare O'Brien)*

This captures an era. Midnight Oil with friends and early road crew at 77 Albert Avenue, Chatswood, Sydney, having a break during our first (of many) photo shoots. Left to right: Martin Rotsey, me, David Binns, Jim Buda, Robyn Kirk, Kate Furlong, Roger Maddrell, Anita Buda, Andrew 'Bear' James, Rob Hirst, Lesley Holland, Peter Murray, Annie Hooton, Peter Garrett, Mark (surname unknown), Shane Fahey. *(Philip Morris)*

Below: A very 1970s-looking werewolf, with my first really good guitar, a Gibson Les Paul Deluxe. In the foreground is our custom-made Midnight Oil sign, complete with inbuilt 40-watt bulb.

Above: Peter Garrett and me in 1979. We must be playing 'Powderworks' or 'Eye Contact', as I'm way up on the fretboard and Pete is playing 'keyboards'. *(Geoff Schuck)*

This looks like Martini's in Melbourne, around 1978. Left to right: me, Peter Garrett, Rob Hirst, Martin Rotsey. I'm deep into my Jan Akkerman phase.

Pete and me at my wedding to Clare O'Brien in Gladesville, Sydney, in 1983. And what a beautiful celebration it was: Irish harps, pork pies, a rented marquee and (just out of frame) a Hills Hoist. *(Beth Noble)*

Being a performer must run in the family. My children, Sam and Alice Moginie, in Lindfield, Sydney, 1992.

With Clare and the kids on a US road trip. Dad had just died in 1997, so we took Mum with us and went to see the Grand Canyon. *(Betty Moginie)*

Bushmen searching for a waterhole, somewhere between Kintore and Papunya, NT, on the *Blackfella/ Whitefella* tour, 1986. Left to right: Martin, Charlie McMahon, Pete, me, Peter Gifford and Rob. *(Clare O'Brien)*

Left: It's almost impossible to find any photos of Midnight Oil's manager Gary Morris Vasicek, but even he'd have to agree that this one, with his pet olive python, in Wadeye, NT, in 1986, is pretty good.

Below: When the first tyre blew, we didn't think anything of it. But when the second one blew we started to get concerned. Rob Hirst and Charlie McMahon with his Toyota HJ45, lost somewhere about 150 kilometres northwest of Alice Springs, in 1986.

Some of us became obsessed with cameras during our 1991 US tour, especially using black and white film with a red filter. This is one of my efforts, which could be entitled 'The tyranny of distance and the existential angst of a lonely hotel room in Boston'.

Midnight Oil, aka 'The Bushmen', performing 'My Country' on *The Tonight Show with Jay Leno*, 1993. The other Australian guest that night was Elle Macpherson. Pete got the hug. *(Margaret Norton/© 1993 NBCUniversal/Getty Images)*

Left: Saying sorry when Prime Minister John Howard wouldn't. After we played 'Beds Are Burning' at the Sydney Olympics in 2000, I felt like our mission was pretty much accomplished. *(Rick Stevens/Sydney Morning Herald)*

Below: Our induction into the ARIA Hall of Fame in 2006 was a proud moment, recognising that we'd had a significant influence on the music culture of Australia. Left to right: Bones, Rob, me, Pete and Martin. *(Paul McConnell/Getty Images)*

With Brian McRedmond at Rivett, ACT, on 2 May 2003. This is the only picture I have of me with my birth father.

Above: Waltzing in and creating havoc. On 3 May 2003, I finally met my birth mother, Anne. Here she's examining me in forensic detail as my newfound sister Janet looks on. Everyone was in tears except me. *(Suzy Flowers)*

Right: I'd never thought I would ever get to hug my birth mother. It was no normal hug. *(Suzy Flowers)*

I was then but a twinkle in their eye, but they were a handsome couple, I'd have to say. Brian and Anne at the Queanbeyan Show in 1955. *(McRedmond family archive)*

After I was born in 1956, my birth parents went on to have five more children. This is Anne with John in 1958. *(McRedmond family archive)*

The parallel universe where I might have been but wasn't: McRedmond children at home in Inverell, NSW, in 1970. Left to right: Dave, Paul, John and Janet. My birth siblings have all welcomed me into the family as their brother. How lucky am I? *(McRedmond family archive)*

A 1988 Christmas gathering showing my birth mother, Anne, at left, with all my birth siblings: Dave, Janet, Paul, Susan and John. *(McRedmond family archive)*

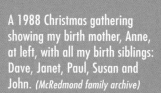

Top Left: After fleeing the Troubles in Ireland, my grandfather Paddy, seen here at Inverell, NSW, found love with Grandmother Rose in Australia. *(McRedmond family archive)*

Top Right: This makes we want to take up boxing to maintain the family tradition. Paddy's brother Dick 'The Boxer' McRedmond in 1930, a giant of a man. *(McRedmond family archive)*

Left: At the Grand Canal, Tullamore, brushing up on my Irish family history with Malachy Spollen after a grand tour of the bogs, rivers and gentle hills of County Offaly. *(Christabel Blackman)*

Exploring the town of Dingle/An Daingean, County Kerry. Visiting Ireland's west coast threw me into the deep end of traditional Irish music, which, unbeknown to me, was already coursing through my veins.
(Christabel Blackman)

With Jim Moginie & The Family Dog we were aiming for a fierce psychedelic sound. Left to right: Paul Larsen Loughhead, me, Kent Steedman and Tim Kevin. *(Mandy Hall)*

Shameless Seamus and the Tullamore Dews. Left to right: Peter Mackie, Evelyn Finnerty, Dave 'Bird' Twohill, me, Alan Healy and Stephen Coburn. *(Catalin Anastase)*

Classical music meets Kurt Weill via Pussy Riot, Hildegard von Bingen and Dolly Parton – the Australian Chamber Orchestra Underground, Sydney, 2016. Left to right: Satu Vänskä, me, Brian Ritchie and Julian Thompson. *(Christabel Blackman)*

The band that kept the wheels greased for Pete's return: The Break at the Commonwealth Games, Brisbane, 2018. Left to right: Martin Rotsey, Jack Howard, Brian Ritchie, Rob Hirst and me. *(Christabel Blackman)*

We always had our best conversations and made our best decisions around a campfire. Midnight Oil at Uluru, NT, for a photo shoot in 2016. *(Oliver Eclipse)*

Not just a lazy victory lap around the wineries. Midnight Oil announce the seventy-seven-date worldwide *Great Circle* tour at a press conference aboard the *Mari Nawi*, in Sydney Harbour, on 17 February 2017. *(Ryan Pierse/Getty Images)*

Playing on the *Great Circle* tour, 2017. This yellowing guitar is the 1974 twentieth-anniversary Les Paul Custom I found to replace the sunburst one stolen in London in 1982. *(Sam Tabone/Getty Images)*

Martin, Bones and me backstage in 2017. We always had a warm-up room so that from the first downbeat we could hit the stage running. *(Christabel Blackman)*

The Makaratta Project is probably my favourite Midnight Oil record, and we took it on the road with a crew including Adam Ventoura (far left); Alice Skye, Leah Flanagan, Liz Stringer and Troy Cassar-Daley (centre); and Andy Bickers, Tasman Keith and Dan Sultan (on the right, next to Rob). *(Robert Hambling)*

During the 'cocktail kit' part of the show one night in Canberra in 2021, Rob called for a rare group hug. In the background is Leah Flanagan. *(Tony Begg)*

Christabel would always climb up on the drum riser at the end of each show and photograph the group's final bow. This shot, from the Vieilles Charrues Festival at Carhaix, France, in 2022, takes the cake. *(Christabel Blackman)*

In June 2022, after coffee in a dixie cup with an almond shot and a pretzel at a truck stop in Delaware, the *Resist* touring party gathered for a group photo. *(Tom Jones)*

Midnight Oil's final show at the Hordern Pavilion in Sydney, on 3 October 2022. Fans would do almost anything to get a ticket, and even the prime minister came — he had his own dressing room. *(Joel Cangy)*

Me at left, joining in the fun at Bollard's Bar in Kilkenny, with Paddy Cleere (centre) and Mick McAuley, Ireland, 2018. *(Christabel Blackman)*

An Irish blessing. With Christabel Blackman at Mount Congreve Gardens, Ireland, 2022. *(Glenn Lucas)*

A pint of porter from Dempsey's Pub on the bridge of the Silver River, Cadamstown, County Offaly.

The Blarney pilgrim. Walking the clifftops at Dunquin/Dún Chaoin, County Kerry, 2018. *(Christabel Blackman)*

camp one evening and played traditional music that, among the whispering desert oak, seemed to resonate with the earth itself.

*

Soon we joined the Gary Junction Road and convoyed on to Papunya where we met Alison Anderson, council clerk of the community. She appeared a formidable spokesperson for her people, fronting up to the ABC cameras, articulating ideas like 'not selling off Aboriginal people for a dollar'. We heard about the ill-fated assimilation of different Aboriginal clans into the town in the seventies, tribes with huge cultural differences being forced to live behind suburban picket fences. It was never going to end well. Within weeks, the houses were on fire and people were abandoning the community. Another case of government whitefella FIFOs with well-meaning but culturally bloodless policies.

We saw the petrol sniffers stumble around the red dirt streets in the daylight like brain-shot zombies, holding tins to their faces and coats over their heads. The introduction of fuel without the chemicals was later successful at stamping out petrol sniffing, but it took a harrowing toll on the population for a good generation or so.

Next day we pushed on to Yuendumu. There's a photograph Clare captured of the band and Charlie stopped by a waterhole, secret knowledge to the blackfellas but shared with him. White men's cattle had fouled most of these waterholes in the early days. A large flat rock was removed to reveal a small pool between other rocks, brimming with crystal-clear, life-giving water. In the photo you can see that we were happily filthy and unshaven, wearing dirty clothes and dusty boots.

The footage taken by the ABC crew that night in Yuendumu also shows the same thing. In 'Helps Me Helps You', Charlie is wildly spinning his didjeridu around in the air, menacing the crowd, the rest of us looking furry and feral, creating a mighty din that ricocheted off the concrete walls of the local hall.

That night, I was asked to join the Warumpis on an embryonic version of 'My Island Home', which I hopped up to play every night from then on. The *Blackfella/Whitefella* tour was starting to live up to its name.

Afterwards, we camped out under the stars just out of town. As an amateur astronomer and scientist, I had never before seen so many colours in the night sky. The magenta of the Magellanic Clouds, the Milky Way like a 3D white streak, the infinite depth and silence of the universe spinning around.

The next morning we followed Charlie in our 4WD back into Alice Springs for a beer and a long-anticipated shower and bed. Our two vehicles took a wrong turn on the way, only realising our mistake a good 200 kilometres too late. Charlie's idea was to go overland rather than backtrack, using the Reader's Digest *Atlas of the World* as his guide. Pretty silly stuff in hindsight, but we trusted Charlie implicitly. We headed through an outstation of sorts and soon were met with sandhill after sandhill in true Burke and Wills fashion. These obstacles had no road through them, just lofty thickets of undergrowth, twisted roots and saltbush. When the first tyre blew, we thought nothing of it, but when the second one blew we started to get slightly concerned. It went on for hours; the vehicles had boiling radiators from the strain of breaking over these mighty dunes and then down again, and all the while the sun was getting lower, as was our supply of water. 'She'll be right,' said Charlie. 'If we find a fence, we'll follow it and it'll meet a road.' Good advice, as it turned out. Soon we did meet our fence and our road, and in an hour or two we were speeding back to Alice, our vehicles casting long shadows before us.

*

When the tour moved on to the Top End, Clare headed back to Sydney and the rest of us flew on to Darwin. In the bar that night, Giffo told me he was leaving. He had been having blackouts and mental health issues and couldn't see a way to be happy with his role in the band. I didn't want to believe him, but he was serious, and within a year he was gone. On the same night, Gary chastised me for wearing a jumper because I had a cold. 'Take it off! If you embrace the cold, you won't get a cold,' he said, grabbing me by the shoulders. What a night. Coming back to relative civilisation seemed to be bringing out all the quirks and grievances in everybody.

We continued the tour in light aircraft. Gone were the Toyotas. The Warumpis were still with us, but various members had stayed in the desert for family reasons, so it was not quite the same band.

Maningrida was our first stop. I lay on a hammock on a tropical late afternoon listening to Neil play 'My Island Home' to George on the lawn between our quarters and the palm-lined cove. Neil wrote it for George, a coastal man from Elcho Island who was now living in the Western Desert. I never could have guessed its future as an anthem, performed at the Sydney Olympics in 2000 by Christine Anu. As the sweet music drifted towards me, I could see Neil was a writer a cut above. He loves a good tune, but there has to be a good story too.

The barge from Darwin was due in Maningrida the night of our show, a supply line that came in once a fortnight. It rode low in the water carrying necessities and many slabs of beer. The locals celebrated its arrival by sculling them down warm, straight off the deck.

The *Big Country* crew were stepping up their documentation of the shows, worried they had too much footage of us and not enough of the Warumpis. We were more relaxed with cameras being around by now and the laconic crew were seasoned veterans. But the pressure was on George to live up to his Mick Jagger status. He had a few drinks before the show, and by the time the Warumpis played, his voice was a mere rasp. In the aftermath, he was in deep trouble from all around – from his band, Gary and the ABC producer. 'This was going to be Warumpi Band's big break!' they all chimed. 'It's up to *you*.' That burden hounded him from one end of the Territory to the other.

Our next stop was George's country, Elcho Island. Pandanus, red dirt, white sand and clear blue water, with laughing women and children wearing brightly coloured fabrics dotted about the community in clusters. But this was no Qantas commercial. We hadn't eaten before or after our show, so we were starving when we woke the next day. The local lads piled us all into the back of a brand-new Isuzu dump truck and took us spearfishing for breakfast. The parallax error caused by the water between your eye and the fish was something to behold – it was virtually impossible to hit your target, but hunger made us go all out. The locals who were with us had no trouble: they threw some nets out, and we gutted and washed the fish in the saltwater and cooked it on an open fire on the sand. It was served on a flat river stone warmed in the sun, and eaten with fingers, and I have never forgotten how good it tasted.

Generally speaking, the presence of missionaries and the influence of mining differentiate the Top End communities from those of the Western Desert. Nhulunbuy on the Gove Peninsula was home to Rio Tinto's aluminium mine. Local Yolngu people received royalties from it until it ceased operation in 2014. Late in the afternoon I went fishing with a now heavily bearded Giffo at the boat ramp. Giant black gastropod sea slugs moved around our feet in the water and we found huge translucent pieces of turtle shell and held them up to the light of the dying sun.

Things became unhinged that night. We played in the school yard, but Lippold had injured his back that afternoon. He was in agony and had to be left in the local hospital for the remainder of the tour. Gary made a big fuss about catching an olive python in the store room of the school and proudly carried it around in a Globite suitcase from that day on.

*

Next stop was Numbulwar on the Gulf of Carpentaria. Flying in was a feast for the eyes: we could see a few bleached demountable houses dotted among the pandanus, scraggly gums and ti trees, some asphalt streets and power lines randomly criss-crossing deep ochre earth. Then, a strip of pure white sand against endless chalky blue waters. There was no generator for our show, so we jacked into the power lines that provided light for the football field, thanks to the ingenuity of Pat Pickett. Most roadies would risk their own life to get the gig happening.

Our old friend Richard Geeves was now a school teacher in Numbulwar. Richard had introduced me to an old Aboriginal man after the show. Dressed in a blue corduroy western shirt with a white Stetson hat, he spoke quietly and said when he saw me playing he realised that I was the spirit of his dead son returned. He was completely convinced, and wouldn't let go of me. This kind of thing would never happen after a show at Blacktown RSL.

I was starting to see that Aboriginal people view the world through a different prism, where family, spirit and tradition take precedence over our own often flawed ideas of success – gathering possessions and seeking fame and recognition – and began to recognise why there was so much misunderstanding.

The tour wound on through Yirrkala, but in Barunga there was much booze flowing with many white people in the audience. We rocked out, of course, because this was the tranquillised environment in which we had cut our teeth as a band. We were no longer experiencing the strict rules of communities like Warakurna. After what we had experienced in previous weeks, it reeked of a cheap thrill, full of sound and fury signifying nothing.

George had pressure on him again from all quarters to be a good boy for the cameras but, in the true spirit of rock, he was not. He had a few drinks with some cousins and his voice metamorphosed into a hoarse whisper again, much to the horror of the ABC crew and, once more, his own band. He hung out with us in a pub the next day in Katherine trying to get away from the other disheartened Warumpis. He was great company, but harbouring him for an hour in the pub got us into trouble with the rest of the entourage, even though we found him, shepherded him onto our plane and took him on to the next gig in Wadeye (Port Keats), where the first thing we saw was a cyclone fence enclosing a whites-only drinking club in the middle of a dry community.

All the Top End pilots we met were cowboys to the power of ten – and you would have to be, flying vertically through monstrous cloud banks and hair-raising tropical storms as part of your daily mail run. Our pilots, AJ and Captain Coop, performed extra duties as a second support band called The Swamp Jockeys. They were sweet but completely troppo guys, gleefully parachuting into town in the late afternoon before the show to thrill the townsfolk as part of the growing circus-like atmosphere of the tour, which included Gary walking around bare-chested, olive python draped around his neck, scaring and monstering all the children. I snapped a picture of him in that guise – pure Tarzan.

We had a cup of tea with the local school teacher at his house. He was burnt out from living in the town and dealing with its problems and isolation. Administration people turned over fast out there.

We went on to Bathurst Island, where I went fishing in the channel by the town of Nguiu, as it was then known. George had shown me how to catch live crabs and put them on the hook, a surefire way to catch fish with a hand line, but on this day I waited for hours by the river with no bites. When I sensed a dark submarine shape pass by in the water, that was enough for me. I went back and was told it was likely to be the Old Man, a seventeen-foot crocodile known to have taken people on previous occasions. Gary decided that he would hunt down the beast solo, armed only with a huge knife. He set out into the darkening mangroves, up to his waist in mud to deliver the Old Man some frontier justice. They never met. I don't like to think which one would have come out second best in a contest to the death. Probably the Old Man.

*

From Darwin we flew to Kakadu for the final show. Captain Coop and I were the sole occupants of our plane, a Beechcraft Queen Air that carried our stage gear. He flew at an altitude of a mere thirty metres and I could see crocodiles wriggling off the banks and splashing into the river. Flocks of brolgas peeled off into the air as we approached. Flying so low, I could spot the plant varieties whose tops we were almost brushing.

At one point, Captain Coop handed me the controls. 'Hey, Jim, mate, take over, will ya?'

A minute later we were cruising at a thousand feet.

'Why did you do that?' he said.

'Fear,' I muttered.

We made it safely to Kakadu. The band were staying and playing at a resort full of white people and tour groups, with beer flowing, and suddenly we were the rock stars we were accustomed to being once again. We joined the Warumpis onstage for a version of 'Blackfella/Whitefella', which segued into 'The Dead Heart', during which we swapped instruments mid-song. The film crew was happy and it was a fine way to wrap up the tour. That night Sammy (whose Fender Bullet guitar always travelled without a case on the tray of the ute) played so beautifully and sweetly. I knew we would meet again. 'Eh! Jim! You and me, brother! We're just the same!' he said. Guitarists toiling in the shadows while the rest of them were all grabbing the spotlight and showing off, as they were born to do.

*

The next day we headed back home in the best plane, a Beechcraft King Air. We flew over the perfect crescent of Bondi Beach late at night and at low altitude. Sydney looked huge, bejewelled, dazzling.

Upon our return, I felt like I had been on a three-week acid trip. I was unable to explain what I had experienced to the uninitiated and could no longer see our country as I had previously. I felt more like a European than an Australian and questioned what it meant to be Australian, what it meant to be white. To be born a certain colour consigned you to one life or to the other, and some were more equal than others. Apart from the sleight-of-hand theft of land they'd suffered, Aboriginal people had shorter life expectancy and poorer health, higher rates of infant mortality and unemployment, and lower levels of education. But the Western Desert, where Aboriginal people had been banished, felt pure, clean and superior to other places. Their art and music, traditions and laws, their humour, the beauty and space of this country-within-a-country we had travelled through all left their mark. This was the real Australia, not the suburbs where I grew up. I had been radicalised.

I soon joined the Warumpis in a Sydney studio to add an organ part to 'My Island Home' and my creative relationship with Neil began – I was the sonic guy to his songwriting smarts.

*

Midnight Oil started writing more songs for the next album. I kept coming back to 'Warakurna'. It had various iterations and I honed the words down over several months:

There is enough for everyone
In Redfern as there is in Alice
This is not the Buckingham Palace
This is the crown land
This is the brown land
This is not our land
Some folks live in water tanks
Some folks live in red brick flats
There is enough, the law is carved in granite
It's been shaped by wind and rain
White law could be wrong
Black law must be strong
Warakurna, cars will roll
Don't drink by the water hole
Court fines on the shopfront wall
Beat the grog and save your soul
Some people laugh, some never learn
This land must change or land must burn
Some people sleep, some people yearn
This land must change or land must burn
Diesel and dust is what we breathe
This land don't change and we don't leave
Some people live, some never die
This land don't change this land must lie
Some people leave, always return
This land must change or land must burn
Warakurna, camels roam
Fires are warm and dogs are cold
Not since Lasseter was here
Black man's got a lot to fear
Some people laugh, some never learn
This land must change or land must burn
Some people leave, always return
This land must change or land must burn

I took it to the band and we played through it once in a rehearsal room in Sydney. Afterwards I realised it needed something else, another chord in the chorus (B minor). I made a demo on a new 8-track Otari reel-to-reel, now residing under my parents' house, and used a primitive early sampler called an Emulator to play the drum part by hand. We pretty much copied the demo when we recorded it for *Diesel and Dust*.

All the songs on the album were honed like that. A lot of the work was done in Giffo's shed in Seaforth. He and I heard simple grooves and the kind of songs that you could play on a long trip on the car cassette player, bumping over the corrugated roads of the Western Desert, dust chasing you in the rear-vision mirror. Hypnotic rhythms, like a ZZ Top record. Then we took them into the new Alberts Studio in Neutral Bay, which was quite small and dead-sounding by industry standards. We lined the rooms with sheets of galvanised iron in an attempt to liven up the acoustics and bring us back to our Western Desert experience. With English producer Warne Livesey, who realised that the limitations of the studio would dictate a smaller drum sound, we concentrated more on the songs, arrangements and vocal abilities of the band members. He added magical keyboard touches and many sounds I could never have imagined. When Rob asked how the final mix for 'Beds Are Burning' sounded, I said 'anthemic', a word I never would have used about our music before.

I always say my life is divided into two parts, the part before the 1986 Western Desert/Top End tour and the part after. Those intense three weeks, whether witnessing the sacred objects in Kintore or being trusted to spread the word of Aboriginal people's plight, also gave us an album, a record we made to unpack what we had seen and felt in Aboriginal Australia. A record we could share with the world.

The closer to the light, the longer the shadow

By 1988, 'Beds Are Burning' had been a worldwide hit, selling hundreds of thousands of records. We'd had some recognition on previous tours, but this time we really had the song and the album to break through in America.

The size of the response was infinitely bigger than anything else we had previously experienced overseas. After a show to nearly 3000 people in Seattle, we were ushered into a cavernous green room full of overwhelmed radio contest winners and people who wanted to meet us. The door opened and they applauded madly, grinning and screaming, 'Oh my god! It's them!'

America! We were a product that they loved and wanted, and scrutinised both collectively and individually. Look what happened to Elvis with all of that sweet adoration. It was claustrophobic, and my reaction was immediate. I turned and headed straight back to the sanctuary of the dressing room. Willie McInnes, our American tour manager, followed me. 'It's okay, Jimmy,' he said. 'I know what to do.' He filled a large dixie cup with ice, poured a big slug of whiskey into it and thrust it into my hand. 'You'll be all right.' Things calmed down in the green room and so did I, thanks to the drop of 'truth serum', as Willie called it. It made me loquacious and seemingly witty, relaxing every muscle in my body so I could do my duty and 'work the room'. The trick was to go in, walk in one direction only – meeting people, shaking hands, signing autographs, getting photos taken – and then leave. It was almost pleasant.

That was the beginning of my love affair with truth serum. As soon as our international career took off, alcohol was everywhere – in tubs full of ice in dressing rooms after the show, on the tour bus, in mini bars in the hotels, when carousing with the record label or in bars on our nights off. The business is awash with it. I veered away from alcoholism – self-preservation would kick in – but drinking became a coping mechanism. There's a line I was treading between feeling good and becoming a rock cliché, but it wasn't possible to perform our music high on anything: I was playing guitar and keyboards simultaneously like an octopus to replicate the more layered sound of our recent records and would never allow myself to miss a cue. For me, it was a deeply mental and physical gig that required every brain cell. The band was like a sports team with performance indices. We were expected to play hard and well – by our crew, our fans and, most of all, one another.

And we had a new bass player, Bones Hillman. He was just what we needed at that point, a ray of sunshine, and someone who was born to tour. On the first day he joined, in 1987, he asked me if I wanted to play some mini golf. I also discovered he had a wicked alter ego. On more than one occasion he dropped his trousers while descending in an atrium elevator in an American hotel, so everyone having their flapjacks in the bistro below could see his arse approaching at high speed.

By now the rest of us were all fathers, which was an eye opener, as it wasn't all about 'you' anymore. Nurturing infants was all about attention to detail, and such a learning curve. This was a parallel universe of nappies, sleep-deprived nights and trips to GPs. Sam was born in 1987, Alice in 1989, and it was wondrous to have these little people in our midst. Bones was amazing with children, even though he didn't have any. Uncle Bones. They would flock to him like he was SpongeBob. He visited our house and devised a trap for birds in the backyard with a cardboard box, a stick, a long piece of string and a piece of lettuce. The magpies weren't fooled, but I'd never seen my children get so excited. I always suspected, though he didn't wear robes (apart from hotel ones), that Bones was a monk who had renounced celibacy.

*

On 30 May 1990 we parked a flatbed truck with a stage on it out the front of the vertical limestone lines of the Exxon building on Manhattan's Sixth Avenue to protest against the 1989 Exxon Valdez oil spill in Prince Edward Sound, Alaska, for which Exxon was not taking their share of responsibility. This lunchtime event, in between our shows at Radio City Music Hall, had been long planned in secret, and the NYPD threatened to shut it down unless it happened in a New York minute. On the day, we slept in unintentionally and awoke to Willie and Gary banging down our doors. We sprinted from the hotel with our guitars to the location many blocks away. Twenty minutes later, without a moment to tune up, we were onstage playing. We blasted away at the building's 750-foot facade. Despite the steep adrenalin rush, it felt right to do this, and the last song, John Lennon's 'Instant Karma', summed it up. The world's media had their cameras and microphones pointed in our direction. In the van afterwards, an exasperated Gary gave the whole band a piece of his mind for oversleeping.

The van rocked from side to side comically as he berated us. When the van came to a standstill in New York gridlock, I jumped out and walked to a café around the corner and ordered breakfast, joined by the others soon after.

The event was televised worldwide on all the news channels, and we all realised we had pulled off a major coup, made our point, played well, filmed and recorded it, and got out alive.

*

On one of the many North American tours that followed, we crossed the border into Canada at Niagara Falls and parked the Prevost tour bus in the adjacent car park. Our driver, Dominic, had a choice of destinations that he could hand-crank onto the bus's roll-sign. In the past it had read Willie Nelson or Timbuktu or Dolly Parton, but today it was Burt Reynolds' turn.

In no time, a queue of women devoted to Burt's oeuvre assembled themselves in a line by the aluminium bus door and requested autographs. Quite a few had Farrah Fawcett hairstyles. Bones welcomed them in, saying Burt was in the back of the bus resting but would be happy to give them his autograph. Pete signed Burt's name dozens of times on pieces of paper, bras or bus timetables.

*

On 7 July 1990 we played the Rock Torhout/Werchter Festival in Belgium. There were at least 60,000 people assembled in a field for a huge bill that included The Cure, Sinead O'Connor and many others. We came on before Bob Dylan. Due to the speed of sound, the back of the field was dancing half a beat later than the front.

After we played, we loosely assembled ourselves near the Bard's dressing room, nonchalantly hoping for a sighting or even a handshake. Someone passed Bob's joint out through the door so we had a toke on it. It was good pot, as one might expect, and when he went onstage, skinny in a sharp black cowboy suit with white piping, he raced through 'Mr Tambourine Man' in two minutes flat while G.E. Smith, the guitar player from the *Saturday Night Live* band, was mouthing the key 'G!' to a terror-stricken and under-rehearsed bass player in front of the biggest crowd I had ever seen. A mutual acquaintance told us Dylan had said, 'Man, that song "Beds Are Burning" is so good you could tour on that for fifteen years.' They call him a prophet, and that's exactly what happened. By 1991, both 'Beds Are Burning' and *Diesel and Dust* had been huge hit records worldwide. Midnight Oil were in full truck and selling pallet-loads of albums and singles with sold-out concerts everywhere.

The crowds were enthusiastic, and we were taken out to dinner by the labels on rare nights off in all the different territories, for fine dining of all varieties. The hotels were getting classier too – we were greeted by concierges in top hats and tails offering to relieve us of our luggage. We travelled on well-decked-out tour buses with televisions, computer games, kitchens and bunks. It was easy to get used to after the discomfort of our beginnings.

We were on top, but it was a perplexing time. I was troubled and uneasy, but didn't know why. There was absolutely nothing to grumble about. I was in a famous band. But where was the meaning, and where was I in all of it? I was in a strange dilemma, confused about who I was and feeling there was something fundamental missing. It was the time of my warring self. I loved the fame but didn't like myself much. All the success and adulation just made me feel desolate. I wasn't one to seek comfort in love from strangers either, using the 'what goes on the road stays on the road' aphorism, a short-term salve.

It was a lonely existence, and my family always seemed thousands of miles away, leading a different life at home in a distant world. Gary's strategy was to be General Douglas Macarthur, working undisturbed anywhere that was far from the front line with a clear head. It seemed like a lot of sacrifices were being made, and anyone could have seen by looking at our touring schedule that we were getting worn out. That's when your emotions are exposed, but we weren't the kind of people to let emotions show. No one was about to let the team down. We knew that if we didn't ride this rocket for all it was worth now, our journey would soon be over.

We had fifteen years of copious touring behind us, seven albums, two EPs, a monster hit album in *Diesel and Dust* and then another slightly-less-of-a-hit album in *Blue Sky Mining*. Music industry people would declare, 'This next record is the one that's going to take you into the big league.'

By now between the band and Gary we had eleven children, born within a three-year period. Clare and I needed more room for ours, and so we moved house to a bigger, grander place further up the North Shore. It was a Federation house, built at the turn of the 1900s, with high ceilings, four bedrooms and four fireplaces. On the day of the move, one of the young removalists recognised me and, at the end of the job, said, 'You know what your trouble is?' He gesticulated around the luxurious house. 'All this!'

I hadn't solicited his opinion, and it irked me that a stranger would judge me and had for the first time in this way. But it was a textbook Australian tall poppy assessment, a 'don't get too far above your station, mate' kind of comment. With international success, and the records being more listenable in recent years, he simply didn't want to watch helplessly as 'his' band went soft.

The truth in it was that we had become men with much on our plates. The band had been working overtime with blinders on, and we were finally making money. There were now endless meetings with accountants, dealing with concepts such as 'notional loan accounts'. I would emerge, head spinning with tax implications. We never went 'offshore' like other businesses or bands. We proudly remained in our country and paid our taxes, built the roads, built the schools. But the climate we found ourselves in at the end of the materialistic eighties was the era of tax evaders like Alan Bond and Christopher Skase, then portrayed as by the media. This feeling of becoming nouveau riche without any warning felt like spiritual bankruptcy.

We drove more expensive cars than before, bought investment properties, renovated. And our film clips now sported stellar budgets and had us starting to resemble a flock of male models with guitars out on location. We had stylists, makeup artists and hot photographers. Hadn't we learnt anything from the experience at that 1985 NYC photo shoot?

The conflict I felt about the success of the band I now look on as laughable, an apparition of middle-class guilt given how high we were riding at the time. This was the Everest of our career. It's a small window of opportunity to have the luxury of the public's full attention, and better to have a song in the charts than not. But the pressure to deliver and the relentlessness of the road up to that point created, for me, a kind of desperation to escape.

Other band members felt the same, so we all agreed to take a year off. Mason Munoz, our man at Sony in America, said this was not an option. People would forget us. 'A year off?! Fuck that. No! Get back over here as soon as you fucking can. Jesus. *Guys!*'

Conventional rock wisdom says: 'Just keep on going. Don't stop. Never retire.' But a year off is what ultimately happened, despite Mason's warning, even though we managed to do some shows and assemble and mix a live album, *Scream In Blue*, in among it.

*

My parents-in-law managed a huge property in Carcoar in Central Western New South Wales. Clare's father, Tony, and I would go for a trip around the paddocks in his ute in the late afternoon to check on things. Once we saw a lone tree that had been hit by lightning a week before, still smouldering. Tony could see and sense a sick sheep on a hillside miles away. He told me the best way to get a mob of sheep to go through a gate: 'You drove them, not drive them. That will just make them scatter. Just move around somewhere behind them in an arc, in the general direction of the open gate, and they will all get the idea to go through.' As if it was their idea. I liked that notion and thought I might be able to use it.

At home, I took the kids to school, worked in the garden and rode my bicycle through Lane Cove National Park just as I'd done as a child. Clare and I reconnected, but we weren't always seeing eye to eye. That would wax and wane. My life, usually full of applause, loneliness and stress, had become so divergent from hers: raising children, with complementary loneliness and working as an environmental scientist. I built a small studio under our big house and I helped Neil Murray make a solo album called *These Hands*. Producing was harder work than I'd expected and paid nothing, but I wanted to see if I was cut out for this kind of work – or any other kind of work. I wanted to be independent, if only for a while.

Was there a world outside Midnight Oil? I'd almost forgotten what the real world looked like.

Turning
that ice
into fire

Even though it was a year off, there was one gig we couldn't say no to. On 25 April 1992, we were to headline the Earth Day concert at the enormous Foxboro Stadium in Boston. Earth Day started in 1970 to honour the rise of the environmental movement and celebrate the achievements of conservation. On the bill were The Kinks, Joan Baez, Steve Miller Band, Indigo Girls, John Trudell and Violent Femmes.

We flew in from Australia and did a couple of warm-up shows at The Paradise Theater in town to prepare. The Paradise was actually a small club to us by now, and the crowd felt close and vital like in the old days. Before the second show, I went into the mobile truck parked outside and helped the engineers mix the gig from the previous night for a radio broadcast. We hadn't played for a while, so the cobwebs had been somewhat loosened.

We awoke on Earth Day to a rainy Boston and single-digit temperatures. The weather report was grim and snow was predicted. Some of us were still jet-lagged from our trip halfway around the globe. At about 1pm, the band and some of the other wives (Clare had stayed at home) piled onto the bus to the stadium, which was all concrete bleachers and metal hoardings with no roof, built for sports games. It could hold 30,000 people.

We had toured with John Trudell in 1988 and it was good to see him again. John was a Native American poet, a friend of activist Leonard Peltier, and had been at the occupation of Alcatraz. John had a tough life. His Nevada house had burnt to the ground, killing his wife, three children and mother-in-law. He was a former national chairman of the American Indian Movement but had retired from politics in 1979. Bob Dylan had called Trudell's privately released cassette the best album of the year and compared it to the work of Lou Reed and John Doe.

I made a comment about the cold to John; we had come from an Australian summer, and this Boston weather was a bit extreme. He grabbed both of my shoulders and shook me. 'Jim, somehow you've got to turn all that ice into *fire*.'

The Kinks came on just before us. Clearly used to English weather, Ray Davies had dressed appropriately with coat and scarf. They were very relaxed and strummed through 'unplugged' versions of their hits on acoustic guitars with sunglasses on. Even though he played 'Apeman', the finest environmental song ever written, it felt very laidback. The crowd weren't responding, some wandering off to the shelter of the hot-dog stands. Until they played 'Lola'. They busked a folky beginning to the song and then, *bang*, the curtains opened in the middle-eight to Dave Davies doing the splits. Mick Avory's drums thundered in, the sunglasses and coats came off, and Ray prowled the stage with all the showmanship in the world. It was fully rocking, and the PA got ten times louder. We had been lulled. The cheer from the crowd was deafening. Then they played hit after hit: 'All Day and All of the Night', 'You Really Got Me', 'Waterloo Sunset', 'Dedicated Follower of Fashion', 'Victoria', 'Tired of Waiting for You'. A band flying off the pages of the history books to get right in your face. The crowd leapt to their feet and didn't sit down again. A hard act to follow, as Tim Finn had once said about us.

As we were about to go on, Steve Miller came up to me behind the curtain and introduced himself. 'Man, I saw you guys at The Paradise the other night and you rocked! Fuck me. Best guitar sounds I've ever heard. Good luck out there, man,' he said, pointing to the gathering tempest.

We walked out into the cloudy daylight onstage, our hands barely able to move in the cold even with fingerless mittens, and the sound seemed to just fall out of the speakers onto the floor, too thin to project to the 30,000 people. Lots of ice but not much fire.

By the time Steve Miller came on it was actually snowing and getting dark. He wore a giant skiing-outfit suit, a bulbous Michelin Man playing guitar with almost boxing gloves. His band played like bosses as the blizzard swirled around the stadium.

We flew back to Australia, tails between our legs, ready to fight on another day. Ray Davies and Mother Nature had definitely whipped us on Earth Day.

Easter
Island
statues

'I don't like to be intimidated on my own show,' said David
Letterman after one of our appearances on his *Late Show*. 'They're
bushmen. They scare me.'

We might have projected that look with our hats, boots and
stubble, but Charlie McMahon was the real bushman among us.
He was also a good man to have on the road, inviting us to have
billy tea in his room at all hours when we toured the US. 'Yanks
can't do tea,' he declared. He was referring to their default setting,
a tea bag afloat in a glass beaker of tepid water. Tea-making was
to become a Midnight Oil tradition after that, a surefire morale
booster. A suitcase with enamel teapot and cups, tea cosy, strainer,
leaf tea and wooden board to keep the pot warm travelled with us
from then on – a homesickness remedy, not unlike the burning of
eucalyptus leaves.

In 1992, Charlie proposed a squat near the motorcycle
dealerships on Goulburn Street in Sydney's CBD as the location
for a Midnight Oil jamming and writing room. It had a nice and
seedy owner–builder atmosphere – motorbikes, old mattresses,

and bits of 4x2 leaning against the wall. We spent weeks there putting together the songs for the next record.

Then we moved to Megaphon Studios to record demos. In the first few days there, Rob was outside the control room strumming away on his guitar, perfecting his songs for what seemed like hours. Previously he would have melodies and a basic chord structure, which I would refine and flesh out and add music to, but now the tunes coming through the soundproof door were complete and perfect as they were. And Pete wasn't around. He was getting involved in the political world and it was starting to encroach on his availability. It was a natural evolution, but it didn't feel much like we were a team anymore.

Music journalist Ed St John wanted to interview us but as band members individually, which was unprecedented. Pete, Rob and Bones usually did all of the media. Gary called a meeting in our inner-city office at 63 Glebe Point Road to control the party line. He said it was important to relay the message that Midnight Oil was not a band, it was a movement. To me, this sounded like the self-importance and megalomania that accompanied fame. All that music, all that time on the road and in the studio as musicians. My heart sank. A movement?

It took us a year to write and demo the songs for the record. The pressure went unspoken, but we all tried to be light-hearted about it, afraid to loosen our grip on the success we had earned over so many tours, records and years. The radio-friendliness and safer melodic nature of our newer music started to reflect that fear. There was nothing Dionysian about the situation. Too much craft, not enough catharsis. We were afraid to fail or disappoint when everyone was depending on us to deliver the goods.

On hearing the demos, Gary berated us for being soft and demanded that we start again from scratch. The track 'Outbreak of Love' is a case in point. We played it live at the Palais in Melbourne while road-testing new material during our 1992 gigs.

Daryl Braithwaite, at one time Australia's King of Pop, went out of his way to mention he liked it. That should have been the sign that things were heading off the rails.

Soon after these shows in 1992, Clare and I took the kids, now five and three, to Belongil Beach in northern New South Wales for a week's holiday. On this exclusive section of coastline near Byron Bay, the ennui returned. I thought Midnight Oil was becoming a victim of its own popularity, brought asunder by the lure of a dollar and the corporate world. But I couldn't figure out exactly what to do about it now we were up to our necks in it. 'Outbreak of Love' was being bandied about as a strong single contender. I thought there was something overbearing and unrelenting about it, but what did it matter what I thought? We were a movement now, a touring juggernaut.

I talked about the issue with Clare, who listened calmly as usual. Then I went for a walk alone to think about it. I headed up the beach in a northerly direction towards Mount Warning and the estuary, past the roped-off bit of sand where the little terns were hatching and nude men were doing vigorous tai-chi gyrations. I decided to be Buddhist about it, let 'Outbreak of Love' rise or fall on its own merits. Let it go where it wanted. The band was a partnership; it wasn't going to worry me. I'd ignore the industry and just get on with my part of the job. I came back to the house lighter in spirit. But my identity was being swallowed up by the need to be faceless men – Easter Island statues with guitars. I was relaxing my grip on the reins in order to keep the peace, to keep on rockin'.

When we got to making the record proper with Nick Launay, it took four days just to do the backing track for that song, which also should have raised alarm bells. The music we were now making was very poppy in construction, with big choruses. This time it had to be rougher sounding than before, but perfect as well, with the strummy acoustic guitars and big backing vocals – that was our winning formula. Sounds impossible, doesn't it? Everything still had to conform to the rules of radio. Ironically, most of the tracks ended up as long as ragas, some more than six minutes. We spent five months in the studio doing just eleven songs. We added backing vocals, then Nick and I spent a couple of days filling the sound out, Beatle-ing it up a bit, adding organs, mellotrons, mandolins, pianos. But it probably all sounded better raw.

For the first time in our self-governing and long history, the record label became entangled in the making of the record, where previously they had been banned from the process. A rough mix of 'Truganini' was sent to Sony in the US before we'd finished recording. It sounded pretty good, so, consequently, when the proper mix was sent, they rejected it. 'One hundred and fifty retailers in the boardroom were grooving to the snare on the old mix,' they said.

Nick tried to incorporate their changes. Then, when we mixed the whole record, he was so unhappy with the sonics of the desk in the studio we used that he remixed it all again in London – after the album was released. The new version became a running change in the production master, but early copies have the original mix.

The schedule was so tight that we found ourselves doing videos for the songs before we'd even finished recording them. One glamorous two-day shoot was in Broome, on the other side of the country, with film crew, cinematographer and stylist.

An album launch and press junket was held in the hinterland of the Gold Coast. All the journalists had to go on a bushwalk with us. It was funny to see these chain-smoking, hard-bitten types grumble their way up and down the steep slopes of Mount Tambourine.

I noticed the media treated us with a reverence that had been missing before. We were asked our opinions regarding a new Australian flag and whether Australia should become a republic.

The politics were now at the forefront of how we were perceived. We were spokesmen for a movement.

A world tour was planned in 1993. We were offered Lollapalooza, a big new alternative music festival in the US featuring Alice in Chains, Dinosaur Jr, Tool and Rage Against the Machine. Our inclusion would have introduced us to a much bigger and younger American audience. The live power of Midnight Oil would have stood us in great stead on those stages alongside those bands. I can't remember the exact reason why we turned it down, but we opted to do our own headlining shows in the US with Ireland's Hothouse Flowers instead. The reality was that we were now embarking on a tour that was struggling to sell tickets. Politically correct, we stood in a world bursting open with catchcries of angst, nihilism and irony – never Midnight Oil's strong points. I liked contributing to album artwork, and Martin and I found a photo of a Native American in full regalia standing in a typical suburban driveway next to a big American car. It summed up the music we were making somehow, and it had irony. Gary would increasingly police the perimeter and destroy such ideas, claiming he alone knew what was required in the market. The cover became some Mexican indigenous art printed on recycled paper.

The album was named *Earth and Sun and Moon* after one of my songs, written after seeing the 1990 IMAX film *The Blue Planet*. Unfortunately, *Earth and Sun and Moon* as a title was a death sentence in the hippie-loathing, Seattle-grunge America of 1993. And America was all that seemed to matter.

Months later, the album wasn't doing the business everyone had been anticipating. Riding in the back of a white Cadillac limousine somewhere in the US after a long flight from somewhere else, Gary said, 'We have to change the album title. The artwork too. It sucks. People don't want to hear this PC stuff anymore. The kids don't like it.'

I felt like a fart in a spacesuit, barking into a vacuum.

The A&R department at Sony, in Manhattan's Black Rock building on Madison Avenue, rejected our video for 'Truganini'. It was 'those Aboriginal people again, the bush hats, the red dirt. Fuck that. That worked for "Beds Are Burning" five years ago, but it ain't gonna work now.'

Single releases changed at the last minute. 'Our polling was wrong; we're going with another song.' And so we rushed off to the Mojave Desert on a day off between shows to do a frantic video for 'My Country' among the fuselages of ruined aircraft. It felt as if we had the wobbles up, were running scared, spinning off the lazy Susan. Explosive meetings between Gary and Sony president Don Ienner were commonplace. Alpha male confrontation was negotiation 101 in the Black Rock, but it didn't get anyone, including the band, very far.

Songs were being edited for radio play and 'Outbreak of Love' was to have its guitar solo (mine) removed. I loved the solo, but Rob left it to me to approve its removal, which I did, taking one for the team. How could I possibly jeopardise the song's success after all the work that had gone into it? That was a challenge to my ego, but by then I wasn't sure who or what was steering the ship. The video that accompanied it was almost styled out of existence. Gone were the bush hats and R.M. Williams clothes. The brief was 'psychedelic'. I wore a billowing multi-coloured silk shirt and purple Lennon-style glasses, Rob wore a waistcoat over his shaved chest while brandishing maracas and Italian waiter sideburns, and Pete swam bare-chested in a pool made to look like mercury. What would the removalist have to say about that, I wondered.

In the rejected 'Truganini' video, we were depicted straining and sweating as we attempted to drag a prime mover with ropes through a grassed paddock in Castle Hill in north-western Sydney, an unconscious but perfect visual representation of our career at that point. At the label's insistence, we reshot the video in New York, at huge expense. We ended up with a lavish depiction of

Americans dancing wildly around a Hollywood fire blazing beneath the Brooklyn Bridge. Nothing to do with the life and times of Truganini. To Rob, it felt like we were dancing on her grave.

It wasn't all doom and gloom, though. We did a lot of American late-night television shows – *Late Show with David Letterman*, *Saturday Night Live* and *The Tonight Show with Jay Leno*. Wynton Marsalis was the Leno show's musical director, so the house band was seriously cooking. Backstage, Bones had been asked to do an interview and a technician turned up in our dressing room with a DAT (digital audio tape) machine and microphone. He was a shortish guy, a bit older than us, sporting a ponytail and a loud Hawaiian shirt. He said, 'Here's the gear for the interview. So who's the new guy?'

I looked at him and laughed in recognition. Bones was our new guy, five years into his tenure – and the one who was still happy to do interviews.

'Yeah, sounds like the new guy,' he said and set up the gear.

'You have to be in a band,' I said and introduced myself.

'Hey, Jim. I'm Poncho Sampedro,' he said. 'I play guitar in Crazy Horse.'

Poncho was moonlighting as Wynton's assistant. I'd been listening to Neil Young and Crazy Horse's recent live albums *Weld* and *Arc* and ate up the gnarly guitar sounds.

'Oh, man,' said Poncho, 'you like that? The first mixes were the best! The ones on the record suck. It got mixed to death.'

I could relate. We went out to the stage where he spotted our little tweed Fender Deluxe amps in the backline.

'We use those,' he offered.

I knew that but kept quiet.

'We mike them from the back as well. There are tricks to make them sound huge,' he said.

I liked him and his quick wit and could see what role he played in Crazy Horse – emollient.

With our bush hats and stubble, the Oils then performed 'My Country'. Another guest on the show, Australian supermodel Elle Macpherson, appeared onstage at the end of the song. Pete got a hug as we all looked on with envy.

*

Ten months of touring followed, pulling that prime mover for all it was worth to get back on track. We were signing CDs after gigs, sometimes for hours, as fans formed long queues in the cold after exhausting shows – a panicked record company strategy to get the guitar solo-less 'Outbreak of Love' to chart. It didn't.

As 1993 progressed, *Earth and Sun and Moon* stalled, so we toured even harder to compensate. On the final leg, we zig-zagged all over Europe in the freezing cold and gloom of winter in a claustrophobic double-decker bus. It had dirty brown carpet on the walls and low ceilings. Our driver was a pedantic Englishman who never took it over thirty miles per hour and insisted on a tea and fag break every two hours. We all learnt chess to pass the time, but it felt like we were endlessly marooned in a bleak submarine.

Our long-time production manager Michael Lippold, who would say 'Have fun!' every night as we walked onstage, was sleep deprived and stressed, with a fierce workload and the job of keeping some of the bigger personalities of the crew, and us, in check. The band cut him loose, but I felt like we were cutting off our right arm. He was our man, he knew what the word 'Oil' meant more than most. I should have piped up and said, 'I need him; he's not going anywhere; let's just cool down and give him another chance.' But the machine silently rolled forward. Every night from then on I missed his 'Have fun!' The fun was draining out of it.

The worst part was it didn't matter how much work we did for the label – the endless list of gigs or after-shows or handshakes or radio interviews; it was a chasm that couldn't be filled. Anyone can tell you, when things start to go down like this, there's no way to stop the freefall.

Near the end of this tour, after a show we played in Berlin, I asked our Australian Sony A&R man, John Watson, what he thought had happened.

'The world turned left, and you guys turned right,' he said.

It all came down to poor record sales, and Midnight Oil were no longer a priority for Sony in the US, or anywhere. They had new bands, new priorities.

*

My youngest, Alice, didn't recognise me when I got home. I felt I was a bad father, letting down the family, the band, the label, the team, the world. That made me want to run away back to the road even more, and when on the road I wanted to be home again. I was pretty much annihilated – a product of everyone's expectations but my own.

The band demanded so much from one another, silently and not so silently. I was operating behind the united front, the Easter Island statues where the party line ruled, a moving segment of a corporate caterpillar. We had become Gary's 'movement', and there was no one else to turn to in our codependency. No one could leave. I loved my family, but the demands of fatherhood were there and I didn't feel I was up to that either, often on the back foot trying to keep the peace with Clare, who was finding sole-parenting tricky.

Around this time I had a few strange experiences. As I walked down Fifth Avenue in New York, I felt I could sense each person's life story as they passed by. It was like the noise of millions of voices in a confessional speaking simultaneously, and I couldn't turn it off – I was empathising with the imagined anxieties of complete strangers on a case-by-case basis. It was exhausting and started to happen everywhere I went. Sometimes I would curl up in a ball in my hotel room paralysed by the noise of my own unravelling, going into a foetal position to calm down.

I'd had another strange experience back in 1990 on the 'Forgotten Years' film shoot in the French town of Verdun, where in World War One hundreds of thousands of soldiers perished in one of the costliest battles of attrition in history. We were given permission to mime the song in front of the Douaumont Ossuary, where the bones of French and German soldiers are stacked. Some of us walked up to see them through the small windows. They filled the building. The lone voice of a gardener yelled out, 'Vous ne montrez pas de respect et vous devriez partir!' He thought we were being disrespectful and should leave. As usual, there were cameras everywhere, and even a helicopter buzzing about filming. No time to debate the morality.

Later that day, among the countless crosses of the nearby Meuse-Argonne American Cemetery, we were literally dancing on the graves of the glorious dead. I thought I could see the worms turning in the earth, hear the sap moving in the silent trees. I had to cut out early as the fog descended. I went to the bus to sleep. The experience had finished me off and I slept for the next twenty-four hours.

(My Uncle Bruce, Mum's brother, the veteran who had served in World War Two and worked for Legacy, later rang me to say he really appreciated the song's sentiment that 'these shall not be forgotten years' and the imagery of the video clip. He said it was dignified and a valuable message that needed to be heard. It made me feel what we had done was worth it.)

When we played in Mulhouse, France, I walked straight off the stage and out into the street in a daze without saying goodbye to the band, making my way to the hotel via a few bars. My reserves were down but I found a place that made cassoulet, an impossibly rich French stew that partially snapped me out of my poor state of mind.

In 1994 we flew straight from Australia to Belgium to play on a metal festival called Graspop. We were sandwiched between Biohazard and Motörhead. The audience was reacting like grunting animals dumbstruck by the all-day barrage of heavy rock. We did our set but it didn't connect that well with the metalheads. On the way back to Brussels on the bus I got drunk, and when I reached my hotel room, I removed all my body hair (except on my head) with a Bic disposable razor. Acts of self-harm, smashing numbness by arousing sensation, attempts at relieving emotional distress – all seemed possible and acceptable as I was slowly surrendering to something I couldn't control or understand.

Another time we flew out of Amsterdam en route to Zurich. The crew had purchased some hash (they always loved going to Amsterdam) and in the security queue at Schipol Airport I was surreptitiously offered some to dispose of in a pot plant or some such. I swallowed the whole block. The first thing I did in Zurich was walk out of the hotel into a shop where I bought a ridiculously bulky and expensive Swiss watch with a built-in compass and metal silver band, which I never wore again.

*

Through the eighties and early nineties, we had been offered lucrative tours of South Africa but had always refused to play Sun City. In our numerous and lengthy band meetings, we all stood with the UN-sanctioned boycott: only if apartheid ended would we go. The death of activist Steve Biko in police custody had been news everywhere, and news of Nelson Mandela's conduct in prison was getting out to the world at large. Mandela displayed forgiveness, compassion and dignity in the face of brutality. He was a human being like anyone else, not an automaton. From this came his humility, and from humility came his strength, like the

Kipling poem that I was fascinated with as a child. 'If' could have been written just for him.

After twenty-seven years, Mandela walked free in 1990. He became the country's first black president in 1994, and in the same year we toured South Africa. The first gig was at Ellis Park, a giant football stadium in Johannesburg, with Sting, Lucky Dube and Johnny Clegg. The crowd was at least 30,000 strong.

It was a surreal experience. Everything was becoming surreal by that point. Instead of feeling part of this historic event, I felt increasingly disconnected from the act of playing music, even the love of music itself, and was lost in the hours and days between gigs.

We came back to Australia, and the first show we played was at The Domain in Sydney at an outdoor concert called Triple M's Big Backyard Concert. I had bought a six-foot-high wooden sculpture of a bird from a roadside stall near Durban and brought it back to Australia in one of our road cases. As I sauntered off to my car after the show, carrying it by the neck, I heard someone say to Bones, 'What is it with Jim and the bird?'

'Oh, he's been carrying that thing around with him for years,' said Bones.

*

I saw that I had abandoned my wife and children to go on an odyssey to conquer the world. I was now thirty-eight and increasingly disconnected from my family. Clare and I were serving two different masters, and that caused anger and misunderstanding. But there was something else I couldn't quite grasp. I couldn't see myself at all. I'd never really known who I was. Was I the estranged adopted adolescent at school, the infant left in an orphanage?

I didn't have the words to describe it, the wherewithal to confront it, and it would have been weakness in the culture of empire building that surrounded me to even mention it.

Karekare

In 1995 we undertook a national tour of Australia called *The Breaking of the Dry*. At this point in our career we could fill big venues with a multi-band bill but not on our own. So we went out with Crowded House and Hunters and Collectors.

We knew the Hunters well as touring buddies from the *Blue Sky Mining* tour a few years before. A night off with them would always end up in a hotel bar at 3am with all of us sitting around a table overloaded with empty green beer bottles, laughing at one another, or at nothing at all.

We all loved Crowded House. Neil Finn, like his brother, Tim, is a stellar singer and songwriter. Drummer Paul Hester had left a while before so they had a session man filling his place who was doing fine, but the chemistry wasn't the same. Everyone missed Paul's comedic and musical presence, but the band soldiered on anyway and won the crowd every single night of that tour.

The Finns and Midnight Oil had woven around each other's careers for years. As an eighteen-year-old, I saw Split Enz at a free concert on Manly Beach on New Year's Eve in 1975 as the tide was coming in. Eddie Rayner was a god. I was blown away by their power, theatrics and musicianship. Split Enz were very supportive to us even before I met them, singing our praises on *Countdown* (of all places) just before both bands played 1981's Tanelorn Festival.

Our histories were mysteriously intertwined, and there was much mutual respect, love and healthy competitiveness there. Rob had found Paul Hester for them when they needed a drummer, and when Giffo had departed in 1987, Neil had found Bones for us.

The three bands got reacquainted around the time we hit Townsville. The trucks coming from the previous show in Adelaide had become bogged on unsealed roads due to a deluge, so we had to delay the show by a day. Some in the entourage hit the casino or the bar downstairs. I disappeared into my suite, where the phone rang immediately. It was Neil asking me to come up to his room for a chat. He said Crowded House was coming to an end for him, especially now that Paul had departed. 'Do you want to get together and do something?' he asked. Just like Neil to get straight down to business.

I thought it could be, at the very least, a welcome shake-up. I was not thinking of jumping ship, but our music was becoming too much like our organisation: precise and safe. We were about to have some time off, so I said yes, and Neil and I celebrated with some truth serum.

Weeks later, Neil came to my basement studio, which was under the main bedroom of the house. By now I had an Amek board and a used Studer 24-track tape machine, and I loved the challenge presented by so many tracks of blank recording tape.

Clare had gone on a health retreat for a week, so we could make noise any hour of the day or night. Neil would arrive around 9pm, after the kids were fed and safely in bed, and we'd play on to around 3am. It felt pure: his voice could melt a city of hardened hearts. We made music up out of thin air. Some wacky and some great ideas popped out. I made a cassette of them for him to take away.

We soon reached out to each other again and I winged my way to New Zealand, his homeland, to expand on these little seeds of songs. I stayed with the Finns in Parnell, Auckland. They are a warm and friendly bunch – Neil, Sharon and their sons, Liam and Elroy, who were only young then. The next day we picked up some supplies, including an old Roland bass guitar synth from a bloke on Karangahape Road called Bungalow Bill, and headed out to New Zealand's East Coast. Karekare is a prehistoric and ancient place with active volcanoes, frequent landslides and even quicksand. It's deathly quiet compared to the cacophony of the Australian bush. The land is mountainous, running down to black-sand beaches, with winding roads and steep inclines where you could lose your footing in the dark, careering over the edge in a second. The leaves of the plants are large and deep-toned – moss green, Prussian blue and ink black, hailing from the Ordovician era when the earth was young and still cooling. There's a giant bay called the Cauldron where you can crouch behind a monstrous wall of rock in safety as massive waves thump into the other side, creating something akin to a sonic boom.

We arrived at a house owned by Neil's friend Nigel, who welcomed us. Crowded House had made their last album, *Together Alone*, here. We had a spiky-haired engineer called Paddy Free who Neil described as 'a good man with a loop'. Paddy recorded the proceedings on a small desk with a domestic digital 8-track. We spent five or six days there, writing and recording fantastical original music. Nothing was pre-conceived – it all seemed to come out of nowhere.

In the general spirit of things, I took mushrooms after midnight one night, which just made me really cranky and not stoned at all. Neil wrote the words to 'Addicted' the next day, using what I had apparently said sprawled across the sofa at 2am, something about drugs and how I'd had enough of them.

We performed, recorded and conceived the song in one take, using a loop of a taiko drum and a shaker made from seed pods, with Neil on piano and me on acoustic guitar. It's all on the final record: the writing of the song is the performance of the song.

Something major had gone down in Karekare. There was talk, drink and much laughter. I smoked roll-your-owns, enjoying them for the first time. What Neil smoked I don't know, but we got high on the music and played our hearts out.

I mentioned I was adopted and Neil said, 'Well, of course you're Irish. You act it, you look it. You're a wild and crazy Irishman, Jim.' I just looked at him. Neil has deep Irish roots and you'd assume he'd know an Irishman if he saw one.

Touring the US with Ireland's Hothouse Flowers in 1993, I had found myself on a night off at a bowling alley on their team and really seemed to hit it off with them. We despatched balls down our lane with much hilarity, facing backwards, lying down, any way except normal, celebrating being completely rubbish at the game.

On Neil's recommendation, in 1994 Midnight Oil stayed at an Irish traditional music castle near Galway where the bodhrán (Irish drum) and the Uilleann pipes were taught. I didn't partake in the lessons but remembered being moved by sessions in the pub where the patrons may well go quiet for the singers, local people who felt ownership of songs that would be unknown fifty kilometres away. While some in our company made light of the 'diddly-aye' aspects, a video exists of me staring with wonder, trying to understand what made this enchanting music tick. I wanted to dance and weep at the same time when I heard it.

On the last night in Karekare, Neil asked me to join whatever new entity was brewing in his mind. I was tempted, and in some ways it would have made more sense than staying with what I believed was becoming a besieged Midnight Oil. But I knew I would end up being a sideman to Neil. In Midnight Oil I was a musical powerbroker of sorts, and I wasn't about to give that up. Loyalty won out in the end and I'm glad it did. But Neil and I would keep working on his first solo album, *Try Whistling This*, during another ten-day visit to Auckland and an afternoon session two years later in New York City, and it's a record I love dearly.

I felt like a new man when I got home from Karekare. All the years of care and duty slipped away, replaced by a sense of adventure and freedom. It was completely joyous. Music without the marketing, a holiday from the heavy lifting of the last few years. I realised that my career had become a construct, and to nourish a creative self from this moment forward was the job at hand. It was like I was a teenager again, sitting at the piano and just letting the music carry me along with a sense of play, without guile or judgment. Joni Mitchell calls that feeling 'the blarney', and I felt like before Karekare it had been beaten out of me. I'm eternally grateful to Neil for plugging me back into it, the thing I thought was lost.

A streetcar named Malcolm

By 1995, a tall poppy backlash was beginning to grow against Midnight Oil in Australia. Successful bands, less successful ones, journalists and even a knot of venue owners were starting to take coordinated potshots. 'Here come the Oils, every year: the Christmas shows, the album, the big clean-up. Yawn.'

Later that year I was with my family at a house we had just built on the South Coast along with Nick Launay and his now wife, our old friend Nadya Anderson, and their two children, who were the same age as ours. I was digging holes with a mattock behind the garage. The ground was stony and I needed to put two uprights in to make an old-fashioned clothesline. Nick came out to where I was working for a chat. I'd given him a cassette with about thirty ideas for songs I'd written. He'd noticed this backlash against the band and suggested that I make a noisy solo EP from some of the material he'd heard. He said it could lead the camp out of oblivion.

After a canoeing trip to Lake Durras, Nick and I drove home in the dusk, bumping along the forestry trails of Murramarang, avoiding the potholes and fallen timbers of the hinterland. We were listening to a new EP by Geelong's Magic Dirt very loudly. Adalita had a strong voice and the band were tough and rocky. The car sped up accordingly, spotted gums and burrawangs flying by.

We called the project Fuzzface, after the iconic circular guitar pedal. Within weeks, we adjourned to my little basement and added guitars, drums, vocals and weird effects to the recordings I'd already started. It sounded so great to me: my frail voice against a wall of guitars and trippy sounds. It took a couple of months on and off to make, but we had an EP mixed and ready to go.

It flowed effortlessly. The lyrics were impressionistic, not at all political. Psychedelic in places and not so literal. These songs didn't have to serve anyone – or anything. It was nice to not have to make sense for a change. John O'Donnell, previously a music journalist, was supportive and agreed to put it out for us on his new label, Murmur. It was a triumph of music over business and a reclaiming of my identity. I found I could survive outside the cloistered halls of Midnight Oil. I had pushed the reset button. The year was proving to be fun, liberating and life-saving.

*

At the end of 1995, Midnight Oil went to a guesthouse in Leura in the Blue Mountains to have a summit about our collective future. We were all blasted by the endless touring since *Diesel and Dust* and didn't quite know what to do next.

Everyone had a solo project. Rob had an album out as Ghostwriters; I had Fuzzface with Nick; Martin was involved with Bones in The Hunting Party, a project with Melanie Oxley and pianist Chris Abrahams (a wonderful musician who had toured with us in 1993); while Pete was doing his activist work as a member of the international board of Greenpeace and as president of the Australian Conservation Foundation, and becoming a powerful environmental lobbyist.

We sank into the soft furnishings of the guesthouse to discuss our destiny. Mountains of scones and tea were delivered. We did some cursory bushwalking, returning for more tea and carbohydrates.

The only thing we really decided was to sack our absent member, Gary. The guesthouse meeting might even have been his idea, to 'give the guys some time to get their heads together'. Perhaps we were fed up with the touring grind, the need to be family men, the whole thing, and had to lash out at someone, anyone, and make a change just for the sake of it. It was a strange move, an unleavened assessment, especially as we had no plan B. It might have been the carbs or the tea talking. Days later we were corralled into our Glebe office, where Gary demanded his immediate reinstatement in no uncertain terms. He accused us of holding a star chamber in the mountains without him. The walls reverberated with his anger. Scolded, we acquiesced and put him back at the helm. He would, from that time, remind us of this betrayal. 'That false council of Oil.'

We were, by now, in a long-term codependent relationship, which others outside the band saw clearly but we did not. It was true he was on the front line, the bull bar between us and the real world, and he was a master strategist, but the pressure started to show as our chart positions fell. It seemed we could never measure up. Band conference calls became Gary monologues: you could put the phone down, go to the shops and come back with your absence unnoticed. If you dared to say 'Excuse me', he barked back a terse 'Shut up!' and the diatribe continued unabated.

Another thing we decided to do among all the carbohydrates in the mountains was to make another record. We had met the renowned Canadian musician and record producer Daniel Lanois on a tour across Canada called *Another Roadside Attraction* in

1993. The acts involved (Lanois, Hothouse Flowers, Crash Vegas, The Tragically Hip) made a charity record for Greenpeace on our night off in Calgary, recasting a song of mine and Rob's called 'Land', which Lanois produced. The issue was the logging of the very last remaining coupe of old-growth rainforest in Clayoquot Sound on Vancouver Island, where Midnight Oil had just participated in a tense Greenpeace action. Our van, with the band and Gary's eight-year-old son, Aaron, inside, was nearly rolled by timber-industry workers, who understandably thought their livelihoods were being threatened, even though the work was only going to last a few more months. They crushed our CDs in front of the windscreen as we rolled from side to side, growling, 'Take yourselves and your fucking shit music back to where you came from, fuckers!'

The long night in the studio lasted until 10am the next day. I loved Lanois' working methods up close: the smile of appreciation on his face through the glass when I did a guitar overdub in one take using his Stratocaster and vintage tweed Fender Deluxe amp, the way he dealt with people, the way the music flowed out of him, and his sense of loving purpose in getting the job done. It was a night full of magic, etiquette and mojo.

But Dan was world-famous and as busy as a Canadian beaver, with U2, Dylan, Emmylou and the rest. He did recommend his engineer and fellow Canadian Malcolm Burn. Malcolm had produced records that we enjoyed the sound of and he flew to Australia days after we invited him. We moved into a rehearsal room called Darling Harbour Studios, made from recycled materials and across the road from the Powerhouse Museum on Harris Street, Ultimo. With some of my recording equipment and some hired gear, we started work on *Breathe*.

Malcolm had big round glasses and unblinking eyes like an owl, and was skinny and geeky with protruding teeth. He was drinking a lot at that time in his life, and after our sessions he would listen to playbacks of his own solo album, *After Dinner Mints,* sometimes whistling along, laughing, crying and generally acting strangely.

It was interesting work. If you put down your instrument and went for a piss, Malcolm would pick it up and be playing your part, or another unrelated part of his own making, when you came back. There was nothing corporate about this guy. It was a chaotic way of working and that stirred the band up. I enjoyed it immensely, probably perversely. It was as loose as a goose but had a great feel. There was spill and atmosphere all over the recording.

We moved to Lanois' studio, Kingsway in New Orleans, to complete the record, but there was no Lanois. He had fled the city in a dawn evacuation for reasons unknown. Kingsway was an antebellum mansion on the corner of Esplanade Avenue and Chartres Street, with a wide staircase, parlour rooms and Lanois' vintage instruments everywhere. He liked to make records in houses to bypass the controlled nature and sterility of recording studios.

New Orleans was like a slow-moving Nosferatu film: nocturnal; above-ground cemeteries below sea level; air thick with aromas and spices; Spanish moss hanging motionless from towering oak and cypress trees, not a breath of wind; jazz and soul music floating out of shuttered French windows opening onto the street all day and night. It was a city of ghosts and haunted atmospheres, and that worked its way onto the record. The spirit of Lanois was flying around the place, and I was channelling his guitar playing on 'Home' as if my hands weren't even playing it.

People mentioned that Kingsway was haunted. We were told that when Emmylou Harris was recording there, she awoke one night to find the ghost of an elderly woman dressed in an antique black dress sitting on her chest. It was said the owner a century ago didn't like having other women around. Emmylou fled, never to return.

On hearing this, Grant Pudig, our one-man crew who organised everything to do with the transport and maintenance of the equipment for the sessions and also assisted in the studio, was clearly frightened. So, as he slept one night, Bones put a lampshade on his head and stood completely still in the corner of his room. Grant woke up and screamed like a banshee. He had the same reaction on another night when the French doors in his room flew open but there was no one there. It was just Rob trying to find the bathroom in the middle of the night.

The summer days were humid and hot beyond belief. We worked at night from 6pm to the early hours and lived on garlic pizza from the French Market. Some of us had discovered that melatonin and beer combined made a good cocktail. We hung out with some bohemian people at a local bar outside the tourist areas, played pool and listened to rare soul music singles on a jukebox at Miss Alberta's in the Lower Ninth Ward. Alberta was a beautiful African American woman who cooked soul food for us at her home.

In the studio, Malcolm would wear silly hats, do impressions of dumb Canadian sound men, steal beer out of the fridge and bang out some great manual mixes through an amazing vintage API console that was set up in one of the living rooms. I became very fond of him and his strange ways. Music would drift up the big staircase at all hours. It was the most free-spirited our band had ever got. I loved it. It brought us back from the corporate rock we had been disappearing into. Pete's vocals were superb, his best, I think, and the record had a cinema verité quality: it sounded like people playing music in a haunted room.

Experimentation was in the air when the band recorded 'Home'. The original version was fast, but we slowed it to a molasses tempo, exorcising any traces of rock. Malcolm asked Emmylou Harris, who was in Sydney playing some shows, to sing the song with Pete. I knew her duets with Gram Parsons and her work on

Paul Kennerley's album *The Legend of Jesse James*. She came over the night before the recording to hang out, relaxing with a red wine and singing a few songs, accompanying herself on one of our acoustic guitars. Her voice was like an old leather book with beautiful crevices in it, pure but perfumed with the aching wisdom of years. I played guitar and bass, Martin mandolin and Bones acoustic guitar. Buddy Miller played guitar and Daryl Johnson djembe, both from Emmylou's band. It was exactly what the song needed.

Malcolm pulled something out of us we didn't know we had, and *Breathe* stands as one of my favourite Midnight Oil records. It's pervaded by a dark ambience. Not the political pop our fans, the label or even we were expecting. People didn't recognise the first single, 'Underwater', as even being by Midnight Oil. We had wandered off into totally uncharted territory. So musical, so freeing, such good creative results. But not in the marketplace. The record bombed.

Things were going south, but to me they were going south in a good way. They say failure can teach you more than success. In failure, my strength was returning. I was getting my integrity back, and I couldn't have been happier.

Three

Nobody's child

By 1997 my father couldn't walk. Diabetes was claiming him; a long-term leg ulcer had turned septic and life-threatening. I visited him in a private hospital in Chatswood and he looked beat. The fight was leaving him. Once he was back at home, I moved him in and out of bed with a hydraulic lift. He was very heavy by then and way too much for Mum to handle. One day in the living room I had the chance to thank him for being a great dad, acknowledging how challenging it was, being one myself by then. He gave a rare smile and said, 'Thank you.' I'm so glad I had that chance to express my gratitude to him.

He went into hospital on his eightieth birthday and never came out. Naturally, the band were working again, this time on our album *Redneck Wonderland* in Melbourne, from Monday to Friday, week after week. I thought Dad might last until the weekend when I'd be back home in Sydney, but he didn't.

No time to grieve; gotta keep pulling that prime mover. The day after my father's funeral I flew to Brazil for another tour. I walked off the plane and straight onto a stage in Rio de Janeiro to play to 9000 people. The more you do this kind of thing, the more it feels normal.

*

My identity as an adoptee was already playing on my mind after the conversations with Neil Finn and the chambermaid in Ireland, who had both seemed convinced I was Irish, and a sense that I had a singular affinity with Irish people.

I had a birth certificate with my adoptive parents' names, Betty and Paul, but I craved information about my genes. I wanted to fill in the gaps about my identity like never before, not just for myself but for my children. They say sometimes an adoptive parent has to die first to give their child permission to search for their birth parents, and Dad's death was all the permission I needed.

In 1990, a law had passed in New South Wales called the *Adoption Information Act*. It allowed adoptees to access certain documents relating to their birth families. So I went straight onto the adoption register with the Department of Community Services (DOCS) and got my real birth certificate.

Father's name: [blank]
Mother's name: Susan Dymphna Maloney.
Born: Queanbeyan.

I searched death registers and birth registers, and sat down and looked at all the information I had gathered like pieces of a puzzle. My birth mother would have been twenty when I was born. Knowing that women change their names when they get married, I thought I'd seek out her marriage certificate. Sure enough, she had been married to a Brian Joseph McRedmond, so I sought out his details. The records showed they had married in late 1956, just six months after I had been born. They'd divorced twenty-two years later. The good news was that both Susan and Brian were still alive and in their sixties, so there was hope that I might meet them. If I could find them.

Incantation

By the late nineties, I had made work my number-one priority, pretty much thinking it was more important than any relationship. Escaping reality, essentially. Staying late in the studio, obsessing over mastering, mixes and arrangements, doing quality control. Pete maintained that it was my choice to stay the long hours in the studio, but I was 'looking after the shop' when they went home to their families. Gary told me once that between his demands and Pete's, my marriage never stood a chance.

In between Midnight Oil dates, I even began working with other artists. I was working with an old friend of Pete's called Suzy on a record she was making. She had a beautiful singing voice and was a good guitar fingerpicker. From the arts and the healing professions, she was also a counsellor, naturopath, yoga instructor and painter. One thing led to another and I fell for her. At this point, beauty and sensual fulfilment felt like the only things worth pursuing in life. Part mid-life crisis, part shamanic conversion. But the idea of staying safe in the marriage had become more painful than the danger of engaging with an unwritten future. Without doubt it was a selfish and hurtful act, but I was seeking some kind of healing and moved towards where I thought it might come from. I knew I was the architect of this situation, but for some reason I was unable to continue to live life as I had known it.

*

Divorce somehow became linked in my mind with adoption as 'things to get to the other side of'. However, I was met with a brick wall on my search for my birth parents. I couldn't find anyone with the names mentioned in the documents concerning my adoption with any degree of certainty. The Department of Community Services mailed out the *Adoption Handbook,* which I read cover to cover. They suggested I try to find Brian, my mother's husband, on the electoral rolls available at any local library, then write him a letter paraphrased from the handbook. Something neutral like, 'I'm looking for Susan Maloney. I believe you knew her in Sydney in 1956. I wonder if you could put us in touch.' Carefully chosen words that wouldn't scare him off. Sometimes unearthing the past can make people get angry or simply vanish into thin air.

Eureka! There was just one Brian Joseph McRedmond on the electoral rolls, living near Gympie in Queensland. I followed the DOCS guidebook carefully: be vague about the details. I sent off my letter. No reply came, and the search for my ancestry slipped off the radar for quite some time.

Five
rings

In 2000 Midnight Oil headed out to the Todd Tavern in Alice Springs to do a support for Nokturnl, an Indigenous band who had won Band of the Year at the Deadly Awards. As we were already there, we thought we'd travel out to Papunya to reconnect to where the 1986 *Blackfella/Whitefella* tour happened, before 'Beds Are Burning' and international fame. We borrowed some of Nokturnl's gear, threw it into the back of a LandCruiser and, with Gary in another LandCruiser, we pushed on to the APY lands.

We played at the Papunya school. I operated the small PA from the side of the stage as I played, so it was very low-key compared to 1986's barrage. Sammy Butcher had become an Elder by this time. It was wonderful to see him again. If you needed the oval graded for Saturday's football game, Sammy would make it happen. He was also teaching music to young people.

We camped at a spot up in the hills above Papunya with his permission, with fresh water and a view down the valley back towards the settlement. The band and Gary stood around the campfire and spoke of all kinds of things in that quiet country: the internet, which was only beginning, family, politics, music. We slept in swags in the open.

We had been invited to play at the Sydney Olympics. The theme was 'Iconic Australia' with Elle Macpherson, Kylie Minogue, Slim Dusty, INXS, Yothu Yindi and Christine Anu. Various ideas about what we should do were thrown around, but it was Gary, in that environment that had meant so much and done so much for all of us, who suggested the song 'Beds Are Burning' to make the point that Prime Minister John Howard had done nothing, and was going to do nothing, about reconciliation, and had made no apology to the traditional people on whose sovereign country we were now standing for the stealing of their land, for the lack of a treaty and the genocide of their people. So we decided we would make the apology for him, with 'Sorry' written on our clothes, and send that message to the whole world. It was a moment of inspired clarity. We were going to give this dog and pony show some balls. This was 'Oil'.

Of course, it all had to be planned in secret. It was a protest that had the potential to alienate sponsors, committees and stakeholders. We could be sued. I prepared a track at Alberts Studio to mime to, as nothing could go wrong at such a massive scale. Only Pete's vocal would be live.

I was staying with Mum at the time, and on the morning of the show I ironed my 'Sorry' suit inside out so even she wouldn't see the 'Sorry'. We had to wait around for most of the day in a nondescript green room high up in the stadium where we could watch the live audience of over 110,000 take their seats. It was good to chat to Slim Dusty, who talked about growing up on the land and his lifelong habit of rising at dawn. I was about to chat to Kylie when the Lord Mayor of Sydney, Frank Sartor, cut in on me.

The event seemed to be running smoothly and, as our turn came, we put plain black overalls over our 'Sorry' suits to make the long walk around the stadium to the arena. We were beyond overwhelmed with the emotion of it, like we were astronauts about to board an Apollo mission.

We took off the black overalls at the base of the stairs to the stage. A mighty roar came up from the crowd as we appeared, and everyone stood up and started running towards us as the three-chord volley that introduces the song thundered around the stadium.

It was over so quickly. Bones jumped into the crowd to party with some Canadian athletes. As the event was televised in parks, hotels, houses, even around the Opera House, people all over the country were dancing to the song, celebrating what it meant to be Australian. Apparently John Howard and his party were the only ones not to rise to their feet.

The next day the shock jocks went into hyperdrive, blasting through their anti–Midnight Oil monologues, saying how disrespectful and un-Australian we were with the *Sorry* message as they waxed lyrical into golden microphones on radio stations they were now part-owners of. That was good too; they would place themselves firmly on the wrong side of history.

This moment connected the dots in the band's mission statement. My feeling was that this was the real Everest of our career, not record sales or world domination. We had made our point on the international stage, all the way from our humble beginnings at the Royal Antler Hotel, with a song that we wrote to seek justice for those without a voice in Parliament, in a moment that was both political, cultural and musical. People could dance to it as well as get the message. By the year 2000, we had become good at that. I felt like our mission was, in one way or another, accomplished.

Ever decreasing circles

I'd read Xavier Herbert's novel *Capricornia* from cover to cover at least three times. It was like a boys' own adventure story that touched on everything about the Australian experience: Aboriginal dispossession and the brutal treatment of them, colonial misbehaviour and white privilege that led to calamity, and above all, the beauty and cruelty of the landscape and its power to shape human destiny.

I had been working on a conceptual album based on the novel for a few years, which would have included a film, but in the end the band weren't interested in such an ambitious project, so it was scuttled for its best songs. Management breathed a sigh of relief and only the album title remained.

We were signed to Sony in Australia who had been loyal for twenty years, but our stakes had plummeted overseas so much that we released *Capricornia* in the USA with fledgling label Liquid8. Their other signing was rapper/pro wrestler Vanilla Ice. Our friend and favourite label man Mason Munoz was working for them, but it was owned by a corporate liquidator who knew nothing about music, so despite Mason's best intentions, it was a train wreck by year's end.

We mounted a bunch of tours overseas, with three sojourns through the US and a few European dates. Back in Australia our agency had the band playing pubs and clubs, and the venues shrank each time we did a lap of the country. Even though the overseas gigs were well attended, they hadn't made money. There was only enough to pay our crew and airfares. We had worked all year round for nothing. Not that it is always about the money but, as Pete said, we couldn't make the books balance anymore.

On the tour bus in the US, while the 2002 Australian federal election was being fought, Pete was on the phone consoling and cajoling his friends in politics back in Australia, in truck stops and on freeways, from California to New York State. This was no surprise as he had run for the Senate seat in 1984, but now he prowled the corridor, mobile in hand, a man possessed. 'That is one political animal we have cooped up in here,' I thought.

Rob was writing a book at the same time about the band touring the US in the wake of 9/11. He had installed himself at the only desk on the bus and was recording our conversations not so secretly in an exercise book hidden under the table. This activity would continue at restaurants. Even though he had a firm deadline, and I understood this was his way of getting the job done, we all thought it was comical and sometimes fed him lines for fun.

One day in the Midwest in 2002, I was trudging upstairs to one more anonymous hotel room with my guitar in one hand and suitcase in another. I'd had enough of this so-called glamorous life on the road, the relentlessness of it and the idea that it would never end. I paused to exhale in the corridor and said to myself, 'I really can't do this much longer.' It was a moment that I'd thought would never come, but there it was.

*

Towards the end of the same year, the *M1* tour of Australia beckoned, stadium shows sponsored by one of the major radio networks. They asked us to play on a 'new music' bill with Garbage and The Tea Party. Gary said that the networks had promised they'd play our new single on the radio if we did the shows. It was sold to us as 'the big radio networks airing alternative voices', the concerts booked into huge arenas. We soon realised we'd been shafted. It became an oldies show with Billy Idol and Nickelback. Garbage and The Tea Party remained on the bill, but not as headliners. And radio didn't play our new single when we desperately needed them to. They still played the old stuff. The tour stiffed and they were forced to give tens of thousands of tickets away. Worse, any goodwill between the bands and the organisers evaporated. We headlined, but there was never a soul left backstage by the time we finished.

The morning after the Adelaide show, we had a day off and Pete asked me to ride with him in the hire car over to Melbourne. As we reached Adelaide's outskirts, heading over South Terrace, Pete, who always drove, said, 'Jimmy, I can't do this anymore. I'm giving you my resignation.'

He explained other things were calling him, and calling him loudly. I suggested we cut back the Oils' schedule to incorporate his extra-curricular activities, but he shook his head. I felt consternation mixed with relief, something like butterflies, knowing that we had officially run out of road.

I told the others over airport coffee two days later, flying back to Sydney from Tullamarine. They were angry, disbelieving. 'He can't. He has no right.'

'You should talk to him,' I said.

We had yet another national tour coming up. We were going from A to Z in Australia one more time, in even smaller venues, and going west to east in ever decreasing circles, starting in Geraldton, Western Australia, and ending at Twin Towns, Coolangatta, home of club and variety acts like Gerry and the Pacemakers. It was decided that no announcement of a final tour would be made. Some thought it would reek of a cash-in, or that Pete might have a change of heart if no one said anything. We swore to each other that we wouldn't tell a soul, but those close to us could see in our faces something was terribly wrong at the shows. There was a grimness about the proceedings. Half the band were accepting, half were angry. I've always thought the best shows are where everyone feels the same, whether tired, happy or pissed off. We were a band that could always fire up under pressure; we never got creatively stuck on anything. If something didn't work, we'd move on without sentimentality. It was an alpha environment where you had to argue your corner – very competitive – but we were all team players. Call it chemistry, but I knew that the potential to experience it again would remain as long as we were all alive.

We made the announcement on 2 December 2002. It was instant front-page news. I didn't feel too bad, and I told friends and acquaintances that when they called to offer support or sympathy. I knew I would miss the onstage hours, the life of backstage riders and rock privilege, but there was so much in the background that I wouldn't miss. The unending touring, the indifference of radio to our new music, the shrinking crowds, the disconnection from family, Gary's combativeness and, most of all, our own impossible expectations of one another.

Residuum

In the aftermath of the break-up, I played the Bob Dylan album *Time Out of Mind* on a loop. The message was 'I'm fucked, I'm old and I don't give a shit'. Especially the song 'Not Dark Yet'. It suited my mood. It was like aural Mandrax.

I thought I might need help with the end of the band, my impending divorce and the fact that I had also decided to continue the search for my birth parents, so I started seeing a therapist called Mary. She was of Polish descent and quietly spoken. She had me revisiting early experiences. I wasn't keen to relive infant trauma. It seemed like a cobweb-covered rabbit hole of intrepid exploration under crumbling earth. But my hunch was that it informed my behaviour in adult life. I could see it acted out: fear of not rocking the boat, fear of being abandoned, fear of confrontation. An inability to trust myself. Maybe there was a missing cog in my anthropoid clockwork. Unable, as an infant, to understand the abandonment consciously, I had simply absorbed it. I've always been sensitive, an INFP personality type in the Myers-Briggs sense. I recall catching Gary and Pete share a stolen glance in London in 1983. I can't remember the context but it was something like, 'Oh God, is he tough enough to take the news?' As if I wasn't even there.

I could still hear Dad's voice: *If you trust yourself when all men doubt you, and make allowances for their doubting too ...* I wasn't the father figure, the younger brother, the strong adult he had wanted me to be. *Yours is the Earth and everything that's in it, / And – which is more – you'll be a Man, my son.*

I was a wreck, and utterly disoriented after each session with Mary, but it felt like I was slowly making progress. I did some reading on the subject of the trauma that adopted babies experience. In the womb, child and mother have a nine-month chemically and emotionally linked relationship, even sharing the same psychology. If that bond is severed at birth, the limbic system, the part of the brain that deals with fear and flight, would have to be traumatised – stress-related hormones like cortisol would flood the brain, possibly affecting emotional responses for life. The emotional effects might include avoidance of situations reminiscent of the trauma – symptoms similar to post-traumatic stress disorder. The mother-directed gaze, if absent, is a known cause of disconnected behaviours, reduced emotional capacity and lack of remorse or empathy. Had I manifested that in leaving the marriage, dealing with Lippold or those strange experiences in the early nineties?

My cousin Patti had been there, aged ten, the day Mum and Dad brought me home from the orphanage I'd been sent to after my birth. She said I appeared to be a withdrawn and frightened infant. She used the word *traumatised*. Was it programmed from the day I drew breath? Missing maternal comfort, the oxytocin produced by hugs and cuddles?

I was rescued from the orphanage, and I know Mum would have made up for a lot. She would have felt my distress and held me close. I'm told I cried easily and often. Early photos show me as a bit clingy, always next to her, sometimes looking stressed or spooked, holding a hand over my eyes if the light was too bright. My brother, Kim, in contrast, always looks content, confident, a boss.

When Mum and Dad adopted us, appearances mattered. It had to look like we were related. Adoption agencies used to match babies to the adoptive father's hair colour. Dad's was reddish and so was ours.

Mum mentioned in passing that the adoption agency, the non-denominational Benevolent Society, had told her I was 'special', but I never found out what 'special' meant and imagined it was something they said about every baby. She would sometimes call me Seamus, the Irish equivalent of James, when we were alone or the conversation became quieter. And once, after she'd had a gin and tonic, there was a passing mention of Queanbeyan.

My last
afternoon
as myself

I had begun to wonder what my birth might have been like for my biological mother, Susan, having to let me go. In 2003 I sourced the medical charts of my birth. In a handwritten manila folder were my mother's name, time of admission (3am), temperature chart, blood pressure and other vital signs, her last menstruation before pregnancy, length of labour (nearly twelve hours), the time of birth, my weight, length and the doctor's name.

There was a Sydney address for Susan on the charts. The house backed onto an oval near Manly Lagoon. I drove down there and sat outside, soaking up the atmosphere in a rather desperate way forty-five years later, looking for answers where there were none. The trail was cold, the participants had moved on.

Sitting in the car, I tried to imagine what the hospital would have been like for her. Under no circumstances were mothers allowed to form bonds. Babies marked 'FOR ADOPTION', as I was, were hidden from them by a sheet and whisked away at birth. The nurses saying, 'It's for the best,' while just trying to deal with the brutality of the situation.

A helpless newborn, untouched and un-nurtured by its mother; a young mother unable to touch or comfort her own child. Then the clip-clop of sensible footwear and the rumble of the trolley on linoleum as the baby is wheeled away. And the poor mother sobbing in an empty room after this brutal bisection, the smell of disinfectant in the air.

The charts said my mother was discharged five days after the birth. The paper had yellowed and the ink was beginning to disappear. 'FOR ADOPTION' was indeed written in capitals at the bottom of the page. I had been kept in hospital and bottle-fed for nineteen days until I was deemed 'Satisfactory, free of congenital defects and fit for discharge'. From there, the Benevolent Society records show I was taken to the Scarba House orphanage in Bondi, where I was kept from 5 June to 18 July 1956, before a home was found for me. Two months seems like a long time to have been left alone without a mother. It's something I'm glad my own children didn't experience.

I checked the electoral rolls again. Brian Joseph McRedmond had rematerialised, this time in the ACT. I wrote him another letter on a Thursday and sent it off. The following Tuesday night, my kids were over at my place. We'd cooked dinner and were settling in for some TV when the phone rang.

'Hello,' I said.

A gruff voice spoke. 'Hello. Is this Jim?' A radio played talkback in the background.

'Yeah.'

'It's Brian.'

'Who ...? Brian!'

'I got your letter. So,' he asked curtly, 'what's all this about?'

The *Adoption Handbook* kicked in. 'I'm looking for Susan Maloney. I believe you knew her in Sydney in 1956. I wonder if you could put us in touch.'

'Oh yeah. Why?'

I took a breath. 'She's my birth mother. I was adopted out in 1956.'

Silence for a few seconds. I could hear my heart beat and Brian's radio.

'Well now,' he said, 'I'm your father, and you've got five full-blooded brothers and sisters, and they've got eleven kids between them.'

I felt faint. I was leaning against the doorjamb in the kitchen, looking outside. I slid down onto the floor.

I could hardly speak, but I heard myself say, 'Can I meet up with you? I can come down to Canberra tomorrow.'

I had to drive down to Victoria that week to play at the Apollo Bay Music Festival with Neil Murray. I thought I could detour through Canberra on the way.

He coughed. He didn't sound too healthy.

'Nah. I've got something to do. Don't call me. I'll call you.'

He hung up.

I sat there on the floor for a while holding the phone, looking at the garden I had alternately tended and neglected for years. Azaleas and inch plants were doing battle among the asparagus fern on the embankment. Someone in the units nearby was playing a flute.

I walked into the lounge room where my children were sitting on the green sofa watching television. I told them what had happened and they said, 'That's so cool, Dad,' especially when I mentioned the eleven new cousins. They went back to what they were watching. Ah, that Dad, always full of surprises.

The next day I headed down the Hume Highway with my mobile charged and on, expecting Brian to call. In my self-doubt, I also imagined that he was never going to call, that I was a can of worms he wouldn't want to reopen. That doubt was rewarded. I stopped in Rutherglen for the night in one of those drive-up-to-the-room motels. There was no call.

In Apollo Bay I did the gig with Neil Murray in one of the bigger tents with my phone onstage beside me. If Brian had rung, I would have put my guitar down and taken the call there and then. Again, no call came. Afterwards I heard that the sound man hadn't even put my guitar into the mix.

Our flute-playing friend from way back, Richo, now lived in Apollo Bay. He had started to perform as Howlin' Wind, taking the name from the violent winds that blast through the region. He's a force of nature as well – opinionated, inspired, a proper lunatic and a great coach. He has been important in my life.

Everything about my adoption had been shaken up, like solids in solution, and I was grieving my marriage. It was two years since it had ended. We talked long and hard and walked along the beach. His motto was, 'If all else fails, good old Doctor Music will never let you down.'

By the time I headed home, Brian still hadn't called. 'Yeah, that'd be right,' I said to myself. 'I probably deserve it. They gave me away and he doesn't want to know me now either, so I double-deserve it.'

At least I was beginning to understand where that voice came from.

*

Brian did finally call a few weeks later. He sounded healthier. The radio was on in the background again. He'd been in hospital but was vague about the details. I organised to meet him at his home in the suburb of Rivett in Canberra. Suzy travelled with me and waited at a hotel in town.

I was in no hurry now as I cruised and lurched around the avenues and roundabouts of the national capital. The pieces were all on the chessboard. I arrived in a quiet cul-de-sac. The house was more like a tiny cement hovel – government-issue besser block.

It was one of a cluster and seemed like a place where people just ended up. I checked my reflection in the rear-vision mirror. I was wearing a white Levi's shirt with an orange T-shirt underneath and jeans with R.M. Williams boots. I got out of the car and headed for the door. I heard only gravel crunching underfoot.

I knocked on the door. There was some coughing and shuffling. A gruff voice said, 'Coming.' The door creaked open and I laid eyes on my father for the first time. He had a round unshaven face and yellow teeth. The door opened wider and I saw he was still in his pyjamas at 2pm. The first thing he said was, 'Go down and get me a couple of packets of Marlboro Reds, will ya?' He pointed out the shops down a paling-fenced passageway between two houses. I obliged, and when I returned we sat down to talk.

The place was small and sparsely furnished and the radio was on, murmuring by the bed. There were clothes draped all over the room and another room full of messed-up laundry. It smelt of stale cigarettes. At the back there was a screen door and a couple of broken chairs. We headed out there.

After Brian had lit up, he relaxed and said, 'Yes, I'm your father.'

He said that he and my mother had never told another soul. She'd gone to the family doctor when she found she was pregnant at nineteen. It was the 1950s, and being unmarried and with child in a Catholic community in a semi-rural town like Queanbeyan was no joke. The doctor admonished her. 'This news will kill your mother. She has a heart condition; you must under no circumstances tell her. Now you listen to me, young lady. I'll tell you what you are going to do …'

Marriage was the bedrock of society and babies were not supposed to be conceived outside it. You couldn't even discuss it. But 'decency' had a price. A whole wing of the Royal Women's Hospital in Paddington was dedicated to the industry of delivering countless illegitimate children.

'Your mother was christened Susan, but everyone called her Anne right from the start,' said Brian. When she'd started to show at seven months, late in the piece as pregnancies go, Anne had travelled to her sister Kit's place in Manly, the same house that I had sat outside in the car. Five days after the birth, Anne went home and returned to work the next day. It was a huge secret to wallpaper over, but that's exactly what my birth parents and my Aunt Kit did from that moment on. And then Brian and Anne went on to have five more children together: John, Janet, Paul, Dave and Susan.

I was reeling at all this information. I snapped a couple of photos of Brian and me together, the only photos I have with my birth father.

The shadows got longer and the cold came on, as it does in Canberra in May, so we moved inside. My eyes scanned the room. There was a yellowing pine dresser collecting dust, with lots of family photos, but none were of Anne. A photo of my sister Susan, who looked the spitting image of my daughter. In all the faces there was a similarity to my own. They were all in groups, smiling and happy. The brothers looked kind of beefy, just like me.

Brian sat on the bed, ready to tell me more. He told me he was sixty-seven years old. I pulled up another worn-out chair, this time with no arms. I noticed the floor under the bed was littered with cigarette butts and ash. He was clearly not looking after himself, a walking advertisement for self-neglect.

He started to get emotional. 'We should never have given you away,' he kept repeating. 'I shouldn't have left Anne. She was the love of my life. Everyone had mistresses in Canberra in those days – it was the seventies, you know? I should never have left. We should never have given you away.'

I tried to console him. 'It's okay, it's just the way it is. It is what it is.' It was the best I could manage. 'We can't change it. It happened, you know? It just happened.' I gave him a clumsy hug.

I wasn't expecting this reaction, even though all the reading said 'expect the unexpected'. Yet here I was dancing into this man's life creating havoc. The father I'd been searching for was finally before me and was now weeping uncontrollably. I found out later that he had sold his mother's home in Yarralumla to buy a place in Gympie a few years back with a new woman who already had children. The relationship quickly soured and ended badly, and my brothers and sisters had had to pull him out of there. He allegedly lost all his money and possessions in the process and had only recently returned to Canberra, humiliated and broke.

He said my mother had remarried and was living in Goulburn. With a grin, he said he didn't get on with her new husband, Neil. He suggested that she was too vulnerable to receive any surprises and wouldn't want to hear from the likes of me. End of subject.

It was sunset now. It was so cold I could see my breath in the air in front of me and a low orange light crept through the dusty curtains. I could smell a wood fire burning in the neighbourhood. A lone dog barked in the next street.

I thought I might have overstayed my welcome and should go, but something made me stay on for a bit. We chatted more about his life. Brian had been an electrician, a miner, had once run a childcare centre and had even had a business making fertiliser from worm castings. It was a life path full of jerky left turns, guided by gut instinct. Perhaps he could have been a musician like me and travelled the world. I think he would have taken to it. The life of a gypsy would have suited him, never being in one place for long. He loved a smoke, a punt, a drink and a yarn. A rock and roll guy without the rock and roll.

There was a sudden movement outside the window, a flash of white.

'That'll be Dave. He lives round the corner.'

The man who poked his head around the door looked so similar to me that I couldn't breathe. It could have even been me.

He stepped into the room holding a plate of food for his father and looked me up and down.

'Jim, this is Dave,' said Brian.

'G'day, Dave,' I said.

'G'day,' he said, staring dead at me. 'Who is this bloke?' was written all over his face. From the government? Community services? I was wearing my white shirt and afterwards he said he thought I was some kind of medico. He looked bewildered and a little toey.

'Christ, you should know him, Dave,' said Brian. 'He's your brother.'

'What?' said Dave. He stood frozen, eyes fixed on me. 'Bullshit!'

Brian turned his back and retreated, giggling, to his vantage point on the bed.

I gave Dave the unedited story. He lived up the road and had only come to check on his father. After fifteen minutes, listening as I quietly explained, he sat shaking his head. 'God, I never knew. Unbelievable. Just … unbelievable.'

When I told him I had been in Midnight Oil, he said he'd seen us in 1983 at a benefit show at Penrith Oval called One for the Kids. 'I didn't even see you,' he said.

I explained that was my spotlight avoidance syndrome, heard and not seen behind that bald fellow running around at the front of the stage distracting everyone.

Brian was enjoying himself as he listened and lit up a few more smokes.

'I'd better call Janet,' said Dave.

In the photographs, Janet, the eldest sister, looked like the organiser of family events and was probably the key to meeting my mother.

He dialled and I could hear a lively youngish voice through the receiver. 'Hi, Dave. How are you?'

'Janet, are you sitting down?'

'Yeah, no, well yeah. What is it?'

'I'm with Dad, but there's three of us here. There's a bloke called Jim with us.'

'Okay. Yeah?'

'He's our brother.'

I heard Janet say, 'Our brother? Dave, have you been drinking?'

'No, really. There's a bloke called Jim here.'

'Like … an imaginary friend?'

'No, he's real. He's our brother.'

'Oh, fuck off, Dave.' Then there was a click. She'd hung up.

'That went well,' said Brian.

Minutes later the phone rang. It was Janet.

'What the hell is going on? What have you been drinking?'

'You'd better talk to him yourself.'

I got on the phone and spoke briefly, but Dave took over and I could hear Janet saying, 'You'd better come over. And bring this Jim fellow with you.'

I went to go with Dave but felt bad about leaving Brian in his gloomy cave. It was now dark outside. 'Off you go,' he said with a big grin and a firm handshake. 'Go meet your family.'

We headed to Janet's. It was a good twenty minutes away and I followed closely behind Dave's car. I ran a few red lights keeping up just in case I lost him. I still thought he might try to do a runner. We pulled off the main road into the maze of winding crescents and tree-lined streets of Red Hill. Janet's place was a smart house down the bottom of a bamboo-lined driveway.

A tall and lissom redhead waltzed to the door, smiling. My sister. I could see the likeness in her face again. She welcomed me in, and I met her husband, Andy. They couldn't have been more friendly. Suzy arrived half an hour later and everyone warmed to each other straight away. A bottle was opened and there was lots of talk as we all tried to come to grips with this new reality.

We examined some old photographs including some of Brian and Anne's wedding. I mentioned that the *Child Welfare Act* document indicated that Betty and Paul Moginie adopted me officially on 29 November 1956. On 1 December, two days later, Anne and Brian were married in St Gregory's, Queanbeyan. In the wedding photos, they look radiant and happy.

Seeing Anne's picture for the first time did something to me. 'Is there a chance I could meet my mother?' I asked. Writing a letter to Brian had got me a positive outcome, and I wondered if the same approach might work with her.

A couple of ideas were bandied about, but it was Andy who said, 'Nah. We won't be able to keep this a secret. Word will get out. Janet, myself, Dave and Susan will drive to Goulburn to see Anne tomorrow. You follow an hour behind. You'll be on your way to Sydney anyway. If she wants to meet you, we'll call you. If she doesn't, just keep driving.'

I had to get back to Sydney the following day to sit in on a gig with Neil Murray at the Harp Hotel in Tempe. Andy would meet Suzy and me at the Big Merino in Goulburn if I got the thumbs-up.

We were refuelling at Collector, about fifty kilometres out of Canberra, the next day when I got the call.

'Come on down, Jim. She wants to meet you. See you at the Big Merino.'

I may be an
accident of
energy and
matter

We took the divided road to Goulburn and everything looked
different, felt different. As we approached the turn-off, as if on cue,
John Lennon's 'Woman' was playing on the local radio station.

It made me think about the many fanciful notions that
surround parents who give up children for adoption. For example,
the idea that they should forget all about what happened and
just let bygones be bygones, or that they didn't love the children
they surrendered; that the mothers are fallen women, or that they
wouldn't get a decent husband if the truth were known. There's
still shame and scandal today, but nothing like fifties' shame and
scandal. The woman I was about to meet had had to endure all of
this. The song brought me to tears.

The Big Merino loomed in front of us. The car park was
deserted, with that menacing three storeys of faux sheep-shaped
concrete looking down on us with eyes like black holes. We waited

for a while for Andy to arrive. 'Are you sure this is the Big Merino he meant?' said Suzy, cheerily.

An expensive sports car came screaming into the driveway in a sheet of gravel spray, 'Kosciusko' blasting out of its stereo. Andy was chortling like a hyena and brandished the CD cover of Midnight Oils' *Red Sails in the Sunset* out of the window, singing loudly and doing donuts around the empty car park. After a few twists and turns, following him through suburban Goulburn, we arrived. There was a tall privacy hedge between us and the property. I got out of the car, heart beating fast, and went in through a gate. I felt utterly alone. Time stopped.

As I rounded the hedge, the house appeared: Tuscan red brick, roses in the garden, lawn well maintained. I saw a small woman standing outside the front door on the other side of the yard. Dave and Janet stood apart from her. She was more fragile than I had imagined, with an expression on her face that looked happy, scared and frozen all at once. This was the person who had given me life forty-six years before. But all I'd had until now was her name and vital signs recorded on those impersonal birth records. She was shivering, a bird fluttering. I walked up the path with eyes locked on hers and hers on mine. There seemed to be light radiating out of her in all directions.

When we hugged on the porch, it was no normal hug. It was complete relief. I pulled back to look into her eyes, holding her hands. She was wearing a pinky-purple cashmere jumper, a shiny silver necklace and black slacks. She had neat greyish hair cut short and a couple of dimples. I towered over her by nearly a foot.

Anne looked at me intently, my arms, freckles, my fingers. We hugged again. People were taking photos, all through tears. Everyone was crying except me. I was just totally happy.

Inside, we sat together on the couch. She ran her hands up and down my arms, noticed the veins on my hands, touched my face, looked into my eyes, examining my features in forensic detail.

Andy said that Anne had hung her head and cast her eyes to the floor when her children had all confronted her about me. There was no way to break this news without it being brutal. 'Mum. WE KNOW,' they'd said in unison. It became apparent that she hadn't told anyone else her secret, including her second husband, the barrel-chested Neil, who was now firing up the barbie and throwing snags around. Suzy had ushered him outside to placate him, away from the communion happening inside.

'I thought we didn't have any bloody secrets!' I heard him say.

I was oblivious, only dimly aware of the growing storm out the back. Anne and I sat close and spoke softly. She hadn't tried to find me, she said, as I may not have known I was adopted or might not have wanted my life disrupted in such a way. She had felt it would be okay if I contacted her because then it would be my decision and not hers. After all, she was the one who had given me up. It all seemed quite logical.

'There wasn't a day I didn't pray for you, or a birthday I didn't think about you,' she said.

My brother Dave, sister Janet and brother-in-law Andy were all listening but looking down, heads shaking in disbelief. Susan, my sister and the youngest, arrived looking, as she had in the photo, uncannily like my daughter, Alice.

The barbecue on the outside patio was finally ready. Around the table we looked at all the photos of our respective families. A beer or two had thankfully loosened us all up.

After lunch, more group photos were taken, phone numbers exchanged. I could have stayed there all day, but there was that gig at the Harp with Neil Murray to attend to.

I couldn't get behind the wheel to drive after all of this emotion, so Suzy drove the two hours or so back to the city. I fell asleep at once in the passenger seat, totally exhausted. It felt strangely like the sleep of a metamorphosis or a transfiguration. When an actor takes off his mask he reveals his true identity. What I noticed in the ensuing days looking in the mirror were my facial features. I saw myself differently. I saw Dave's earlobes, Susan's eyes, Brian's nose ... it was as if I wasn't carrying my old face anymore. It was totally odd, but not unwelcome. The face had finally relaxed.

The next week, even Pete observed, 'Your face looks different.'

New grass

My decision to find my DNA was having a domino effect on others. Mum had given her blessing when I'd started my search. 'You should,' she said. 'What took you so long?' But she didn't want to meet my new family. 'It might change the way I feel about you,' she said of this redrawing of the family tree in the shape of a triangle. My brother, Kim, didn't have the same interest in finding his biological parents. He was content to let sleeping dogs lie.

The range of attitudes made me think of some of the myths that surround adopted people. Like the idea that searching for birth parents means their relationship with their adoptive parents wasn't important to them, or was troubled or toxic; that those who don't search aren't curious about their origins; or that people from good adoptive families shouldn't care about their identity or where they came from.

For my biological mother, I think it was a relief to find me, but I could see in her eyes that it had been a heavy burden to carry for such a long time. Her life was like wisteria wrapped around a wooden post: once the post rots away, the wisteria holds the same shape, formed around a secret. She was young when she got pregnant and endured the whole trauma of having to give me up without emotional or psychological support. A certain amount of amnesia is needed to get on with life after an event like adoption. Forgetting as a survival mechanism. Silence, too.

I now knew for sure that I was genetically Irish, with some northern Italian from my grandmother on my father Brian's side, Rose, from Grosio. Anne's parents, the Maloneys, hailed from Corofin, in the heart of County Clare. Brian's father – my grandfather Paddy McRedmond – and his family were from Cadamstown in County Offaly. This was the part of the family I went on to meet for the first time in Ireland in 2008.

Cadamstown was to become a key discovery for me. I have since visited the area many times and experienced an iron-clad connection. At the foot of the Slieve Bloom Mountains, below the town on the Kilcormac road, the family farmed the curragh (Irish for 'marshy ground') by the Silver River at the bottom of the hill.

Paddy McRedmond came out to Australia in 1924 to escape the bloodshed that preceded and followed the birth of the Irish Republic in 1921, after it gained its independence from Great Britain. As a young man, Paddy had been despatched to shoot a British soldier as he walked up the hill to his barracks in Cadamstown for lunch. This was his initiation into the local branch of the IRA. He waited all day in a field for the soldier to come up the road, insects buzzing around him from his sniper's position, crouched behind a thicket and a stone wall. But the soldier never appeared. It was all too much for Paddy, so he decided to go to Australia at the invitation of his Uncle Dick, who was farming around the area that was to become Canberra. It was there he met my grandmother Rose.

Paddy's brother was known as Fighting Dick McRedmond, the Rock of Dunamase, or, around Cadamstown, just Dick the Boxer. Dick was giant of a man at 193 centimetres tall, with a reach that exceeded his height. He became the Australian heavyweight boxing champion in 1929, going on to fight the Italian Primo Carnera at Ebbets Field, Brooklyn, in 1931. Dick wore his signature green shorts with Irish gold harps embroidered on them, and someone in the crowd yelled out 'Cadamstown!', which momentarily made him turn his head. In that split second Carnera knocked him down for eight with a hard right. Dick never recovered. Boxing experts say he would have beaten Carnera if he'd weathered the first round. Carnera soon went on to become world heavyweight champion.

I went to see Brian in Canberra a few weeks later for morning tea with Sam and Alice, by then teenagers. They took on the McRedmonds with admirable politeness and excited curiosity. But Brian wasn't looking well. A few months later, he moved to a nursing home at Batehaven on the South Coast. I spoke to him on the phone and was making plans to see him, but prostate cancer had overtaken him and he died on 27 June 2004, roughly a year after I met him. It explained his absence in the weeks between our first conversation – that trip to hospital. The timing of our meeting was uncanny. If I'd waited any longer, I would never have got a sense of him.

On occasion, I felt I was *becoming* him, especially given some of my behaviour at the time, like leaving a marriage, using alcohol as a coping mechanism, recent issues with fidelity and being an absent father. Brian knew he'd erred and perhaps realised too late what he'd given up. Catholic guilt had not ascended to any kind of constructive contrition for Brian, and it seemed to me his past pained him. Perhaps I was able to be more Buddhist about it. Our reunion had set us both free somehow.

*

It was a full church in Canberra for Brian's funeral. My newfound brothers asked me to be the fourth pallbearer and help carry Brian's coffin out to the hearse. It was unexpectedly heavy, and I nearly dropped my corner as I put it on my shoulder.

'Is that man all right?' enquired the priest as I struggled.

I felt Brian slide down the coffin towards me and took the opportunity to whisper, 'It is all right, you old bugger. I'm with you now.'

Although I wasn't formally introduced as part of the family, my resemblance to my other brothers hadn't been missed by some of the congregation. Afterwards, when asked where I fitted in, I offered, 'I'm a friend of the family.' The word was that Brian had got around a bit, and that I was his love child. At the cemetery I stood next to Anne as Brian was lowered into the ground. The priest sang in a sweet and tremulous voice, waving his incense about. As we looked down, dropping clods of loose earth gently onto the coffin, she quietly whispered to me that Brian was the love of her life.

My brother Dave wanted to show me something. We walked across the cemetery to an area shaded by trees. There was a small grave. I didn't know, but his son Timothy had been stillborn only months before.

A flock of red-tailed black cockatoos landed in the trees above us, snapping off pine cones and calling out.

'We lost Timothy,' he said, 'but we got you.'

*

I kept in touch with Anne, dropping in to visit her on the way to the South Coast or Canberra. I bought her a little piano because she told me she'd loved playing songs from sheet music when she was a girl, like 'Camptown Races'. I did the same thing when I was young, and I was curious about us having that in common.

I told her about growing up, my career and of course about my children, whom she had now met. She wanted to know every little thing. We were content to be in each other's company, interested to discover what we had missed out on in each other's lives, both bemused about the situation. There was still a respectful and unspoken distance between us, the years lost that could never be reclaimed.

She told me she'd grown up on a farm near Tidbinbilla, about fifty miles from Queanbeyan, with two sisters and a brother. She pointed out they didn't have much but never lacked for anything. There were no local schools in the vicinity, so she did her schooling at St Brigid's Convent, Queanbeyan, as a boarder. The girls would rise every day at 6am for Mass in the convent chapel and fast before Sunday Mass at St Gregory's, which they walked to across a suspension bridge. In the convent, there was no heating in winter, and water pipes, taps and wash basins would routinely freeze over – she had the chilblain scars to prove it. The boarders had a bath once a week. Colds would be treated with castor oil. A recycled boiled lolly soaked in kerosene was used to treat coughs. They would eat woody pumpkins that grew in the convent's open drains, melon and lemon jam sandwiches twice a day, and sometimes soup made from that morning's leftover porridge.

She said that after my birth she had flown straight back to Queanbeyan – a recollection different from Brian's, who'd thought that they'd driven back from Sydney together. As flights were expensive then, and Anne would have been in a delicate condition, I tend to believe Brian, but I'll probably never find out the real story. Memories can shift over time, and sometimes they'll set in concrete. None of it really matters, because giving me away was their plan all along. I had been a slip-up, so the stage was set for my life to unfold differently. Brian and Anne were able to have a trouble-free fresh start.

*

I didn't expect I would lose my birth mother again quite as soon as I did. I knew she travelled with a respirator, but she didn't make a big deal about it. Her heart gave out on the couch watching the football with Neil on a Saturday night. He looked over, and she was gone. It was 27 June 2009. Five years to the day after Brian died.

Suzy, Alice and I drove to Goulburn for the funeral. It was held at St Peter and Paul's Old Cathedral, a magnificent gothic building with high vaulted ceilings. My brother John spoke first and began, 'When Anne had children, the first one to arrive was Jim.' The words flooded through my veins like hot whiskey.

Suzy and I sang the spiritual 'Life's Railroad to Heaven' and my brother Dave and I sang Slim Dusty's 'Looking Forward, Looking Back' (penned by Don Walker). Anne had loved Slim's music.

It was a great day in many ways, as funerals can be. I felt very much welcomed into the fold, a grafted-on part that was taking root. Afterwards we followed my brother Paul to the cemetery in our car but got hopelessly lost in the Goulburn streets. We arrived at dusk just as the grave was being covered.

Our paths had been different but thankfully had joined up. I felt more grateful to Anne than sad. Maybe that's because I never really knew her like my new brothers and sisters had or got to love her in the way that they did. But what I really mourned was all the things we'd never got to talk about.

Big
tree
down

Mum was now eighty-nine and in a nursing home after falling and breaking her hip. With great gusto she demanded to be taken home every time I or anyone else visited. And go home she finally did, against conventional wisdom and doctor's orders. But soon she couldn't come to the phone, and adventures with dementia were coming on strong. I had my studio in the garage behind her house and would do production work with artists and introduce them to Mum, who loved that, or work alone and spend tea breaks with her. I was there most days. In September 2009, I had the chance to take her to the South Coast, away from the rigours of home nursing and grumpy matrons. We went for three days and she lay in bed in the mornings listening to the wattlebirds and the ocean. 'How lovely and peaceful,' she'd remark. She always had something positive to say. 'Jamie, the sky is a particularly beautiful colour today.'

She walked around the house by holding on to strategically placed furniture, Margaret Olley–style. I made her favourite meals – roasts, natural oysters, macaroni and cheese, Vegemite on toast. We caught up, laughed and emptied a huge bottle of Bombay Sapphire gin. We talked about Dad and her childhood growing up in Hurstville, where her father, James, had a double block complete with well-tended vegetable garden and tennis court. She spoke in the voice of a young woman, the one who used to pick me up from school in the Falcon 500 at Gordon train station.

'I'm okay, you know. I'm not afraid of dying,' she would say. I was stunned that anyone could get to a point where they could say those words with conviction, and I could sense that she was letting go.

Within weeks she returned to hospital. She was off her dementia medication and was clear as a bell. 'Now, sit down and tell me all about yourself. Is everything okay in your life?' she asked, looking me straight in the eye. This was the mother I grew up with, not dulled by anti-anxiety drugs. Life was full of my usual dramas at the time, so I lied and said everything was fine. But she could see through it. Her favourite saying was always, 'Jamie, you're not making history.' She didn't even have to say it this time, she just gave me the look.

She was seeing visions in the hospital room. There was a generic framed print on the wall of three children playing by the seashore. She thought the figures were moving and that it was my children and Suzy's son on the beach. Another time I was sitting next to the bed holding her hand and she woke, round-eyed, with a start. 'Oh! I was at home with my mum and dad in Hurstville. They were in bed, by the fireplace.'

On 8 October I got caught up in the studio for a few hours on a project deadline. Mum's companion dog, Ellie, was with me, placidly napping as I mixed, but around 1pm she started barking hysterically.

Ten minutes later the phone rang. Mum had died. Trish, her neighbour, had been there visiting when Mum suffered a quick and fatal heart attack.

This woman had brought me up selflessly since I was two months old. She'd got over her beloved husband's death with dignity. And with her neighbours, a few visitors, and her home, garden and dog, she'd lived in a small world at the end of her life, but it was rich and nuanced. Her boundless optimism was a mighty influence, and it got me through childhood, the sometimes-gruelling years of Midnight Oil, and a divorce. I will always carry her optimism with me.

Two mothers gone in one year. And two fathers already gone. It was a time in my life now to count what I had lost but also reflect on how much I had gained. I still had my old family and had found a whole new one.

The pepper tree

Christmas of 2009 saw both of my families come together at my house on the New South Wales South Coast, near where I would holiday with Mum, Dad and Kim when I was a child. Thirty-three people gathered from all over the country – including Kim, his wife and their son – circulated and sat in ever-changing groups, and talked over the days. Some were strangers at first but soon played games, watched Test cricket and the Sydney to Hobart yacht race, drank cups of tea, broke bread.

Everyone seemed to accept the new situation, which doesn't always happen when meeting your biological family. Every family is an unfinished symphony, a work under construction. Janet told me that when they were kids, the whole McRedmond family, including grandparents Paddy and Rose, had moved to a four-room house on a 3000-acre property near the small town of Inverell to prise Brian away from the loose crowd he was running with in Canberra. Anne had brought up the five children, who went to the local country school. They were poor and Anne had to clean the house continually, as dust was always finding its way in. But Brian soon headed off to his nearby sapphire mine, or his tin mine in Glen Innes, or his opal mine in Lightning Ridge, all initially successful but over time a disappearing mirage of fortune. And there were women, which finished off the marriage for Anne.

I imagine swapping places with my alternate self, the one I would have been if Anne and Brian had kept me, lying in the shade of a giant pepper tree near a stockyard, dozing in the afternoon. I can see a tyre swing and a machine shed. Hearing the sound of my younger siblings rough and tumble it out on a patchy lawn, red dust encircling the funky four-room homestead. Wondering about the whereabouts of my father, who was a good father to us when he was there, imagining him heroically swinging a pick way down a mine hundreds of miles away. Hearing my mother tinkling on an out-of-tune piano in the distance.

Country life would have been good for me, I would have enjoyed the open spaces, infinite skies and closeness to the earth. Doing physical work would have been expected, riding horses and dealing with animals, repairing motors and fences. And being the older brother could have been empowering; the things you say and do as an older sibling have a profound effect on the little ones watching. Who knows how that would have played out?

If I thought about the life I didn't have, that parallel universe of remote possibility, the one where I grew up with them, the McRedmonds, I didn't so much yearn for it as catch myself wondering about it. My life as a Moginie was comfortably suburban in comparison, and my parents were always together. Even though I'm sure the love in both houses was equal, I never had to deal with the anathema of a father with a wandering eye and a mother often left alone. I never had to go through divorce as a child like my birth siblings and my own children. But relinquishing parents can have similar problems to adoptees – trouble forming and keeping relationships due to lingering feelings of guilt. Brian and Anne filled the loss quickly by marrying and having more children but would never have dealt with their feelings about my adoption in any conscious way.

The *Adoption Handbook* warned that when you meet your birth family you should keep your expectations low and not think it will make you happier or solve your personal problems. It's not about filling gaps, or finding yourself, or chasing happiness. It's about finding equilibrium, laying to rest some existential questions, and perhaps confirming something about yourself that you instinctively felt but had to prove. Something along the lines of truth-telling leading to reconciliation.

In this hypothetical reality, I would have been the same person, but perhaps more comfortable in my own skin. But I did learn that two of my brothers had also stuttered at school, just as I had when I started high school at Shore.

Both of my Irish grandfathers played the fiddle. I was told by her sister that Anne accidentally burnt her grandfather Maloney's fiddle, thinking it was just an old box she was throwing on the fire. I saw this as a strange metaphor. Instead of music being passed down in the family naturally, it returned to them from outside, with me.

My children played music too, Sam the drums and Alice the piano. For me, music dives down deep to the blarney in my genetic code, and I'm acting that out, whether on jaunts to Ireland to reconnect with my people, improvising madly on the rock stage or composing music. My brother-in-law once quipped that I stole all the musical talent from my birth brothers and sisters. I was brought up with that 'you can be anything you want' mantra of the middle classes. I don't know if my siblings felt they had the same permission to dream and think big.

The
Blarney
pilgrim

The roads in Ireland are tangential. They may start off running parallel, but soon one imperceptibly veers off. Five miles down one road you may meet the other road, but you probably never will. It will look like it's the first road, but it's not. Horses and carts full of hay block the impatient tourist.

Traditional Irish music twists and turns too, and never really repeats itself. But if it does, there's a deadly variant that makes it sound like it's not repeating at all: magic, shape-shifting, tricky.

At the heart of traditional Irish music is the session – a communal event where local musicians turn up to play. These are usually held in a place where drink is served, on a quiet mid-week night to drum up extra patrons.

There is etiquette attached to the best sessions. When the storytellers and solo singers are called by name to perform, someone will quell the chatter with a booming, 'Silence for the singer!' You could hear a shamrock drop as the performance takes its place in time.

I visited Dingle in County Kerry in 2008. A fellow named Michael invited me to sit in on his group's nightly session. All I had with me was my old Martin ukulele, a rare sight in traditional Irish music, but Michael didn't mind, and I joined him and his button accordion (or box), a guitarist from Killarney, and an all-Irish champion bodhrán player (and yes, they have national competitions for playing that kind of drum).

I have a certain pride in being able to pick up music quickly, learning by ear on the fly, over what some might say is a distinguished music career, with a few pointy ARIAs collecting dust on the shelf. But I couldn't keep up. The music eluded me like a quick fish to a slow spear. If there were rules, I didn't have the manual.

And it didn't get better. Later in the night, an Irish woman with a fiddle asked to sit in and, despite never having met before, they played dozens of tunes as if they'd been playing together forever. Then there was that Irish lilt in the singing and the playing, mysterious and heartbreaking. For five nights in a row I could not grasp one tiny thing. I realised with horror that I couldn't hide here like I could in rock music. It was a mighty kick in the arse.

I went back to Australia and immersed myself in traditional Irish music. A gauntlet had been thrown down. I formed an Irish band called Shameless Seamus and the Tullamore Dews and scoured YouTube for the better versions of the tunes. My Irish friends in the band guided me towards seminal performances and records, and I discovered many of the masters: Willie Clancy, Planxty, Turlough O'Carolan, Tommy Peoples and dozens more.

I took lessons from Dennis Cahill, the minimalist and exquisite guitar accompanist to fiddler Martin Hayes. Going back to that very same pub in Dingle in 2011, I had more of an idea. Armed with a cheap bouzouki, I kept pace with about a third of the tunes. That was enough to set me off, travelling for hours up and down meandering Irish roads to find any well-regarded session. It was a heady time of self-discovery. And Dennis's two rules: don't get in the way of the melody if you're accompanying, and never lose the groove. Which is the same in all music.

In Ireland, there's a wonderful expression: 'Music is no load to carry.' Literally, because it's acoustic, you just turn up with your instrument – no lugging of black boxes. Children are expected to play from a young age and do, gladly because they're led by example. Almost everyone plays, but even the listeners know the difference between good and bad. The serious musicians eschew the drink and stay on the water all night, creating a lock into a pure magic and mystery that runs through the body like a drug.

Evelyn Finnerty, who played the fiddle in Shameless Seamus, was brought up in Blarney, near Cork City. She wanted to play the fiddle as a child but her father said, 'There's a perfectly good piano accordion sitting over there; learn that. It's all music.' There are no pennies to waste in those big Irish families. He didn't play, but he would whistle her the tunes so she could pick them up. Decades later, the fiddle she ended up with was her grandfather's. If you show some aptitude, you get the heirloom. The sport-obsessed brother will get grandfather's hurling stick. Which is no small thing either, especially if he was a county champion.

Music runs deep within the culture. I'm inspired by Steve Cooney, the Australian-born guitarist who bought a one-way ticket to Ireland in the early eighties. Through living with Aboriginal people, and studying the didjeridu in northern Australia, he was taught there were five things to learn in a culture – the language, the music, the dancing, the poetry and the magic. Applying this to his own Irish background, he learnt its traditional music so well and so deeply that he is now called the Maestro.

Irish traditional music is the source for me, the pure form. It can wake up the muse. I did more than keep up with it in the end.

I don't know if I could ever move to Ireland permanently and be bathed in the light of it all like Steve; maybe that's what it would take to receive the holy gifts, hard earned as they would be. But I drink from the fountain and join in the song that paves the roads that run like tangents.

Sentences
of
childhood

I've known many restless summers
The sand dunes I imagine
A place without a postcard
Flower people were so beautiful
But straight and loud's the way
Good luck the beatnik spirit
The talk of politicians
The sentences of cynics
And the sentences of childhood
Midnight Oil, 'Brave Faces'

It's in the adoption literature: a lack of attention to important things, insecure attachment, reckless behaviour, an inability to go deep or trust anyone for fear they will abandon you. Issues with loss, rejection, shame, grief, identity, fidelity, intimacy and self-control. Mea culpa. Hurting myself, hurting others.

My decade-long relationship with Suzy and other relationships I had after my divorce ended, usually by my hand, and I did the abandoning. Understanding the connection between adoption and my behaviour, somehow, was forcing me to confront these feelings of unrest and crystallise into something more solid. I hope one day I'll get to see the fog lift, crawl out from beneath the sentences of childhood and stand up straight.

Four

The Gympie
International
Film Festival

After Midnight Oil split in 2002, it took a while to get my bearings. I was asked to join several outfits but none of them felt right. I thought I had to wait and see what my options were. I was still writing songs and had some left over from my time in Midnight Oil so decided it might be best to record an album. John O'Donnell, now the head of EMI, was supportive again, as he had been with Fuzzface. I released *Alas Folkloric* in 2006.

It took me some time to figure out how to play live. My inaugural gig, as Jim Moginie & The Family Dog, was in Katoomba in 2005. I was so nervous, not frontman material at all, but felt a sense of authenticity in delivering my songs: old songs, Oils' songs, any songs I felt some connection to. It went over surprisingly well and I knew I'd get better if I stuck with it. My voice needed strengthening, so I attended singing lessons: the first thing the teacher said was, 'Jim. Please. You have to open your mouth to sing.'

As soon as I started down this road, Pete was parachuted into the safe Labor Party seat of Kingsford Smith as a federal politician. There were some Midnight Oil reunions for good causes – the first in 2005 to aid earthquake relief in Aceh and other places hit by the 2004 Boxing Day tsunami. These reunions were akin to being abducted by aliens: suddenly there were roadies, lights and a huge audience. I had become used to playing clubs to seventy patrons and lugging my own equipment. The gig at the Sydney Cricket Ground was attended by over 50,000 people.

If it was accompanied by mighty adrenalin levels, the aftermath was a mightier anticlimax. I was driven home in the van at 3am with empty beer cans rolling around the floor. The door opened and I stumbled and fell onto the nature strip from the slowly moving chariot of rock, the Toyota Tarago, followed by a few dead cans. The door closed to the sounds of a unison 'See ya, mate' and it accelerated off into the night. I lay on the dewy grass looking at the stars circling above for a sign. In the subsequent weeks there was a rapid decompression and unscrambling of what had just happened.

Soon I was able to resume normal duties. I now chose to do what interested me and follow the voice that was impossible to hear during the uproar and constant travel of the Midnight Oil years. The smaller but no less important job of being a musician, a writer and a producer.

We came together for the second time in 2009, playing to 80,000 people at the MCG for a bushfire benefit, and the next day, with the same sense of crashing back to Earth, I fell out of a different Tarago onto the same nature strip.

A week later, I attended the Gympie International Film Festival as a judge. What possessed me to agree to such a thing I don't know. I was dramatically unqualified. I had become one of those people who said yes to everything.

I was strangely drawn to Gympie, like I was to the Yallah Roadhouse in Wollongong. Gympie is where Brian lived for a while and where all the guns that John Howard couldn't get back after the Port Arthur massacre in 1996 were allegedly buried. It was the birthplace of Darren Hanlon, who I think of as Australia's indie answer to Slim Dusty, and it is where they have an annual gathering called the Gympie Muster, where country and blues acts, and cattle, presumably, all get together and kick up a stink.

I was flown up to the Sunshine Coast but there was no one to pick me up at the airport. No celebrity should have to endure such a humiliation! Eventually, a taxi was summoned and I was spirited through the once volcanic, scenic hinterland and dropped off at a guesthouse, an old Queenslander with bougainvillea, frangipanis, shutters and lattice adorning wide and shady verandas.

The other judges were a local male journalist, ABC presenter and journalist Caroline Jones, and the actors Tony Barry and Noni Hazlehurst. In antipodean terms, I was in exalted company, and any feeling of being out of my depth was quickly alleviated. I realised that even though we came from different backgrounds, we were all 'luvvies'. Left-leaning empaths, fierce defenders of all expressions of art and the right to create it. They were people just like me who had been drawn to this curious fixture on the Gympie calendar.

Tony Barry quipped that he had been typecast as a cop or an Irish priest in every Australian film ever made. These people all had vulnerabilities and matters to contend with like anyone else. I hadn't realised that there were kindred spirits out there, coming as I had from the cloistered ranks of Midnight Oil. The band really was like an army, distrusting of mostly everybody, touring the globe and existing in a monastic bubble – Easter Island statues on wheels.

After the Midnight Oil split I'd made more solo albums – surf music with Rob, Martin, Brian Ritchie from Violent Femmes and Jack Howard from Hunters and Collectors as The Break; Irish music with Shameless Seamus; and psychedelic rock with Jim Moginie & The Family Dog. I played with the Australian Chamber Orchestra and some of its satellite ensembles, with my own Jim

Moginie's Electric Guitar Orchestra, made film soundtracks and composed for art installations. I started an equipment-hire business and then a fully fledged commercial recording studio with some recycled materials, some mates and my bare hands, Oceanic, which opened in 2009 and is still in business. I worked on many sessions as a musician or producer, with Kasey Chambers, Silverchair, Shane Nicholson, End of Fashion, Lyn Bowtell, Bill Chambers, Mick Hart, Sarah Blasko, Kate Miller-Heidke, Jimmy Barnes, Huckleberry Swedes, The Fauves, Angie Hart and others, and discovered that there were other people outside the world I had known. All operate in little ragtag communities with satellites circling them (managers, sidemen, partners, agents, crew, friends), doing great work, not with the big gestures Midnight Oil had been dealing in but in smaller, more homespun ways. Not to denigrate our achievements, but to see people like these win crowds with the humble power of storytelling, moving hearts with song, was like witnessing a miracle. I was learning a raft of new skills. I began to believe in the idea of the troubadour, the grand tradition of a life in music, no matter what the reward. The way forward became as simple as taking one step after the other.

I had watched the film festival's entries in Gympie, and the other judges and I had some heated discussions about their strengths and weaknesses. I told Noni Hazlehurst I really enjoyed her recent film *Little Fish*, and I found out that the presenter of *Play School* could swear like a stevedore. I liked her immediately. Working with Sarah Blasko, my son, Sam, Martin Rotsey and Wayne Connolly, I had put together a version of the Cold Chisel song 'Flame Trees' for *Little Fish*. It came out as a single in 2004 and did well, winning a few awards.

But this film festival award ceremony was held on Saturday night at the Gympie Racecourse. The room was only half full. You could see the running rails of the track and smell the bain-marie from the stage. The sun went down behind the course and shone in my eyes. I played some songs on my ukulele with a local radio personality.

For the finale, Noni led us in a version of 'The Hokey Pokey', bringing the crowd to its feet to dance, relaxed by an abundance of alcohol, a sense of the absurd or just the desire to be part of a community.

One step after the other. One foot in and one foot out. By now, that's what my life was all about.

A
great
circle

Tim Finn once said to me that being in a band can keep you being a child forever. Once the band splits, you have no choice but to grow up. I was forty-six when this occurred.

Just when I had come to terms with Midnight Oil's demise, the band was resurrected. It was at a lunchtime meeting at Martin's house in 2016 when I caught the news. Rob brought a bottle of his father's red wine, something like Penfolds Grange but not as expensive. Pete arrived on time. The four of us sat on the veranda looking out towards some bushland and Martin talked about the snakes that lived around the paths below and sometimes got in the swimming pool.

The whole idea of a tour was one of those things that was going to happen when it was going to happen, on Pete's timetable. He led the meeting towards the conclusion, the chairman, droving and not driving us towards the open gate of reunification. I knew it was going to be a steep climb to work our way back to form, blitzing the audience and leaving quickly. I didn't say no but didn't really say yes either. It felt preordained, and there was no sense in throwing myself in front of it.

'So, Jimmy, when are you going to start your fitness regime?' Pete enquired soon after. There was that directness I had been missing for so long. I'd put on a few kilos and he had a point. But a slow diet wasn't what I embarked on. I wanted something fast and effective, that required zero visits to the gym. I went to the Chinese herbalist who had helped politician Malcolm Turnbull lose weight when he was about to run for the Liberal leadership. The good doctor was not shy about his association with Turnbull. I told him that I played music. 'After your treatment, you will live until 101 years old. Your mind will be able to focus. And your music will be AMAZING,' he said.

I signed on immediately.

In the coming weeks there were more rumblings. Bones was living in America now and was keen to come on board. The tour was planned in secret, like a panzer attack, by John Watson and Melissa Chenery, now our managers, and their company, Eleven, that looked after many great Australian acts.

It's funny what eating nothing will do for your waistline. I was looking forward to the promised reintroduction of food after three weeks of starvation (well, herbs, black tea and water were the whole menu) and was told I could now have half a cucumber each day. I was very spaced out with this and wasn't feeling any pain. After a few more weeks I had lost twenty kilograms. A friend said, 'Hey, Jim, you look yellow. Have a steak or something, will ya?' That's when I pulled out of the program.

Bones was told that he had to learn the whole Midnight Oil catalogue, not just the hits. I thought, 'If we're going to do this, we'd better get right into the nitty-gritty of our music and the deep cuts in the repertoire, and change the setlist every night.' Weeks later we flew out to Uluru for a photo shoot. It was the first time in years we'd all gathered in one place. It felt a bit awkward being thrown together for the cameras like this after so long. We sat around a fire and were filmed talking about the band. I don't think any of us were that comfortable, but Rob and Pete were their usual media-savvy and articulate selves. I mumbled a couple of things that the boom microphone didn't quite pick up. I brought my Irish bouzouki with me and then realised, with its unusual tuning, that I couldn't play any Midnight Oil songs on it when asked to.

I had a weird feeling of dread about the tour, like I was going to be killed or something. It rose up like a panic attack the day before the big announcement. This hesitation to join my brethren, the threat of gazing through the eyes of an Easter Island statue once more, was getting the better of me. But letting the side down was unthinkable. Rob said that he felt the power of the band when we reunited at Uluru. I knew what he meant. It felt we were being assembled to see if it still worked, but of course it was going to work. Midnight Oil always had an unstoppable quality, like a force of nature, a tulip bursting through the ground seeking sunshine, a meteor crashing to Earth, an avalanche obliterating all in its path.

The band had been my other family, giving me direction, determination and discipline. But I'd forgotten that being in a band is work. It's sitting in a plane looking at the back of people's heads, or in a van getting lost in a strange city in the rain with your body screaming for food, sleep or the toilet. It's tolerating the rantings of racist and green-baiting American bus drivers, and standing on a stage and looking at the corporate boxes at the back of the auditorium. It's feeling a hard bump on the shoulder in the middle of a noisy guitar solo and a tall body glistening with sweat would be upon me. Arms around my neck, knocking me off my game, and my grin of feigned annoyance all part of the show. It's dealing with Bolshevik housemaids who knock on your door at 8am with the dreaded word 'Housekeeping'. There's microwaved food in diners, and bed bugs in hotels, and conversations with addled A&R men who really believe in you in the hotel bar at 3am, and drunk punters who sway wildly while their drink remains motionless, shouting in your ear and projecting saliva onto your face as they regale you with their experiences of, well, you. Touring was like being a soldier, demobbed and sent into the battlefield to fight the good fight. In a way it granted me Dad's wish, encoded in 'If', and in his words, 'What you people need is a bloody good war.'

The band started to have more meetings. Pete was the chair. He had spent the last twenty years on boards and in government, striving for consensus when there was none. Getting farmers, politicians, environmentalists all sitting at the table to agree. He was more the pragmatist and CEO since leaving politics in 2013. The non-accountability of rock, the Valhalla of the deafened, and brain cells wired for entitlement was not something he had come across recently. It was much harder to get consensus from us, but to deal with that he had John Watson to unite with and form a Maginot Line of reason.

It was a heady time. I met Christabel Blackman through my friend Stephen Coburn at a party. Both are children of Australian art royalty. Our friendship turned into something more around about the time I renounced the Chinese medicine. Christabel was a strong, funny and smart woman who understood me, and I her, and we just clicked in a way that took us both by surprise.

*

The *Great Circle* tour was announced on 17 February 2017 at a press conference on the *Mari Nawi*, a boat owned and run by Aboriginal people. We dropped anchor just off Lady Macquarie's Chair where the silent protest happened at the 1988 Bicentennial. Everyone in the media seemed to be there. We all wore slimming black and stood on the rear deck in front of the Aboriginal flag in all its glory, with the Sydney Opera House and the Harbour Bridge shimmering in the background. It was filmed and broadcast worldwide. The questions were many and various. Martin got seasick and had to go below.

The world tour sold out in twenty-four hours. We were now to undertake a seven-month, 77-date jaunt that would take us everywhere, including South America, USA, Canada, UK, France, Germany, Finland, Sweden, Norway, Belgium, Holland, the Czech Republic, South Africa, Singapore, New Zealand and Australia. I knew from that first day at Martin's that this was never going to be a lazy victory lap of the Australian wineries.

The rehearsals started in a vast production room in Sydney's Inner West near Sydenham train station. All our gear was wheeled in and we were there for months, re-learning our songs. It had been seven years since we had played the 2009 benefit show, but fifteen years since we had done a world tour like this. I still had my muscle memory for all Midnight Oil music. Bones struggled a bit at first, healing from a dislocated shoulder; Pete was sensitive to volume; while Rob and Martin looked like they were falling off a log. I had to figure out how to make my keyboards work again and use a new piano that controlled all the sounds. Rob jumped on arrangements when they were wrong ('We play this part three times, not four') and didn't say anything when they were right. It was a daunting list of songs, but there was plenty of power.

Jack Howard from Hunters and Collectors and The Break joined us on trumpet, flugelhorn and keyboards; production and tour managers were hired; and, by the end, even before we set foot on a real stage, we were going full steam ahead again, like Midnight Oil had never stopped. I felt the imposition of the razzle-dazzle elements and high production values, but enjoyed the authenticity of presenting our career in retrospect and in depth to audiences around the world.

My premonition that something bad was going to happen came true. At the Myer Music Bowl in Melbourne, four dates before the tour's end, I slipped over and tore my hamstring tendon clean off the bone, an avulsion that required a nasty bit of surgery to reattach and months of physiotherapy and recovery. Even now, it's still not quite what it was. I played the remaining shows in a high-backed seat and was wheelchaired onto the stage with much pomp and ceremony by the road crew, dressed in medical white coats emblazoned with the Midnight Oil hand.

Our fifteen-year absence seemed to have made hearts grow fonder. Everyone in the band brought to the table what they had learnt in the missing years. It was a humbling experience to stand in front of so many audiences that remembered us and the music we created, and an honour to be alongside my brothers in rock once more. Now the job was done, the circle was whole. I thought we'd completed any unfinished business we'd had between us.

The
Lobbyist

After Pete had gone into politics in 2002, Bones left Australia, sensing the band wasn't going anywhere. I saw him again for the 2005 WaveAid and 2009 Sound Relief benefit shows, but only for a few days each time.

In 2014 I was touring in the United States as guitarist with the Australian Chamber Orchestra and flew from New York to Nashville to visit him. He was at the airport to meet me. When my suitcase came off the carousel pulverised by baggage handlers, he frogmarched me over to the Delta counter for compensation. Unsurprisingly, none was forthcoming, so he made it his business to traverse many faceless Tennessee malls until I walked out with a sale-priced Delsey.

We visited a gun store, where acres of floorspace are dedicated to the extinction of every species imaginable, and where you can purchase a bottle of raccoon urine, pour it over yourself to attract raccoons of the opposite sex and blast them as they break cover with a gun you could buy with just $10 and a Tennessee driver's licence. All of this amused Bones greatly.

I tagged along when he was doing a session at RCA Studio A, where Elvis and Chet Atkins had recorded, and we sat around many a table joking and talking with his wife, Denise, usually all convulsed in laughter.

After the *Great Circle* tour in 2017, Bones settled down with his dog. He and Denise had split up but remained close. The tour bought him a house, and they both relocated to Milwaukee, living minutes apart, looking after each other's dogs when needed.

*

I couldn't quite believe it when Pete and Rob both agreed, late in 2018, that we should make a new album. They don't always agree, but on this they were unanimous.

I had nothing prepared. I'd assumed 'job done, point made' after the *Great Circle* tour. The idea of regrouping in the studio made me uneasy because we had changed as people, myself included; that was clear from the last few years of touring. I'd been lucky enough to do whatever maverick musical projects felt good in our hiatus, regardless of their success. I was independent and used to getting my own way. More bohemian, less of the company man, the Easter Island statue formerly known as ... But as soon as Rob played his songs 'First Nation' and 'Gadigal Land', I felt the higher purpose. We talked about asking First Nations artists to contribute. Rifling through my songbooks, I found some ideas that fell into the broad brushstrokes of Midnight Oil subject matter and style. Pete had some complete songs too, and Rob and I then finished a few incomplete ones. It was game on.

I'm all for getting things done fast and avoiding perfectionism, but in making two albums simultaneously we rushed the recording process on a few songs, while devoting perhaps too much time to others. Groupthink is always tricky. Bands always dictate boundaries. On many occasions during the recording, I felt it was a case of 'don't want to follow, unable to lead'.

But there were moments of brilliance. When Martin played the freakish one-note solo on 'Reef', or when Dan Sultan let out a scream from the depths on 'Gadigal Land', or when Alice Skye sang the beautiful 'Terror Australia' and moved us all to tears, or when we pushed up the fader to hear Frank Yamma on 'Desert Man, Desert Woman' or Gurrumul's cry from the heart on 'Change the Date' or Kev Carmody and Sammy Butcher on 'Wind in My Head' or when Pete made the hair on my arms stand on end when he first sang 'Nobody's Child'.

Meanwhile, Bones was counting the days, wanting to go home to his dog back in Milwaukee. It was 'thirty days to go' or 'fifteen-and-a-half days to go', but we needed to overdub his voice on the as yet unfinished recording. Uncharacteristically, he wasn't going out at night much either. I badgered him to redo some bass parts, which annoyed him at first, but he played them graciously and beautifully. He wasn't quite himself the whole time and I couldn't put my finger on it.

Earlier that year, the band had played in Paris at the art deco Le Grand Rex on Boulevard Poissonnière, and two days later we were heading north to play at the Festival Retro C Trop in the grounds of the Château de Tilloloy. I saw Bones outside the lobby, necessarily with cigarette, watching the passing parade of humans and animals. He could be out there for hours before lobby call, observing the progress of a three-legged dog making its way haplessly down the boulevard, giving homeless people money or striking up a conversation with a stranger. He seemed to be treasuring the passing world more than ever. We christened him 'the Lobbyist'.

He and I walked to a restaurant for lunch, crossing the bridge above Jim Morrison's resting place in Montmartre. It was a typical French restaurant with carafe wine, gingham tablecloths and a blackboard menu. Bones generally felt more comfortable travelling and dining with the crew, feeling the band wasn't as much fun, so this was a rare moment.

As we relaxed, I heard myself say, 'Mate, I really can't do this much longer.' The words from the Midwest hotel corridor in 2002 came back. I'm not sure I believed what came out of my mouth completely, because all of us would just keep going despite ourselves anyway. To not let the other guys down. To earn. To win the applause of a crowd. To keep on rocking. To drink from the fountain of youth. But the words felt truer than ever.

Bones surprised me by saying he felt the same, shooting me a look I hadn't seen before, a desperate expression that said that he, at least, did really mean it. Looking back, I recognise now that he had an inkling that he was dying.

An hour later we were on the bus to the festival. As we arrived, I heard The Zombies playing. Colin Blunstone and Rod Argent had recruited some younger players to fill out the sound. It was fantastic. I walked to the side of stage during 'Hold Your Head Up' and 'Time of the Season'. The crowd was lapping it up. It was a long summer day, and the audience was assembled in a giant tree-lined field. Beyond, the country rolled on in the late afternoon, canary-yellow fields of wheat, heat haze and animals foraging.

Walking towards the dressing room in the chateau, I noticed there were bullet holes in the walls. We were in the Somme, the location of a brutal battle in 1916 between Allied Forces and the French Republic against Germany, waged amid mud and much loss of life. Maybe Gary was right about us being a movement. The higher purpose that Midnight Oil could reach, to make sense of the world, to respect the good things and call out the bad. Rob introduced 'Forgotten Years' in fluent French, saying that here, on this very soil, Jim's grandfather, Bones's grandfather and relatives of the others had fought side by side with French countrymen to keep peace and order in a world where tyranny was out of control. 'This song is dedicated to those deeds not ever being forgotten.'

*

There was enough magic to get the two albums made thanks to the combined efforts of the band and Warne Livesey's stellar production, engineering and mixing skills. There was rock but also spoken-word pieces, folk offerings and ambient sounds, and *The Makaratta Project* is probably my favourite Midnight Oil record. Martin said the albums were a successful amalgamation of all the things we'd done previously, plus what we had done as individuals in the 'missing' years between 2002 and 2017 – Pete's craving to be passionately re-involved in music after politics; my bringing the influence of Irish and guitar orchestra music into the fold; The Break's two albums and much touring, which had importantly kept Martin, Rob and me a creative unit; Rob's ascendancy as a songwriter of real breadth; and the fact that Bones's Nashville session years had been so beneficial to his playing. Warne said, 'The one thing I've noticed is that every member of the band has become even better as musicians, singers and writers.'

Reviews of the albums were a long way off because Covid-19 crashed onto the world and knocked back our release dates by over a year. Silence descended on the best-laid plans.

*

Bones hadn't been returning calls, and by mid-2020 Rob had wrung out the confession that our bass player was having a skirmish with cancer. He placated everyone by saying he was going in for a biopsy, but he didn't.

I spoke to him a few times. Sometimes he was hilarious and other times startling. He was unwilling to be the skinny bald guy attached to drips and machines in hospital, with friends and family standing by helplessly as he wasted away. I assume it was because he had watched Buster Stiggs, the drummer from his former band The Swingers, descend into the maelstrom of terminal cancer with so many painful and ineffective treatments. 'That's not me, Jimbo,'

Bones said. I respected his wishes, but the thought of him using the cover of a pandemic to waste away, smoking pot, drinking cough syrup and getting bedsores from lying on the couch at home alone in Milwaukee for months irks me to this day.

Denise discovered the truth and was there with him for the end, making him laugh, fielding the phone calls of the bewildered and sorrowful, diverting them from turning up at the door, watching films with him, communing with their dogs, organising palliative care and a hospital bed in the downstairs living room.

On Saturday, 7 November 2020, I called to tell him we had a number-one record with *The Makaratta Project,* and also to celebrate the end of the Trump era, but the Lobbyist had just checked out.

I had probably spent more time over the years with Bones than my partner, parents, siblings or children. There was so much love, codependency, brotherly friction, shared knowledge – so many storms weathered. I stood beside him on thousands of stages. He was a man who never had a bad word to say about anyone.

Bones bequeathed his guitar strap to me. With the help of a leathermaker, he had incorporated into it the war medals earned by his grandfather and father as part of the New Zealand Army fighting in the two world wars. It was his special possession among not many others. I took it as a measure of our friendship, for all the mini golf, the waiting at airports, that shared sense of the absurd to balance the serious business of Midnight Oil's advocacy, or for whatever restless type of creativity I brought to the table.

Bones lived for the moment, for the wisecrack, the perfect note or golf ball hit, and he was the life of the party. It will always be terribly difficult to comprehend his absence.

In the service of others

Touring had already been booked in for 2021 and it was coming closer, an earthbound comet. We were facing up to the cold reality of keeping the Midnight Oil enterprise upright, to pull that prime mover for all it was worth. But there was also the need to grieve yet undertake an endeavour to touch the celebratory and the divine with everything we had.

In 2020, drummer and singer Declan Kelly brought along Adam Ventoura to my studio for the day. We'd never met, but it was a productive session and he played his bass nimbly. The thing we were doing involved a lot of guesswork, playing to a sinuous keyboard part that came from a friend in New York, but Adam clearly knew music.

When he auditioned for Midnight Oil, there was primal power and dexterity that exploded from him from the first note. Martin and I approached, and as it progressed we were bunched around him like a couple of car thieves as he played the ending of 'Only the Strong' that was pure Giffo. I knew he was our man.

I spoke to Leah Flanagan about singing with us and handling Bones's crystalline vocal parts, and she brought along Liz Stringer to sing and play acoustic guitar. Andy Bickers played saxophone for all those iconic horn lines.

With this lineup we embarked on the *Makarrata* tour in February and March 2021, with guest singers Dan Sultan, Alice Skye, Troy Cassar-Daley and Tasman Keith. Bunna Lawrie and Frank Yamma joined us at the Womad performance in Adelaide. Covid let us get away with it, opening the door for three weeks before it once again slammed shut. The tour had played out well and made a well-founded point in favour of reconciliation and the Uluru Statement from the Heart. We had always written from an Australian perspective – about the dispossession of Indigenous people and the cover-up that followed, the prison empire in the wake of the First Fleet, the influx of migrants and the possibility of a multicultural nation despite the ironies of the White Australia policy: Australia as both work in progress and beacon of hope. Even if, for me, it was always more about the music.

*

But what now? We had watched other bands soldier on: one member there for the music, the other for the money; one is fat, and one is in remission from cancer; one recruited from a cover band to replace a leaving or deceased member. One is there for the partying; one doesn't want to be there at all but doesn't want to let the side down. All of them trying to recreate something that's gone, a journey to a past glory. It's a codependence that has few counterparts in other professions.

The questions for me were many. Could we surpass our work as twenty-somethings on huge albums like *10, 9, 8, 7, 6, 5, 4, 3, 2, 1* and *Diesel and Dust*? Should we even try to get an album played on the radio in an auto-tuned world that idolises youth, where no one buys music anymore?

How about a nostalgia tour, rafting up with other bands of a similar ilk as part of *A Day on the Green* or the *Red Hot Summer* tour, trundling through songs that were hits more than forty years ago? Not to denigrate the bands that keep on rocking this way, but Midnight Oil were cut from a different cloth – there would be little challenge in it, no motivation to keep it going. Or another lap of the clubs and the pubs? We'd been down that road, that vanishing point to the horizon where parallel lines meet, before Pete left in 2002 and we'd disbanded.

Now there was an ex-politician in the band, of the Labor Party variety, and shaped by that culture. His experience as a federal minister was a hen's-teeth moment in the rock world. Someone who talked the talk outside Parliament had actually passed through its doors, walking the walk. I was as proud as a mother of his achievements, his maiden speech and the dignity with which he handled himself in that undignified cat-house. Yet it begged another question: 'What kind of political band were we now? One that could not support anything outside the Labor manifesto?' This was no longer the browbeating Midnight Oil of old. Climate change, Indigenous rights and environmental degradation were still issues for us, and we rightly wrote about them in our new work as we always had. But were these merely centrist issues now, with no gauntlet thrown down to the powers that be? It was as if we *were* the powers that be. In our absence, the internet had become the primary information and disinformation source. The world had vehemently swung right, with the left on the back foot, even migrating to the ultra-right where anti-authoritarian beliefs run riot, including people from the traditionally left-leaning wellness industries, gorging on likes and shares, the dopamine hits of an algorithm. Had our message become mainstream with the passing of time? Some said we were needed more than ever, but were we even relevant?

Then the pressure to be a pop group snapped back. My song 'Rising Seas' was the first single and had to be shortened to qualify for radio airplay. I loved our version, every gnarly and soaring moment of its six serpentine minutes, and the endless repetition of the riff for me was the song, building the climate-change argument and driving the message. Apparently, and quite reasonably, radio and the public would not go along with such a lofty conception. So the song had to undergo radical reconstruction to romp in at around the requisite four minutes. I simply found this unnecessary and, worse, uninteresting. Bands. Formats. Compromise.

I dealt with it philosophically, but at what point would we turn into our own cover band? Where Midnight Oil become The Oils, and the audience yawns as the tempo slowly grinds to a halt. Where is the line that you cross before it gets tragic? Who actually knows where that line is? Would anyone tap us on the shoulder to tell us? Would anyone care by then?

Now one of us had actually died. I didn't want to turn around and find that my whole life had disappeared in the service of others. It was my turn to pull the pin.

To air this heartache, I made the three hardest phone calls I've ever had to make. But no one tried to talk me down; there was no pushback. Maybe the words hit home. I'll probably never know. I assumed they would soldier on without me, but they didn't.

In late 2022, we announced the final tour. In interviews, I made an effort to have a nuanced conversation about a band wrapping it up, but it was a hard sell with journalists who mentioned the endless farewell tours of Farnham or Elton. The ocean in which we swam. Some who were fans said, 'You can't end now.' Some shrugged understandingly or sighed cynically, while others appeared relieved at the prospect.

The only way to progress was to stop. And the only way to stop was to go out with a bang.

The
listener

Announcements were made. 'RESIST: THE NEW ALBUM. THE FINAL TOUR.' Hearing those last three words, a feeling of dismay rolled in like a morning fog over South Head, a creeping realisation. This really was the end.

'What the actual fuck are you guys *doing*?' Adam Ventoura said. As if we were unsound of mind to stop the enterprise that our newest member assumed was a sure thing.

But there was history. The audience would buy the tickets, the trucks would rumble out of the depot, the ushers would shine torches on the seat numbers, the risers and stages would be scaffolded and un-scaffolded.

Many weeks of rehearsals followed. The band adjourned to Rancom St Studios in Botany, an airport-handy suburb in the process of generational change. Industrial warehouses were being skittled in favour of clusters of townhouses, but the huge chemical refinery, working container port and stevedoring watering holes meant the suburb retained its authenticity, character and working-class reputation. On a detour to work I saw that Dad's Karbonkraft factory, with its sawtooth roof, remained.

My second adoptive family was about to break up, the brotherhood of Midnight Oil, where I had learnt much and grown more. The grief was going to be prolonged every single night in every country we had an audience in around the world. A celebration of an illustrious career full of creativity and great music, but also a drawn-out death.

So it felt like a dream walking into Rancom on the first day of rehearsals. In this familiar asymmetrical room, a giant sign saying *SHERBET* is festooned along the longest of the brick walls. Garth Porter, the keyboard player of Sherbet, owns the studio. As a teenager, I would catch the train to lots of their concerts because they usually played outdoors for free and I didn't have any money, but I did like their songs.

Our crew – Alex, Kenno, Kellie and Ben – set up consoles, in-ear monitors, amps, cabling, microphone stands, all buzzing around equipment that was being rigorously finessed. Martin had a new pedalboard that looked very modern compared to my five-foot-long analogue one. My keyboard rig was monstrous by modern standards: Akai drum machines and samplers from the 1990s and a borrowed Hammond organ, an indication of my assumption that anything that works after thirty years of use is still worth using. Adam respectfully used Bones's old bass amplifier, which was very powerful, and again Andy Bickers played saxophone and Leah and Liz were back to sing Bones's vocal parts. Four old hands and four new ones.

We played through the new songs, knowing that we could only squeeze in five, or at the most six, a night. The obligation would be to do audience favourites so, in true Midnight Oil fashion, we decided to rotate the new songs democratically and fairly over the tour.

It all sounded great, sinewy, dynamic, vocally strong. Don't you always love something more when you're about to lose it? Standing in the middle of it, I felt a colossal sense of pride accompanied by a liberal dose of melancholy. I could only stare at the concrete floor. The noise bouncing off it was such a joyous racket, all of its glory and internal chemistry on full display, and yet listening to it was just making me sad. But it had to end before it got really sad.

Australia, Europe and the USA were on the itinerary, and it had been flagged that outgoings were massive compared to incomings. After the nightmare of Covid, freight, hotels and air travel had skyrocketed, especially outside Australia.

Cost-cutting was requested by management, but my heritage keyboard rack just had to be there. Other avenues were explored but we reached similar impasses. Leaving Liz and Leah behind was an option, but they were part of the show now, so they stayed. If the band had decided not to bring them, Rob would have paid for them himself because of the anxiety it would cause him if he didn't hear Bones's vocal harmonies coming back at him through his drum monitor.

We needed them, because this final part was going to be hard.

It's the end of the beginning, but still we go on

The ripples of our decision were now turning into big waves. In this altered state of consciousness, the tour began in Newcastle to over 6000 people. The audience participated differently, not going ballistic to the beat, but watchful, circumspect and drinking in every drop of what was coming off the stage. It meant that every note had to count, every song had to translate, every gesture had to be meaningful. We played in front a giant video wall containing footage from the protest movement, Great Barrier Reef, open-cut mining and pristine Tasmanian forests.

Soon we were in Orange, where the parks are filled with deodars, crepe myrtles, London plane trees, oaks, duck ponds, aviaries and sunken rose gardens. Midnight Oil fans inundated the town for a last chance to dance, but life outside the tour persisted. Men from rural properties still parked their utilities at a 45-degree angle on Summer Street and strolled into Blowes Menswear in their moleskins looking for the perfect Akubra. I watched a twelve-year-old boy in the Kmart car park smash the coin tray of a shopping trolley with a wooden mallet as his mates looked on. Inside, a young girl stared blankly at a row of automatic teller machines opposite her checkout counter. Outside the window of our apartment, a slim teenager stood in the shade of a specimen street tree by a galvanised iron fence, studiously adjusting her fringe in her phone for a good half an hour, checking out the form, or garnering approval from an admirer.

We played at Heifer Station winery. The set, fast and furious for a cold night, was the John Trudell invocation of turning that ice into fire. Nine thousand people can shine a lot of love back at you. Everyone is at their best when they have witnesses. An audience and a band create something together. The ups and downs in the band's popularity resonate with their own peaks and valleys. I went to the microphone to sing the second chorus of 'In the Valley' and choked up. I knew this was going to happen.

For the Melbourne show, we stayed in Melbourne's Parliament district. There was a labrador called Mr Walker in residence at the hotel, presumably to bolster the morale of guests. He lay nonchalant on his day bed or motionless on the front steps. You could even book in advance to walk him. I got lost trying to find the hotel bar. Glazing over at the critical moment when receiving directions, I often found myself in a dead-end or a fire escape. Once I ended up inside a hexagon of six closed conference room doors, like in the video game *Myst*. It was similar to one of my recurring dreams where I'm on the wrong side of the glass at an airport, the rest of the band on the right side, blissfully unaware of my absence, and I have to scramble along endless corridors and dead-ends, hair awry and sweating, to rejoin them, which I never quite manage to do.

On the way to Geelong, Rob wasn't too well and dozed on the back seat of the van. Rain threatened the whole way. The crew hadn't mentioned the weather, but as we walked onto the Mount Duneed Estate winery stage, we saw that the keyboards and pedalboards were covered in plastic sheets and towels. Everything was doused. We played well because of it, the grizzly rock warrior stance kicking in, that defiance to beat the elements shared by band and audience. For us it was a glorious battle; for them it must have been like Glastonbury with drinks.

Rob didn't come up to the front of the stage for very long for the acoustic part of the night that we called the cocktail kit set, preferring to stay dry at the back behind the big drum kit in a heavy coat. His sickness soon transformed into Covid, which meant postponing the next two shows we were there in Victoria to play. So we went home for a few days and waited for the tour to resume. In the garden, I spotted a moth vine growing near the garden tap, an invasive plant that produces white liquid if you break the stem. I was about to pull it out when I noticed one of the leaves covered in hundreds of the tiniest orange and black ladybugs, in a larvae form, a family all being born. I was taken aback by my heavy-handedness, playing God like that, and I was reminded of my own story, how I had been allowed life back in 1956. Empathy is noticing the little things.

Rob came back for the Rod Laver Arena concert on 27 March 2022. Twelve thousand people were there to see us. Melbourne had always been a stronghold. On this night, and any night in fact, standing in the wings watching Rob do his drum solo in 'Power and the Passion' was to admire the musicality, showmanship, fitness and dazzling skill of the man. Every night was a see-it-to-believe-it moment. I was grateful for how much he cared about the band, driving himself way beyond the physical capabilities of any other mortal sixty-six-year-old. We'd been riding alongside each other since we were fifteen.

I felt I didn't give it my best that night. There was a niggling splinter in my left index finger caused by some reckless gloveless gardening. And those in-ear monitors were troubling me, the curse of guitar players worldwide – you can sing perfectly in tune with them, hear the keyboards in brilliant stereo, but electric guitar doesn't have the grunt and bloom. Clinical detail replaced the roar of that lost 1970s Australian guitar sound I pined for. I wanted to change amps for the next show. Equipment and emotion are related.

It was as if I was looking down on someone else playing Oils music. The existential crisis that must be avoided. Deep down, I knew changing amps wouldn't make any difference.

Our
Land's
End

I saw the wave pool from the hotel room. There were plastic flamingos and real lifeguards. It was Darwin outside, but inside it was Greenland. The air-conditioning couldn't be turned off. The artificial environment beneath our balcony was propped up by child-proof fencing, waterfalls, man-made pools and lawn sprinklers. The greenness of the Astroturf was too much information, the so-called Darwinese more used to a thirsty grass of dusty olives and yellows. The humidity would make tough guys and southerners like us succumb, roll over in mute surrender.

Time seems borrowed here. Indonesia and Timor lie close. You're standing on the edge of a cultural precipice. This is our John o' Groats, our Land's End.

It was April Fool's Day, 2022. Pete had a cold, or the beginnings of one, and Leesa Ellem, our tour manager, had her hands full. Honey and lemon, PCR tests and voice rest for the frontman. But she found time to ferry some of us to the art gallery in the eight-seater. Here were the canoes, catamarans and boats that brought so many refugees from Vietnam and other places to this northern gateway to our continent. So handmade, so funky to trust a life to. The gallery was filled with clattering school children and highly excited Midnight Oil fans. We beat a hasty retreat back to town in an Uber.

In much of Darwin, streets are flung down and unresolved, lined with mixtures of gravel and piles of dirt. Sun bounces off asphalt. The poincianas in Darwin are beautiful when in flower, but it was the end of the season now. Their shadows were a relief, a haven for the long grass people. (Darwin's short grass people live behind picket fences and worship Bunnings.) These giant trees hovered over acreages of beaten-down parklands, their buttress roots lifting footpaths and scrambling over the ground like distorted veins. The occasional building appeared until we hit the bayside Copacabana-style resorts, where everything is resolved.

The next day, we woke to the news that Pete had Covid, and so three semi-trailers of equipment heading north from Adelaide had been turned around at 3am. At 8am, the stage built for us at the Darwin Amphitheatre came down. So Leah took us for a drive around her hometown in her mum's car, which was without most of its paint on the roof. A furnace of ultraviolet was too much for blue duco here. Parap Village Markets were a treat, with stalls shaded by bamboo slats and the fragrance of sambals, curries, satays and sweets with coconut cream and mango flesh wrapped in banana leaves. We ended up at the eastern end of the bay lying on a lawn looking across to Mandorah, munching on market fare and talking about the people on tour, family and music. Some long grass people sat just out of earshot. There was shade, a cool breeze and Christabel's ever-present metal water flask.

Forts
made from
bracken

It's lucky I don't believe in luck or else I might have thought our farewell tour was jinxed. Before we even left the rehearsal room, long-time tour manager Sean Richards was struck down with kidney failure and was now on dialysis. Pete and Rob falling to Covid induced the cancellation of the Victorian, Darwin and Cairns shows.

My right-hand man, guitar and keyboard tech Ben Lyons, had flown home from Darwin for a few days to see his family and was struck by a car speeding out of the driveway of a Krispy Kreme donut franchise near Sydney Airport. He had to have surgery to insert a plate between his knee and his shin and we had no choice but to replace him.

Undeterred, Christabel and I became fixated on keeping the touring groove, adhering to the exact schedule of flights and hotels on the original itinerary as if we were still playing our twenty-eight-song list of hits, new stuff and deep cuts every third night. On 5 April 2022 we found ourselves in a fancy hotel in Cairns overlooking the marina with no gig to play.

The next day, with Liz Stringer, we drove north to Mossman to meet the rainforest Aboriginal people, the Kuku Yalanji. They were to be acknowledged as land stewards of their bubu, or country, and of the buyback of other freehold land that was to become part of Daintree National Park.

A speedboat trip was organised. We aquaplaned past mangroves guarding both sides of the Daintree River, where brave souls had built Queenslander-style houses in small cleared areas on the muddy banks, forts made from bracken against crocodiles, mosquitoes and flood. We couldn't help but be humbled by the majesty of Thornton Peak wreathed in cloud, towering over hills that run to the river.

We were accompanied by Aunty Lyn, an Elder from Mossman, as well as an Aboriginal ranger, a boat captain, a photographer called Steve, and Kelvin from the Rainforest 4 Foundation that raises funds for the buybacks. As the boat rocketed eastward, we approached Snapper Island. Aunty Lyn told us it was formed by a dingo taking a bite out of a cassowary. A turtle surfaced to have a look and elegantly vanished, leaving a welt on the water's surface. Lyn is Stolen Generation, and I shared my adoption story. 'That's why you have a heart,' she said. She had an Italian father and an Aboriginal mother. She was taken from them when she was ten. The more time I spend with Aboriginal people, the more I learn about the important things: connection to nature, family, how to live.

A rainforest boardwalk tour followed. Betty, a local woman wearing an 'Always Was, Always Will Be' jersey, introduced us to the candlenut, rich in oil like a macadamia, and told us how to extract worms living in the buttress roots of mangroves to eat. 'Too good for bait,' she said. 'If fruit is picked before it's ripe, thunder will come.' Bush turkey nests lay just off the path, telltale low hills of leaves where the male controls the egg temperature by opening or closing the mouth of the hole.

Betty picked up a half-eaten purple plum just as a cassowary appeared, strutting down the boardwalk towards us. The Aboriginal women screamed and laughed while trying to climb some of the spindly trees by the walkway. We scattered in disarray as the man-sized bird came at us, but it veered off to port side and climbed gingerly down to the stream to have a drink, tossing its blue-plumed head back to swallow the water like a drinking bird toy.

At the end of the boardwalk there was some talk to camera about the aims of the group. I was representing a band well versed in this subject but who were manifestly not present due to the broken rhythm of the tour. I summoned enough words to get by, but it was Andrew, one of the Kuku Yalanji, who had worked on the railways, who stole the show. Missing most of his teeth, he said he loved his mother and that the earth, who is our mother, loves us too. He had been stricken down one day with the feeling of this love, falling to his knees in the rain. He cried when he said it was his mother's land, his uncle's land, his grandfather's land.

The meeting broke up, some autographs were requested, and Liz Stringer and I signed the back of a few of the jerseys. Andrew puffed on a Drum off to one side with a wicked grin. The young daughter of our tour guides hadn't said a word the whole time. Her mother blamed herself for not schooling her in English, but she had her own language. I felt like I never had the right words when I was a kid either, and it must have been daunting for her with all of those cameras, lofty ideas and stakeholders. Cameras are something I've learnt to live with.

I posted some photographs of the day on social media and was accused by some bloke of virtue signalling. I shared my experience to educate people about the struggles of others. Virtue signalling? What a funny world we live in. What a dickhead.

Bluesfest and rain bombs

There were so many new people on the road with us now – video operators, riggers, stage managers and their managers, promoter's staff, caterers. I hardly knew any of them. Mahalia Swinfield, our assistant tour manager, was the next to go down with Covid, and as Leesa had dined with her the previous night, she was now all masks and surgical gloves.

We were going to be playing at the Byron Bay Bluesfest on Good Friday 2022, and as Byron was booked out, we found ourselves staying an hour north in Australia's Florida, the Gold Coast. From our vertiginous apartment, you felt like you were about to drop like a leaf from the parapet. Christabel and I headed up the boardwalk to find a friend's art gallery, dodging holiday-makers on electric scooters, skateboards, bicycles and other contraptions. The tree-planting along the path had only half worked. Stunted banksias struggled, tightly swathed in lime-green plastic stockades, defence against the relentless onshore wind lashing this sandbar interred under skyscrapers. North of the city, there was no shade at 11am, but we discovered an estuary surrounded by trees, an unlikely oasis in the concrete labyrinth. Mangrove roots, muddy water, picnickers reclining under tall trees, peacocks strutting, ducks squawking. School-aged boys were daring each other to jump twenty feet into the muddy water from a pedestrian bridge, and girls with wet hair and swimmers, wrapped in threadbare towels, looked on nonchalantly, pigeon-toed with their paddle pops and sun-creamed noses.

Bluesfest was a blur. We got in and out of there in short order because of the need to isolate, lest the tour take another tumble. Pete ran from the sound mixer to the stage at the beginning of 'US Forces'. The tent was airless and crowded and the stage sound was pretty bad, but it went over well enough. There was a clingy quality to the audience I'd never seen before.

A few days later in Canberra, a meteorological aberration, a rain bomb, dropped on the crowd as the two support acts played, turning the ground into a quagmire. We had our stage clothes on, our in-ear monitors taped in, when Alex Grant, our Scottish production manager, walked in and said, 'They've pulled it.'

The Australian Federal Police shut the whole outdoor site down thirty seconds before we were about to hit the stage. Rain and lightning were one thing, but after the support bands, the ground had deteriorated to such an extent that the delay towers were poised to fall over on the audience. There were so many people knee-deep in mud, all injury risks, and many drunk, that the cops had no other option.

I was feeling a build-up of stress from all of the cancellations. While having a coffee at the National Arboretum the next morning, a disgruntled fan called me out on why the band itself hadn't made the cancellation announcement. I dealt with it and had a measured conversation with him in the end, but my daughter, Alice, now a mother and in her early thirties was there and said, 'He was so rude, Dad. People expect so much from you.'

Sponsor-a-Highway

The concierge lost the keys to our van, so on the evening of 7 June 2022, Midnight Oil were walking downhill from the hotel to our show at the Hollywood Palladium through the night-time streets of Los Angeles.

As we traversed Selma Avenue, a man with trousers around his knees was screaming at a huge metal skip bin. Christabel and I lagged behind the group, my hamstring giving me some grief, but Pete waited like the Good Samaritan he is and ushered us past Undies Man. One of the first times I was in LA, I stood on Sunset Boulevard waiting to cross when a disturbed soul next to me tried to hang himself from the traffic light, noose tight around his neck.

We were swept with a metal detector as we entered the backstage area. In the dim light inside, I spotted the familiar and comforting laminated yellow signs blue-tacked at every show to the doorjambs: Adam/Bickers room; Liz/Leah room; Situation Room (production office); and the sanctum of the 'Oils Compound'. The first thing I noticed was a two-litre bottle of Jameson Irish whiskey. The drinking might have been creeping back.

We had played the Palladium before in 1985. Reminiscent of one of those spacious Gold Coast nightclubs we used to play in the

1970s and '80s, tonight the band had a similar vicious energy that catapulted around the room. We debuted a new song, 'We Are Not Afraid', which I wrote in Valencia in 2017. The trouble was that we were playing to a sequencer track. Once you're playing to one of these things, you can't go off-road with it, so here I was playing the chorus while Pete was singing the verse, and vice versa. No one really seemed to care, as everything goes with everything else in that song.

I watched Pete sing it, coming in late, the music washing over him. Afterwards he remained alone for an hour in his room backstage, nursing a glass of red. He confided the news of the terminal illness of our mutual friend Pammy Swain, a TV producer and long-time supporter of the band. Perhaps the quietude of the song allowed such thoughts some space, whereas guitar rock pushes grief down, distracts, anaesthetises.

The tour progressed to full houses in Chicago, Boston and New York. I always find it exciting to wander these great cities. You see where you've played years before, recording studios you've been in, restaurants you've visited, monuments you've climbed, avenues you've strolled when you were in your twenties.

We'd come to Philadelphia, where Benjamin Franklin invented bifocals, like the ones I was now wearing. He also discovered electricity and invented the postal service. The morning after the show, we were about to move on to Washington, where his statue stands outside the original post office, which is now the Trump Hotel. I wonder what Ben would have made of Trump.

I got a message from Leah. Todd Rundgren was in the lobby, but I'd just missed him. I was moving slowly that morning because the previous night Andy and Adam had come to my room for an Irish whiskey or two.

Band and crew soon headed down the Interstate 95 towards the nation's capital. After a black coffee with a shot of almond milk and an 'original' pretzel at a truck stop, I felt less hung over. The pretzel soaked up the coffee and the coffee broke down the pretzel. We took a group photo afterwards.

It was quiet and respectful on the bus. Pete sat upright, hands folded, taut and disciplined in the passenger seat at the front. There was no Bones to provide the hilarity and bonhomie, but with the way Adam, Leah and Liz filled his absence the band never sounded fuller or better, all Bear-Giffo-Bones-Adam debates aside. It was a different band now, a professional tournament.

The familiar American industrial military complex flashed by, a Home Depot with acres of car park. A yellow school bus sped along an adjacent road then dropped behind some greenery and vanished. In the distance, Baltimore hove into view, all cranes, derricks and chimneys. Rob, Martin and I had pieced together 'King of the Mountain' on a night off here in 1988. A lone hawk hovered and presided over a straight road that looked like an alt-country album cover. A brown-brick church appeared in front of some more greenery. 'Sponsor-a-Highway,' a sign pleaded. A mobile phone tower sailed into view like the mainmast of a Spanish galleon. Then a concrete flyover and a turnoff to Maryland 295. A child dangled an empty chip packet from the rear window of a car, watching it billow with air. I spotted an empty electric-car recharge station.

The next day, we were in the National Mall in Washington when *Roe v Wade* was overturned, upending the right to abortion. Homelessness, a dearth of gun laws, junk food, media misinformation and prescription drugs ruled this place. We were back in the Dark Ages, and I was glad to see the back of America.

Pitch and precision

In Berlin we had dinner with theremin virtuoso Carolina Eyck. Carolina is very accustomed to leading symphony orchestras as a soloist. In her hands, this voltage-controlled oscillator is a Stradivarius, with her innate sense of pitch and precision hand movements that never touch the electronic instrument. You have to be ethereal like a nymph but as grounded as an oak when you approach the field of the theremin, with nothing but complete respect balanced by an equal lack of fear. On a whim, I invited her to join us to play on 'Short Memory' the next night. She obliged, and stunned everyone with her solo.

We headed next to J.S. Bach territory, Leipzig. Leah, Casey Barnes (my new guitar/keyboard tech) and I were standing by the drink machine of Platform 2 at the Berlin Hauptbahnhof waiting for the train, talking about everything from children and crash diets to Sinead O'Connor.

In Leipzig, we met some Powderworkers, Midnight Oil fans, who caught the early train. I look at their Facebook page occasionally but it's a guilty activity, somewhat like peeping through someone else's venetian blinds to look at yourself. I like the fact that they like us, but more that they have found and like one another with us as the excuse.

The number of Powderworkers seemed to increase as the tour progressed. In Leipzig, group after group of them came up as we took in the culture around Thomaskirche, the church where Bach was the organist. The man that wrote the Lute Suites that are burnt into my brain is buried in the chancel. In the presbytery I bumped into a Powderworker named Christian, who let me take a photograph of his many Midnight Oil tattoos.

Outside, there was a statue of Bach that Mendelssohn had built as a tribute to the maestro, whose music he adored, which, in a lovely tip of the hat, one muso to the other, now faced a statue of Mendelssohn himself. This statue had been torn down by the Nazis in 1936 but now stands, remade. The inscription reads: '*Edles nur kind die Sprache der Töne*' – 'May the language of music speak only of noble things.'

Bretagne
to Mundi
Mundi

The last European show of the tour in July 2022 was the Vieilles Charrues Festival in Carhaix, France, to over 55,000 people. Audiences that big don't happen every day of the week, and even though the old hands went into stadium mode, the newer members found the experience completely overwhelming.

The tour was to resume a month later for its final leg in Australia, so Christabel and I headed to Ireland for the break. It was great to reconnect with the place I had always felt an affinity with. I did a few traditional music sessions. Apart from the customary reels, jigs and hornpipes, I'd attempt 'The Band Played Waltzing Matilda' by Eric Bogle, 'Broken Song' by Neil Murray, 'Roll on Babe' by Ronnie Lane, even the de facto Irish national anthem, 'The Fields of Athenry'.

Our friend Mim Scala was a London Teddy Boy, an agent representing Richard Harris and Cat Stevens in the sixties, an associate of the Rolling Stones and many well-known others, and became head of promotion at Chris Blackwell's Island Records in 1972. Mim has a faux-crocodile-covered Selmer Zodiac Twin 30 guitar amplifier that Jimi Hendrix, Jimmy Page and Brian Jones have all played through. With Brian he made the *Brian Jones Presents the Pipes of Pan at Joujouka* album in Morocco. In the sixties and seventies, he often travelled to North Africa in a Land Rover called Shadowfax, both as a jewellery trader and a pilgrim seeking its tribal music. He has lived the wildest and most colourful life imaginable.

'Is there life after rock, Mim?' I asked him. He had retired more than thirty years before, leaving the trappings of London for rural Ireland to become a sculptor, painter, farmer, husband and writer.

'Yes, Jim. There is,' he said. But when I mentioned we were on our final tour, his only response was a terse 'Bollocks'.

We flew back to Australia the day before flying to Broken Hill to do the Mundi Mundi Bash. This is a festival with an encampment of 4WDs and campers, a 12-volt Woodstock, or a Burning Man without the effigies. It's held on the same plains that the 'Beds Are Burning' video was made. We posed for a photo in front of the same dilapidated hotel we posed in front of thirty-five years before, both hotel and band looking somewhat wiser but slightly the worse for wear.

As Leah and Liz couldn't make it, we rehearsed the night before with Missy Higgins and her band in the hotel corridor, deputised as our backing singers for one night only. All took to the stage as the sun sank and the fingers of cold rose up from the earth like stalagmites. Missy's crew fan-girled out, dancing deliriously and singing like angels into a headfirst freezing gale, and Keith Potger from The Seekers made his way backstage. Jet lag, surreal encounters and out-of-body experiences – business as usual in Midnight Oil.

*

Due to the massive financial hit of the cancelled dates earlier in the year, we played the rescheduled Cairns and Darwin shows with a stripped-back setup. The big stage rig would fly to New Zealand for our four dates there, and the smaller 'B' rig would fly to the Top End. It was a move that the crew threw together the best they could.

The band rented a Nord, a generic modern keyboard. These Nords look like a red sewing machine on legs, so I asked the crew to make it more 'Oil' by dressing it with some old rusty corrugated iron. Unable to source such a thing, they adorned a new metal sheet with a spray can to make it look like rusty metal, but ran out of brown paint before they could do a decent job, even though they drilled nail holes and beat it with hammers for five minutes to simulate dents. In no time the faux rusty iron sewing table was set up on the lip of the stage like a Daryl Hall or Supertramp concert. I missed my normal prog-rock warlord setup, authenticity vs convenience. I'm always fighting the latest orthodoxy of minimalist Marie Kondo-ism. Tonight, though, she was victorious.

On our descent into Broome, the ochre earth, white sand and aqua water dazzled us as we circled to land. Four thousand tourists, locals and Powderworkers were about to kick up the dust at the Father McMahon Oval at the Stompem Ground Festival, which has run sporadically over the years. We had played here in 1998 with Warumpi Band. Broome is the melting pot of Creole Australia: Malayan, Aboriginal, Japanese, white and every combination make the place wonderfully exotic.

As we arrived at the good Father's oval, the dulcet saltwater sounds of The Pigram Brothers wafted over the grass to the dressing room. They're an Indigenous band, and all the brothers were present, with an Aboriginal woman – their dancer who is always with them in Broome – swaying to the beat onstage, eyes closed with a big smile. Acoustic guitars, mandolins, dobro and tiples rang out beneath the singing. I admired the Pigrams' unique sound, beach-pebble smooth, nothing in the way of Stephen's smoky voice, and how they sang about what they knew: the blue bone biting, campfires, mangoes ripening and frangipanis blooming. After trying to crack the big cities as a heavy rock band, this sound was revealed to them simply by coming home.

We met the Kimberley Stolen Generation Aboriginal Elders and posed for a photo, the older Stolen Generation people seated in white plastic chairs as the Midnight Oil band members stood behind them.

During the show we were joined by some locals for 'Beds Are Burning'. One wore body paint, another a blue shirt and a big cowboy hat, and we transcended the existential crisis of ageing rock band. It's a gift to have a song that can do that, a lightning rod, a message stick to something higher.

We were invited to Alan Pigram's place the next evening, a large wooden house with big verandas and a giant mango tree dominating the yard. Alan's family and some friends were all gathered, tending children and making salads. Two young women held their babies in front of them while bouncing in sync on a large trampoline. Alan cooked meat on a grill resting on top of a rusty steel drum, which sat in the cast-iron bathtub in which he was bathed as a child.

Alan – woodturner, gold prospector, mechanic, luthier – built his recording studio himself, brick by brick. He has had all the great Irish musicians – Donal Lunny, Mary Black, Stephen Cooney – visit his place. They share the same Irish consciousness, that magic and embrace of sadness and joy, that heart as strong as a mother's.

The next day we piled into some 4WD vehicles and headed north with the Pigrams for a day by the sea. On the way back, we stopped at James Price Point. A woman in a folding chair cradled her dog next to a new Land Rover camping conversion, waiting for the sunset over the Indian ocean with a glass of wine. We asked her if it was nice there. 'Better without people interrupting,' she said.

The rock platform beneath her contained fossils and three-toed dinosaur footprints. In a parallel universe, the band's era, like the dinosaurs, was drawing to a close, a feeling that was heightened by the pageantry and technical wizardry of Queen Elizabeth's recent funeral broadcast. We had five shows left. The next ten days were going to play out differently for each of us. Martin had been quiet, Pete distant and avoiding contact while fighting off a cold, and Rob spent the days in his room recovering between shows. It was a matter of keeping the enterprise upright for as long as we humanly could, so no one would be the one to let the side down. Christabel and I were in our own world, finding solace in each other's company. No one knew what the last show, the last note, the last bow would feel like.

The connection Midnight Oil's music had made to community and humanity was evident as we left Broome. Mark, the founder of Stompem Ground, gave us Stompem Ground beanies, yellow writing on black, and a beautiful hand-carved message stick. Trevor, a representative from the Kimberley Stolen Generation Aboriginal Association, presented us with a seashell, a Broome way of honouring you.

Any doubt I had about the Midnight Oil message becoming vanilla was smashed the night we played the RAC Arena in Perth. The Pete I knew lashed out at energy company Woodside's ambitious plans to drill for gas off the Western Australian coast. 'This is not a sideshow! It is a corporate moral and cultural crime that they are committing, and I use that word advisedly, because back in law school one of the things you learn is that someone is guilty of something if they cause harm whilst knowing what the consequences are. Foreseeable harm!' he roared as we launched into 'Eye Contact', an instrumental written in 1975, with ocean images and protest messages projected behind us, in a venue full of Woodside corporate boxes. 'It's time for Woodside to stop. It's time to put whales and marine life and our future ahead of greenhouse gas emissions and money!'

A similar volley came in Adelaide, with Pete taking aim at energy company Santos, who he queried for extra information on water management strategies back in 2010 as Environment Minister, particularly their effect on the water in the Great Artesian Basin in inland Australia. 'This is not a sideshow!' indeed. This was the Midnight Oil of old, only older.

Two sticks
in the
powderworks

By September, there were only three shows left. The next was at Sydney's Luna Park, the same fun fair and harbourside landmark where I used to go on rides as a child, where the Ghost Train was burnt down, likely deliberately, in 1979, taking the lives of six children and one adult. For this show, titled *One for the Planet*, we played the *10, 9, 8, 7, 6, 5, 4, 3, 2, 1* album all the way through. These themed shows had their advantages – nostalgia for the audience and a painless way for us to knock together a setlist.

In Melbourne a couple of weeks before, we had played a show called *One for the Road* – an extended deep dive into songs from each of our fifteen albums and EPs. On the day, with a drummer with a cold and a singer trying to preserve his throat, the setlist was tweaked to include a couple more slow songs and an instrumental. Although we still played for two-and-a-half hours, the next day the socials thundered with 'Who do they think they are?' and 'Not as good as the Monday show ... fuck! ... what happened?' and the best one: 'What a crock of shit!'

They wanted us to be infallible, the Midnight Oil machine. I wished we were machines, but sadly, we were not.

*

It was Monday, 3 October 2022. By the time it came to play our final show at the Hordern Pavilion in Sydney, tickets had been sold out for months and it seemed people were willing to donate one of their kidneys to get one. The prime minister, Anthony Albanese, was coming – and had his own dressing room.

A sense of clutching desperation surrounded the show, all the ripples culminating into this big final wave. But inside the Hordern in the afternoon, the atmosphere was calm. Most of the crew and management were looking blankly sad or were uncharacteristically subdued. I was wearing Bones's guitar strap and Christabel had polished the medals on it. I offered the mantra of 'sad, elated, heartbroken, triumphant' to anyone who asked how I was faring. Emotions that theoretically cancelled themselves out and left me to walk onstage and just play the music one more time, as if it were our first 'professional' show at the Lifesaver on 10 December 1977.

The set had been circulated and finessed by email for a few weeks. We played forty songs over three hours and forty-five minutes, a scattershot of rockers, ballads, old chestnuts and new stuff. We hadn't played a show this long since one of those dances in the 1970s where we could have breaks and go all night.

A bit numb, I felt at times more like a witness than a participant in that final show, but there was a ferocity to this gig that took me back forty-five years to 1977, when I could never have foreseen what we'd become and where we were now. Blasting through the songs viciously, but respectful of the nuances within them, blitzing the audience as ever, hurling it from the stage in lumps.

Singing the line 'There is something that I will remember' in 'Hercules' as the show drew to a close, I had the sensation that we were setting something free and watching it rise skyward. The collective grief and shared joy between band and audience was palpable. But bewildering also, like a singalong at a funeral.

It was quiet backstage afterwards. We went to open some champagne, but apparently it had been given to the prime minister.

We consumed a few beers together and the inner circle came in one by one. Managers, tour manager, wives, kids, many in tears. Our paths were as interwoven as a macrame owl. Slumped in a wingback chair, the years flashed through my mind in fast forward, a dizzying headrush of every gig we'd played since the Lifesaver. The din of it when the stage ceilings were low, the boom of it when the stadiums didn't seem to have any ceiling at all.

It was all pretty simple, I thought, as the eight-seater glided up to the stage door. All we'd ever done was try to give people something authentic, writing about where we were from and what we cared about in the hope that it would resonate; to deliver more than just a rock show, where the setlist is laminated to the foldback wedges. That unrepeatability meant something to us. It had to feel like it was alive, so we played hard, like it was the end of the world.

Now it really was the end. We'd carried the Midnight Oil message stick around the planet for the last time.

Endgame

Many bands have come to an end before. It's interesting to see how the individuals cope without the adrenalin, applause and nightly approbation of strangers. It's rare that former members completely disappear. They join other bands or re-emerge in another guise, perhaps as part of a music industry body or in academia. There's a need to stay busy: without the structure that a band provides, depression is a common occurrence. (It's the same when army personnel and members of a sports team retire.)

The lure of the band never vanishes. It's a fire just needing a match. Audiences are good at forgiving bands that break up. They love hearing the music of their youth, which reunites them with what they believe are their best selves.

Leaving Midnight Oil behind was like being cut adrift from a monumental ship but still subjected to its wake and pull. In the weeks after the band's finale, the diminuendo and fall from the Tarago to the nature strip felt like dropping off a cliff. Christabel said I was stumbling around the house like a dog that couldn't find where he'd buried his bone. I missed the rhythm of soundcheck and the arrival of the eight-seater. I felt very flat, like long grass under a picnic rug. But when the picnickers go home and the rug is packed away, the grass slowly stands back up again and reaches for the sunlight. One day I woke to find the feeling had lifted, like a vanishing apparition.

The band was my whole life. It was what I was put here to do. It could be the warm feeling of passing by a fan on the street who is proudly wearing a T-shirt, or getting in the car and hearing one of our songs blast out of the radio, or finding an old vinyl record in a vintage shop. It endures, with its own restless life force.

Murmurations

There's a place in County Carlow, Ireland, where the starlings congregate in the trees on winter evenings in the grounds of a mansion house built in 1731. It was once the hereditary home of the Celtic kings of Leinster, now used for weddings and a literary festival.

The birds sound like they're gossiping with a clamorous urgency, reminiscent of the basket wielders in the supermarket opposite. Then they take flight in a massive cloud, writhing, twisting and following one another in expanding and contracting vortexes much like wax does in a lava lamp. In these murmurations, the birds move with a hive mind, like a school of fish. They drop down to their nests only to launch into the sky and reassemble in different formations, again and again. It happens every day just before sunset.

During the 'quiet times' of 2020 as a result of the worldwide pandemic, I started posting daily improvised guitar pieces to keep myself, and hopefully others, sane. The daily murmurations of the birds of County Carlow were in my thoughts as I played, those random movements, often repetitive, echoing nature in the language of a singular guitar. At the end, I had 140 pieces and went into the studio to document the idea.

After Midnight Oil ended, I excavated the *Murmurations* recordings and ran them off to listen to. This quiet music eased the heartache of the big finale, a hushed musical landscape for the mind to wander within. I enjoyed the wayward qualities, the gentle meanderings, the way it lurched and repeated motifs like the Irish roads, never quite going down a path you'd expect. No one knows why the murmuring birds do what they do, though there must be some avian logic guiding them; my music was like that, instinctive, and true to a long-held but blurred belief in making sounds with a sense of wonder. I like to think of *Murmurations* as the late-night party record you play when everyone has gone home.

There is a deliberate vulnerability in some solo performers I've seen, especially in Ireland. You sense a risk being taken to get to the heart of who they truly are. An acrobat on the highwire might wobble and then regain balance, and the audience holds their breath as the chalk particles from their feet drift down in shards into the spotlight below. For me, having nowhere to hide is uncharted land. But music is still challenging me and will always have that enchantment, a way of flowing into the future, luring me on.

The
Silver
River

Christabel and I travel to Ireland for months at a time now. Though still proudly Australian and forever carrying the broad accent of the Australian suburbs, I feel Ireland is my second home and a place to recharge my spirit with the country's deep musical and literary wellsprings. A poet could get right to the heart of being a poet there, but I know from experience that it really comes from within and could happen anywhere.

Many go to Ireland to find their roots, as I did, but I'm beyond any romantic notion of that now. I feel very connected to my blood relatives still in Ireland, who have all welcomed me into the fold. Like my second cousin Mary, and old Jim, who has now passed. He looked after the family's land down at the curragh. It's now a forestry plantation, with over thirty types of timber including Douglas fir, Sitka spruce, Norway spruce, oak, elder, Japanese larch, western red cedar, alder, cherry, beech, walnut, sycamore, maple, mountain ash and Spanish chestnut. 'It's a feckin' lot less work than a normal farm,' said Jim, who could be found at Dempsey's Pub most nights at 6pm for a tipple of black rum.

I have attended many a riotous Irish wedding. Once I was dragged onto the dance floor at 3am, handed a microphone and forced to sing 'Beds Are Burning' with Tullamore's finest wedding dance band. I happily obliged.

My Irish relatives had grown up by the waters of the Silver River in Cadamstown. Now, I walk down to the riverbank from Dempsey's, past the statue of Dick the Boxer, past the ruin of the English army barracks and the old mill, and past local historian Paddy Heaney's house to find the old Cadamstown Bridge fallen into ruin. I reach a leafy glade where the river runs below, under a canopy of trees, and make my way to the river's edge and kneel, watching the eddies and breathing it in. I let the quiet water flowing from the Slieve Bloom Mountains run through my fingers and close my eyes, inhaling the souls of my ancestors, inhaling my own soul.

A
mother's
footnote

I wrote Anne a letter after we first met, and this is what she wrote back in July 2003:

Dear Jim

I thank you so much for your lovely letter, sorry it has taken so long for me to respond. You are so understanding.

Yes, meeting you has been wonderful for me too, it seems like a dream (come true). I often have trouble coming to terms with the decision I made all those years ago & wonder why. Fortunately, our children will never have to make such a decision; with the parental support they know now.

My gratitude goes to your Mum and Dad for the wonderful life they have given you, and as Neil says I am 'very lucky' that you were chosen by such special people & given such a great upbringing, education & fostering your talents in music etc & making you the adult you are today. I thank them wholeheartedly and will be forever thankful to them.

I am pleased your Mum is coping with our reunion, it must be difficult, we respect her concern, but if we can share you 'just a little' we will be happy.

My other children and in-laws have all been so supportive to me, through all this. I always knew I had a very special family, and Neil has been great too.

Yes, Brian's health is not too good, as you saw. Janet, Dave and John are marvellous with him. Janet and David have spent the weekend getting his unit into order, he is spending respite care in a nursing home for a short period. The Brian we see now is not the man he was, alcoholic abuse over the years has taken its toll.

Life has been an experience for me, it certainly had been a challenge, but thankfully I have had good health throughout & wonderful parents-in-law. Brian's parents Pat and Rose were great support in rearing the children. But now I look back and see it was all worthwhile as I have a family I am proud of, & now to have you my life is complete, as there was always sorrow in my heart that you were out there somewhere.

Hopefully we will have more time in the future to spend together. I do love your song 'Home' – it speaks the whole story.

All my love
Your Mother
Anne

CREDITS

Additional photos
Page 55: courtesy of Jan Paul.
Page 225: courtesy of Sean Richards.

Lyrics
Page vii: 'Love of Music' (aka 'Land That Knows Me Well') by Shane Howard, courtesy of Mushroom.

Page xiii: 'Home'
Written by Jim Moginie and Peter Garrett © Sprint Music
Licensed by Sony Music Publishing (Australia) Pty Limited
International copyright secured. All rights reserved. Used by permission.

Page 11: 'Shakers and Movers'
Written by Jim Moginie and Peter Garrett © Sprint Music
Licensed by Sony Music Publishing (Australia) Pty Limited
International copyright secured. All rights reserved. Used by permission.

Page 96: 'Burnie'
Written by Jim Moginie and Peter Garrett © Sprint Music
Licensed by Sony Music Publishing (Australia) Pty Limited
International copyright secured. All rights reserved. Used by permission.

ACKNOWLEDGEMENTS

I started writing *The Silver River* during a visit to Ireland in 2010, as an instruction manual for my children to read, in order to understand their father better. I'd rented the bottom part of a house in Raghly, Sligo, which sat on a rock jutting out into the Atlantic Ocean, and I'd gaze out at the icy grey-green water or at the sheep behind the dry-stone walls in a writerly reverie. There was a pet peacock in the yard that would eyeball me through the window and let out arbitrary high-pitched screams as I was mid-sentence.

As it turned out, I only continued writing when I returned to Ireland, as I often did. It must have been that distance thing: the further away from Australia I was, the easier the writing came.

I knew I didn't want to do an autohagiography or a tawdry 'rock-and-roll-in-the-back-of-the-limo' reliving of an idealised past. I did know I wanted it to be 'writerly' and it became a fun writing exercise, like crafting a good song lyric that might stand the test of time.

Of course it ballooned out of shape, and I spent some time trying to rein it in, which I couldn't have done without the help of Tracy Ellis. For years, she shepherded me through the writing process, turned me on to other writers, edited, questioned, edited more and plain drew *The Silver River* out of me like a splinter. This wouldn't have happened without you, Trace.

Apart from Tracy, many helped on this literary voyage. Thanks to all at HarperCollins for your patience and skills, particularly editors Scott Forbes and Jo Butler and publisher Helen Littleton, who understand everything about writers and writing. Thanks, too, to all the many people I annoyed with questions, and to John Watson, who believed and helped from the start.

Thanks to Christabel Blackman for her steadfast and loving support, and for her photographs that grace this book – words fail me, but I am lucky. Thanks also to her children Pepa, Miguel and Gabriel.

Thanks to Clare O'Brien and Sam and Alice Moginie, for being there for such a big part of my life. You are still there and always will be.

To Suzy Flowers and Josh, for that decade, at Prickle, and by the sea, thank you.

Many in my musical life contributed to this book, and need thanking. Rob Hirst, Peter Garrett and Martin Rotsey have been my Midnight Oil brothers in rock for the last fifty years, and that experience has been a mighty teacher. Thanks also to the many (so many) incredible bass players: Andrew 'Bear' James, Peter Gifford, Bones Hillman, and Adam Ventoura for the finale. And to the wives: Lesley, Annette, Doris, Amanda, Denise, Alex, Marcie.

Thanks to Midnight Oil's original manager, Gary Morris, for his mercurial mind and spirit-level management, without which we would never have got far, and to the team at Eleven Management – John Watson, Melissa Chenery and Skye Nevin – for what you do to continue it. And to all at the Midnight Oil office, especially the wonderful and warm life support of Arlene Brookes, Stephanie Lewis, Di Lindsay, Denise Officer, Paul 'Jonesy' Jones, Craig Allen and many others who passed through 63 Glebe Point Road.

Thanks to our crew people, almost too many to mention, but especially Michael Lippold, Ben Lyons, Casey Barnes, Michael 'Rainbow' Mildren, Oysters, Nick Elvin, Kevin Farrant, Ron 'Worm' James, 'Spanky' Frank Gormley, Michael 'Digger' Kerr, Dave Meyer, Ozzie, Willow, Grant Pudig, Leesa Ellem, Sean Richards, Alex Grant, Willie MacInnes, Mahalia Swinfield, Kellie McKee, Kenno and Colin Ellis.

Wild creatives Howlin' Wind and Nick Launay must be acknowledged for their inspiration; Alan Healy and Evelyn Finnerty for taking me to the trad side, and Stephen Coburn, Michael Vidale, Pete Mackie and Bird for collaboration on the Tullamore Dews and The Tinkers. Thanks to Jack Howard and Brian Ritchie from The Break, the latter for his encyclopaedic musical knowledge, and to Dr Varuni Kulaskera; Kent Steedman, Tim Kevin and Paul Larsen Loughhead from The Family Dog; Michael Trifunovic, Alex Young and Steff Steffen from EGO; Chantal Mahoney; Leah Flanagan, Liz Stringer and Andy Bickers for your MO and Stroopwaffel time; Chris Abrahams, Glad Reed and Michael Russell for all the earlier MO touring; Les Karski, Keith Walker, Glyn Johns, Malcolm Burn and Magoo, but especially Warne Livesey (and Barbara), for your consistent studio brilliance.

Thanks also to: Andrzej Liguz for kindly allowing us to chop up your iconic image for the cover; to Neil Murray and Sammy Butcher for being my Western Desert brothers; to Richard Tognetti and Satu Vänskä for letting me into the classical sandpit; and all at Select Music agency, especially Rob Giovanni. To Declan O'Rourke and Eimear O'Grady, Cornelia and Glenn Lucas, Mim and Janie Scala, Clive Barnes and Luan Parle, Nick Seymour and Nicola McCutcheon, and Neil and Sharon Finn for the Irish thing. To Rick Grossman, Ron Perry and John Carmody, for their wisdom. And to Dennis Handlin, Tony Glover, Damian Trotter and Chris Moss at Sony, for your loyalty to the band and its individuals, and to Van Picken and Clay Doughty.

On the Oceanic Studio side: to Dave Mead, Greg Cameron, Brent Clark, Ted Howard, John Cobbin and Maryanne Slavich, and the many artists I've worked with as a musician, engineer or producer, thanks for letting me be a part of your stories.

Thanks to my brother Kim Moginie for his lifelong love and enthusiasm, and to Frannie and Christopher.

My parallel-universe siblings, John, Janet, Paul, Dave and Susan, you've been so welcoming it takes my breath away. Thanks to Maude for information about her sister Anne. Thanks to Neil O'Neill for caring for Anne, and to Trish Fellows, Patti Ruess and Jay Upton for looking after Mum in her later years. Dear departed Mary, Jim and John McRedmond, I was so lucky to meet you and the extended family. To the Spollens – Malachy, Caroline, Niall, Orla, Pamela, Conor and Mal – you showed me the Silver River and my second country.

Last but not least, my two sets of parents. Paul and Betty Moginie, thank you for giving me a life and for your loving parenting. It was perfect.

Anne and Brian McRedmond, thank you for giving me life in 1956, and for being so wonderful when I burst through your door in 2003. It was what it was, it happened, and thank God it did. I just wish we'd all had more time to spend together. Wouldn't it be great if it all went on forever?